MW00459771

INCREDIBLE
WORLD CUP
STORIES

INCREDIBLE WORLD CUP STORIES

WILDEST TALES AND MOST DRAMATIC MOMENTS FROM URUGUAY 1930 TO QATAR 2022

LUCIANO WERNICKE

sh.
SUTHERLAND HOUSE
TORONTO, 2022

Sutherland House
416 Moore Ave., Suite 205
Toronto, ON M4G 1C9

Copyright © 2022 by Luciano Wernicke

All rights reserved, including the right to reproduce this book or portions thereof in any form whatsoever. For information on rights and permissions or to request a special discount for bulk purchases, please contact Sutherland House at info@sutherlandhousebooks.com Sutherland House and logo are registered trademarks of The Sutherland House Inc.

First edition, October 2022

If you are interested in inviting one of our authors to a live event or media appearance, please contact sranasinghe@sutherlandhousebooks.com and visit our website at sutherlandhousebooks.com for more information about our authors and their schedules.

We acknowledge the support of the Government of Canada.

Manufactured in China
Cover designed by Jordan Lunn
Book composed by Karl Hunt

Library and Archives Canada Cataloguing in Publication
Title: Incredible World Cup stories : wildest tales and most dramatic moments from Uruguay 1930 to Qatar 2022 / Luciano Wernicke.
Other titles: Historias insólitas de los Mundiales de Fútbol. English
Names: Wernicke, Luciano, 1969- author.
Description: Translation of: Historias insólitas de los Mundiales de Fútbol.
Identifiers: Canadiana 20220247129 | ISBN 9781989555958 (softcover)
Subjects: LCSH: World Cup (Soccer)—Miscellanea.
Classification: LCC GV943.49 W4713 2022 |
DDC 796.334/668—dc23

ISBN 978-1-989555-95-8

Contents

Preface   ix

World Cup Prehistory   1

Uruguay 1930   9

Italy 1934   29

France 1938   44

Brazil 1950   60

Switzerland 1954   77

Sweden 1958   92

Chile 1962   104

England 1966   116

Mexico 1970   128

West Germany 1974   143

Argentina 1978   155

Spain 1982   169

Mexico 1986   184

Italy 1990   200

United States 1994   215

France 1998   231

Korea and Japan 2002   249

Germany 2006   268

South Africa 2010   284

Brazil 2014   312

Russia 2018   324

Qatar 2022   335

All World Cup Records   336

Bibliography   353

To my children,
Facundo and Nicolás

Preface

Much has been written about the history of the World Cup. I wanted to tell the story a different way.

Not with a compendium of results and match recaps, but with stories of the people, the politics and the passions—spectacular and strange—that the world's most popular sport inspires. *Incredible World Cup Stories* is a tour of the World Cup from its earliest days, a chronicle of unforgettable clashes and legendary heroes, but also of the entertaining and surprising moments you've not read about or seen before, and would not have imagined were possible.

Some stories are about what happened on the field of play, moments both dramatic and absurd. Some are stories about the fans, in all their devotion and insanity. Others are located a little further away from the stadiums, and will help you understand the historical context behind each tournament. These will explain that certain events, which at first glance seemed to come from the heart of the game, had been born somewhere else.

Politics and world events have influenced and been reflected in the World Cup as in few other sporting events. The tournament was cancelled between 1939 and 1950 because of the Second World War—and Germany was barred from returning in 1950—but the ball kept rolling in the midst of other conflicts, including the Falklands War, when two nations embroiled in conflict in the South Atlantic nearly came to blows on a "neutral" pitch in Spain. Many historians question Italy's triumph in 1934 at a World Cup it hosted under the despot Benito Mussolini, who had players and referees worried for their safety should the result not be to his liking. Others cast a suspicious eye at the World Cup in England in 1966, with its bizarre refereeing, and at Argentina in 1978, played under the watch of a brutal military junta (did that explain the bulging scores, including the host country's 6-0 thrashing of Peru?). Of course, in fairness, in all three of these cases, the winners were truly excellent teams. Still, is it a coincidence that until live television covered the entire planet in the early 1980s, and fans everywhere could see the action for themselves, half of the championships were won by host countries?

But if soccer is a game of political intrigue and a billion dollar business, it is also very much a human game, one of passion, love and nobility. *Astonishing World Cup Stories* tells of players who have refused to leave the field despite having a broken bone. Of a striker who had the guts to face up to Germany's SS by refusing to wear a fascist emblem on his jersey. Another continued playing after suffering a heart attack in the middle of the game, and a defender was killed for preserving his honesty after having committed the sin of scoring an own-goal.

The permanent memory of all those heroes keeps alive the flame that fires the sport. It's a beautiful game, a game of hope, and of humor. These are its best stories.

World Cup prehistory

The roots of soccer, according to the Fédération Internationale de Football Association (FIFA), first took hold in ancient China, during the Han Dynasty in the 2nd and 3rd centuries BCE. An activity called Ts'uh Kuh, or Cuju, was practiced in the city of Zibo. It consisted of putting a leather ball stuffed with feathers and hair into a small net, of some 40 centimeters (16 inches) in diameter, placed on top of a bamboo stalk some ten meters (or 33 feet) high. Players could only push the ball with the lower extremities, and with the chest, back, and shoulders, but not with the hands or arms. It was the first game of foot-to-ball that we know of.

A study by a British anthropologist puts the invention of Cuju even earlier, perhaps as much as 2,000 or 2,500 years BCE. By 500 CE, it had been incoporated into military training. But Ts'uh Kúh is not the only game of its type in antiquity: the Japanese practiced Kemari; the Greeks, Epislcyros; the Romans, Harpastum; the Aztecs, Tlachtli. All combined the use of hands and other parts of the body to push the ball forward, and are considered grandfathers of modern soccer. (And reports of misadventure date back just as long. Marcus Tullius Cicero reported on Harpastum in one of his works, recounting the tragic death of a man who ended up with his

The Chinese game of Tsu-Chu or Cuju is considered an ancient form of soccer.

throat slit after a ball entered the window of a barbershop and hit the knife which, in that fateful instant, was passing along his neck.

It was in England that games played with a ball became the soccer we've come to know. Some assert that the first ball to bounce over Great Britain's ground was imported by a legionnaire who had arrived with Julius Caesar. Others, more romantic perhaps, believe the first ball struck was the head of a Roman soldier killed in combat. Whichever the case, it was there that its rules developed and the game matured.

(Other games involving balls did not evolve quite so much. For centuries, games known variously as "mob football," "mass football," or "football of multitudes," were played in Great Britain. Almost all combined hands and feet, with teams of twenty, fifty, or even hundreds of participants, often residents of neighboring villages. Sometimes a team of married men would challenge a team of single men on improvised pitches in the streets, or in parks and fields. There were usually no goalposts, and not many rules to speak of, the objective being to carry the ball with the hands or kick it to a certain point—a tree, the bank of a stream, or the central square of the town. It was, in essence, an early form of rugby.)

Soccer won favor among the common people, though the ruling nobility disapproved. It was popular in the schools. In the sixteenth century, Saint Paul's school in London highlighted its "positive educational value" and its promotion of "health and strength." Individual schools and universities often devised their own rules and regulations that differed from those of others. As the game flourished, it soon became time to homogenize the rules and, as FIFA suggests, definitively separate "the paths of rugby-football (rugby) and association football."

Delegates from eleven London clubs gathered on October 26, 1863 in a pub on Great Queen Street called Freemasons' Tavern. There, between pints of beer and amid the swirling smoke of fine cigars, they founded The Football Association, or the FA, the first governing body of the sport. In that same conclave, delegates began to draft the first official regulations which, after two months and several meetings, consisted of fourteen rules.

This code served as a cornerstone for everything that would come later, especially its conclusive decision to eliminate the use of hands to carry the ball. Trial and error and unforeseen situations would give rise to new guidelines over the years, and after more than a century and a half, the rulebook remains alive—restless, growing year by year to perfect the competition. Soccer is a constantly evolving sport.

The first international matches

On March 5, 1870, just six and a half years after the formation of The Football Association, the first match between national teams took place. At the Kennington Oval Stadium in London, just a few meters south of the River Thames, teams representing England and Scotland tied at one goal apiece. This inaugural duel is not considered "official," however, because the eleven "visiting" players lived in the British capital and, moreover, had not been chosen by The Scottish Football Association.

The first international match deemed official was on November 30, 1872 at the West of Scotland Cricket Club, on the outskirts of Glasgow. That day, in front of three thousand spectators, Scotland—made up of players from a single club, Queen's Park FC, and dressed in blue club uniforms—fought England to a 0-0 tie.

Outside the United Kingdom, the oldest encounter between countries occurred in 1885, when Canada beat the United States by 1-0 on a pitch in Newark, New Jersey. This clash is also not taken as "legitimate" because the visitors represented the Western Ontario Football Association, and the home side the defunct American Football Association—an entity that, despite its name, had only regional scope. The United States Soccer Federation, the first national body, wasn't founded until April 5, 1913. (The first "official" match between national teams outside Great Britain was played on June 20, 1902 in Montevideo, between Uruguay and Argentina.)

The Fédération Internationale de Football Association (FIFA) was born in Paris on May 21, 1904, when delegates from France, Belgium, Denmark, Holland, Spain, Sweden and Switzerland met in a back room at the headquarters of the Union Française des Sports Athlétiques. The English Football Association, chaired by the Scottish Lord Arthur Kinnaird, refused to send a representative. No matter. That inaugural meeting adopted the English rules and vowed to incorporate other national associations, hoping to set up a tournament among national teams for 1905 or 1906. The next day, FIFA held its first official congress, in which France's Robert Guérin was appointed as president.

FIFA and the failed World Cup

Within a year, England, Germany, Austria, Italy, Hungary, Wales and Ireland had joined. At the second congress, June 10-12, 1905, again in Paris, representatives were enthusiastic about the idea of the first

"World Cup." But they could not decide if it should be played by clubs or national teams, nor could they agree on whether to allow professional players to participate. Nevertheless, the delegates set up group stages and picked Switzerland as the likely host of the semi-finals and the final. The Swiss government even offered to donate the trophy. Economic and logistical problems scuppered the plan, however, and the Olympic Games of London, in 1908, became the first major international competition—the first to feature national teams and be organized by a soccer entity, England's Football Association. After the 1912 Stockholm Games, and with the incorporation of non-European countries like South Africa, Argentina, Chile, and the United States into FIFA, plans for a World Cup sprouted again. The outbreak of World War I in 1914 would freeze that initiative for fifteen years.

Uruguay, the first destination

While soccer gained fans and prestige in the Olympic Games, FIFA held several congresses without actually achieving its primary objective: an exclusive championship for the sport with national representation from all continents. Following the failed attempt in 1906, the Englishman Daniel Woolfall, who would later lead FIFA, said the organization wasn't "sufficiently stable" to pull it off, and suggested another possible roadblock when he stressed "it would also be necessary to have the certainty that all the inscribed teams will keep to the same rules of the game."

It was France's Jules Rimet, who took charge of FIFA in 1921, who renewed the push for a World Cup. With WW I still a fresh memory, he was convinced soccer could "strengthen the ideals of a permanent and true peace."

After many delays, on September 8, 1928, in Zurich, FIFA announced the first tournament would be scheduled for July 1930.

Almost a year later, on May 18, 1929, Spain, Italy, Sweden, The Netherlands, Hungary and Uruguay presented their candidacies to host at the FIFA congress in Barcelona. Uruguay was the favorite because it had won gold in the last two Olympic Games, because if offered to pay for the transportation and lodging of the delegations (something the Europeans could not guarantee, with economic troubles brewing), and because they had the support of all the American continent's representatives, while the Europeans were divided among five hopefuls. The Uruguayan delegate, Enrique Buero, with the help of his Argentine counterpart, convinced Sweden, the Netherlands and Hungary to drop out. Then, arguing that Uruguay's Spanish and Italian community that would support their national teams, he managed the withdrawl of those two nations as well. The honor of being the first country to organize the World Cup, finally, was granted to Uruguay with great acclamation. "We have given everyone a reassuring example of continental solidarity," Buero said in a speech published in Buenos Aires's *La Nación*.

The cup

With the first venue confirmed, FIFA needed a trophy. It would remain in the hands of the winning nation for four years, until the next competition. If a country won a World Cup three times, it would keep prize forever. Jules Rimet commissioned the French sculptor Abel Lafleur, who designed a trophy with the figure of the Greek goddess of victory, Nike, with outstretched hands. The work—55 centimeters high, weighing four kilograms and a costing 50,000 francs—was molded with 18-carat gold and mounted on a base of semi-precious stones.

The trophy, which was put into play nine times until Brazil finally took it home for good after winning in Mexico in 1970, found itself in some curious situations. In 1938, after Italy beat Czechoslovakia in the final of the World Cup in France, the cup was kept in the vault of a bank in Rome. When the World War II broke out, the vice president of the Italian federation, Ottorino Barassi, withdrew it from the bank and hid it under his bed, inside a shoe box, to hide it from German troops in Italy. It is said that a group of SS agents knocked on the door of Barassi's house, in Adriana Square in Rome, to kidnap the trophy. Officers searched the apartment but could not find it, and when they left, Barassi said the Lord's Prayer in thanks.

Almost thirty years later, on March 20, 1966, a few months after the start of the World Cup in England, the golden figure mysteriously disappeared from the windows of the London store Westminster Hall, where it was displayed to promote the championship. Scotland Yard police force assigned its best men to the case, but failed to find a single clue. Desperate to avoid embarrassment, England's Football Association secretly commissioned the goldsmith Alexander Clarke to make a copy to replace the original, which had already been baptized "Jules Rimet" in honor of the French leader. But before the artist finished his work, on March 27, a collie dog named Pickles saved English pride by finding the prized cup, wrapped in newspapers, in a garden in the Beulah Hill suburb. It would later emerge that a dock worker named Walter Bletchley had stolen the trophy. Pickle was immediately declared a national hero and his owner, David Corbett, a 26-year-old Thames River boatman, received a reward of 3,000 pounds. The famous collie died in 1973, mourned by the tears of thousands of fans.

In 1970, the original trophy arrived at the headquarters of the Brazilian Football Confederation (CBF) to stay for eternity. But as the song says, "nothing lasts forever": the cup was stolen on December 19, 1983. The heist had been planned months earlier in the Santo Cristo bar, in the port area of Rio de Janeiro, by bank manager Antonio Pereyra Alves, decorator José Luis Vieira da Silva, a former policeman named Francisco José Rivera and the

Argentine jeweler Juan Carlos Hernández. According to the police, on the night of the robbery, Vieira da Silva and Rivera tied up the only guard and disappeared with the trophy, which was immediately melted down by Hernández. The four suspects in the robbery were arrested and sentenced to nine years in prison. The bars produced with the golden trophy disappeared into the Rio black market. One of the police investigators complained that "Brazil fought so hard to win the cup and it ended up in the hands of an Argentine." Shortly after regaining his freedom, Hernández returned to prison, convicted of drug trafficking. When it learned that the disappearance of the precious object was in fact forever, the CBF commissioned the Eastman-Kodak company in the U.S. to create a reproduction, to be displayed in a showcase of the Maracana stadium.

To avoid further unpleasant surprises, FIFA decided the new cup put into play in 1974, designed and produced by the Italian goldsmith Silvio Gazzaniga, would not be delivered to the winning country. Since then, the winner has received a replica; the original is kept at FIFA headquarters in Zurich. (And what of the replica the English commissioned from Alexander Clarke, but didn't need in the end? It was auctioned off by Sotheby's in 1997 at the request of the jeweler's family. The winning bidder? FIFA, which paid $400,000 and put it on display at the National Football Museum in Preston, England.)

Uruguay 1930

Getting the ball rolling wasn't easy. The 1930 Uruguay World Cup was scheduled for July 15-August 15, to coincide with the summer holidays in Europe. But as the start of the tournament drew closer, one by one, the Old World countries begged off the long haul to Montevideo. At first they claimed money troubles. When FIFA reminded them that Uruguay had agreed to pay all the participants' travel and hotel costs, the argument changed: participation in the World Cup, and the long sea voyage this entailed, would mean their clubs would be without their best players for two months.

With the World Cup threatening to turn into an exclusively American affair, Jules Rimet undertook some high-level diplomacy and persuaded the governments of Romania, Yugoslavia, Belgium and his native France to facilitate matters. King Carol II of Romania, for instance, appealed to the British companies employing Romanian players to give them time off to travel to the World Cup.

Rimet and the delegations from France, Belgium and Romania set sail on June 21 from the beautiful Provence port city of Villefranche-sur-Mer, bound for the River Plate aboard the SS Conte Verde, while the Yugoslav team set sail in the steamship, Florida. The Buenos Aires daily, *La Nación*, reported that, on arriving in the port of Montevideo in early July, Rimet admitted that "the number of nations participating is fairly low, but everything has to start somewhere and this is an encouraging beginning . . . For many Old World countries such a tournament would be of great interest if it were being held within their borders. Interest wanes once it leaves their borders, and plummets when the tournament is so far away. This does not, however, mean that there is no genuine excitement over the World Cup."

At 3 p.m. on July 13, the first ever World Cup matches kicked off between the USA and Belgium, and between France and Mexico. In the nineteenth minute, France's Lucien Laurent scored the first of over 2,000 goals scored in the twenty tournaments up to Russia 2018. Laurent worked for Peugeot and was only in Montevideo after getting time off from his employers.

Uruguay won the first World Cup, beating Argentina 4-2 in the final in a rerun of the Amsterdam Olympics final. The tournament contained no shortage of oddities. It was, along with Brazil in 1950, the tournament with fewest participants in the history of the World Cup, with only 13 teams—nine from the Americas and four from Europe. It was the only World Cup to take place in a single city and the only World Cup without qualifiers. The first round was played in three groups of three teams and one of four, with the group winners qualifying directly for the semi-finals. None of the eighteen matches ended in a draw. The two semi-finals ended with the same 6-1 score, Uruguay beating Yugoslavia and Argentina seeing off the USA. It also witnessed the lowest attendance at a World Cup match, with only three hundred people turning up at Peñarol's stadium for the Romania-Peru tie, even though both were in the same group as the hosts.

A winner on and off the pitch

There were more curiosities, and legends made, at the first World Cup. Andrés Mazali wasn't just a tower of strength in the Uruguayan goal, winning two gold medals at the 1924 and 1928 Olympics. A multi-talented athlete, he was South America's 400 metres hurdles champion, breaking the continental record on five occasions, and a tremendous basketball player, winning the 1923 Uruguayan championship with Olimpia. The legend goes that, because of his speed and agility, he stood out as a forward in his youth but

Mazali was great on the pitch and popular with the ladies

when he made the first team, he had to settle for playing in goal because he couldn't get boots big enough to fit his enormous feet.

As well as making a name for himself in the world of sport, Mazali was a distinguished dancer and, according to contemporary reports, an irresistible ladies' man. So much so that his reputation cost him his place in the Uruguayan team for the 1930 World Cup. One night shortly before the start of the tournament, the goalkeeper escaped from the team hotel to meet up with a stunning blonde who had been at the hotel that afternoon. It appears that the beautiful señorita was either a relative or 'close friend' of one of the Uruguayan bigwigs and, when word of the affair got out, Mazali was kicked off the team. Despite entreaties from captain José Nasazzi and the rest of his teammates, coach Alberto Supicci held his ground and replaced his wandering goalie with Enrique Ballesteros.

The 'Centenario'

When Uruguay was chosen to host the first World Cup, it lacked a suitable venue. The Uruguayan government commissioned architect Juan Antonio Scasso to design a new 100,000-capacity stadium. It was christened the 'Estadio Centenario,' because its official opening was planned for the 100th anniversary of the Oath of the Uruguayan Constitution on July 18th, 1930. Builders set about construction at a breakneck pace and the stadium was up and running in a matter of months.

The planned capacity of 100,000 was reduced to 70,000, but the Centenario drew scathing criticism in Buenos Aires, of the sort modern venues draw today. The *La Prensa* newspaper thought that "a stadium with a capacity for 100,000 spectators in a city of around 600,000 inhabitants is quite out of proportion." La Cancha magazine asked "Where will they find the people in Montevideo to fill the seats?" and in the Argentine capital a play opened with the caustic title "What shall we do with the stadium?" The fans on the other side of the River Plate shrugged off the jibe, retorting, "We'll do what we always do, beat the Argentines."

A few weeks before the tournament's opening on July 13, building work was set back by bad weather in Montevideo. On July 4, La Nación reported that "around one thousand labourers are feverishly at work, some on the grandstands, others on the América stand and others in the adjacent stands, in addition to whom a battalion of army sappers has been scrambled to do their bit." Building work wasn't finished in time, so the first matches were rescheduled to be played at Nacional's Parque Central stadium and Peñarol's stadium in Pocitos, both in Montevideo. When the 'Centenario' was finally opened on July 18, many spectators daubed patriotic or romantic graffiti in the wet cement. Their scrawlings could still be seen years later.

White Lie

The history books of Brazilian soccer say the legendary rivalry between Rio de Janeiro and São Paulo is due to the fact that Brazil's first World Cup team was made up only of players from Rio de Janeiro. The bad blood led to a boycott of the São Paulo clubs against the National Confederation, whose headquarters was in the then national capital. But the Brazilian squad that traveled to the World Cup in Uruguay did have an element from São Paulo: a boy who was born in nearby Santos, named Araken Patusca. A powerful forward who had scored 31 goals in just 16 games in the Paulista Championship in 1927, Araken was so eager to play in the World Cup that, a few months before the start of the international tournament, he told his team leaders that he was going to move to a club in Rio de Janeiro: CR Flamengo. He never did wear the red and black jersey. It was all a farce to dissociate himself from Santos, break the boycott and join the national team that would travel to Montevideo. In the Uruguayan capital, Araken only played in one match, the 2-1 defeat by Yugoslavia, in which he failed to score. After the World Cup, the wayward attacker returned to his São Paulo club team.

An early ejection

José Juan Luqué de Serrallonga had a character as strong as it was shameless. The Spanish coach of the Mexican squad ran his training sessions on the grounds of the Pius IX Salesian College in Montevideo—they were intense, as was his language. Every time a maneuver failed, Luqué de Serrallonga would get angry and out of control, without caring too much where he was. After a couple of days of enduring the high-volume rosary of insults coming from the pitch, the Salesian priests asked the Mexicans to train elsewhere. They noted that the masterful lecture in swearing had been the main lesson learned by the students of the school in those days.

13

Balls

In the week prior to the tournament, the Buenos Aires daily *La Prensa* reported that "Proposals for match balls were reviewed and it was unanimously agreed to use the one made in Argentina." Two days later, the same newspaper reported that "this resolution became a thorny issue when the Uruguayan Industry Minister intervened so that Uruguayan balls without leather straps could also be used. The Executive Committee thus ruled that both types of balls be taken to the field so that captains and umpires could reach an agreement and choose the most suitable ball." The balls were similar, both dark brown leather with rectangular patches and stitching on the outside (which made some players choose to wear berets to avoid head injuries). The only difference was in size, with the Uruguayan ball slightly larger. Ultimately, it was only favoured by the Uruguayan team, with all other teams preferring the Argentine ball. *La Cancha*, in a highly provocative article, reported: "In Montevideo the matches of the first World Cup are being played with an Argentine football. The Uruguayans can hardly accuse us of blackballing them."

Prior to the final between the team captains couldn't agree on which ball to use, so Belgian referee Jan Langenus ruled that two balls would be used, the Argentine ball in the first half and the Uruguayan ball in the second. Many attribute Uruguay's 4-2 win to this peculiarity—Argentina was up 2-1 at the break.

Rebels

Days before Yugoslavia made its debut against Brazil on July 14, a *La Nación* journalist expressed his surprise to Yugoslav coach Bosko Simonovic that his men had not held a single training session since their arrival in Montevideo. "We aren't professionals," he explained, "and have no reason to make any sacrifices. Our lads all rebel against training. Our play won't change much as a result of a few more kicks of the ball and a bit of stretching; it might even stiffen us up." And it worked, for a while. Yugoslavia had a commendable World Cup, winning their group with a 2-1 win over Brazil and a 4-0 thrashing of Bolivia, before ending up on the receiving end of a 6-1 hiding from Uruguay in the semi-final.

Getting a bite

What did the players do off the pitch? Some indulged in hard-fought ping-pong and domino matches, while others lay around reading. The Uruguayans, led by Alberto Supicci, preferred card games like chin-chón, truco, tute cabrero, or listening to tango on the gramophone. One paper reported that "fishing in the River Santa Lucía was one of the favourite forms of entertainment" for the Argentine team. "Our lads," one journalist revealed, "spend hours on end waiting for that twitch in the water that tells them a naive fish has taken the bait." Very different pastimes than those of videogame-obsessed footballers today.

Carlos Gardel

On July 10th, five days before the Argentine team debut, the famous tango singer Carlos Gardel visited the Argentine delegation along with his guitarists to perform for the players. Gardel performed various songs in the dining room of the hotel in La Barra, which was bedecked with Argentine flags. After the show, journalists tried to worm Gardel into touting the team that would win the tournament, but the loyalties of 'El Mudo'—The Mute—were evenly split on both sides of the River Plate. "Football is harder to predict than the horses, and we all know that nobody, except [famous jockey Irineo] Leguisamo, gets it right at the racetrack," he said. "But all the same, and without sticking my neck out, and leaving aside the Brazilians and the Yanks, as I have no idea what they're like at football, I will only say that I think the Rioplatenses will be the hardest to beat and that, if they reach the final, we'll have to toss a coin to decide who wins. They're both good and play wonderful, artistic football, and now that our teams look so happy and decisive, one can only hope that, win or lose, they will do so as good patriots, that is, with all their honor intact."

The day before, Gardel had played a similar concert for the Uruguayan contingent. Gardel had in fact visited both teams before the final at the Amsterdam Olympics, and on that occasion 'El Zorzal Criollo' (The Creole Song Thrush) had told both teams he would not be going to the final because he loved "both teams too much." One story often used to suggest Gardel's preference for the Uruguayan team is that, shortly before the Amsterdam Games, Gardel first performed the tango *Dandy* by Lucio Demare, Agustín Irusta and Roberto Fugazot to the Argentine delegation at the Hotel Moderne in Paris, before they set off for Amsterdam. As the Argentine team then lost to Uruguay, he repeated the 'jinxed' song at La Barra to bring good luck to the Uruguayans. This time, the legend goes, Gardel was careful not to sing the same tango to the Uruguayans.

Prohibition

On July 11, the daily *La Razón* reported that "at the hotel in La Barra there is also a bar selling alcoholic beverages. After a lengthy interview with many of the Argentine champions, it occurred to us to offer them an aperitif as a logical repayment for their courtesy. 'No drinks,' came the unanimous reply. 'When the tournament is over we'll down all the drinks you like. Our obligation now is to stay fit.'" After reporting on this, the newspaper clarified that "we are not motivated by any other interest than to show that Argentine players are willing to prioritize their obligation to defend the good name of the national sport, no matter what the sacrifice."

Emergency goalie

The first match of the World Cup had something of the unexpected. In the 23rd minute of the first half, with France 1-0 up against Mexico at Peñarol's stadium, the famous Red Star Paris goalkeeper Alex Thépot collided with Mexican forward Dionisio Mejía and was knocked out. The Argentine daily *La Prensa* reported on July 14th that "the accident was mainly a result of the goalkeeper's fearlessness, throwing himself into a spectacular save after perhaps considering that the threat to his goal was greater than it really was. Thépot was out cold and unresponsive. He was removed from the field of play with a suspected concussion. During the second half he left the stadium, accompanied by various members of the French delegation, but happily by the evening he had regained consciousness." As substitutions were not permitted, Thépot's position was taken by the midfielder Agustin Chantrel, who was praised by the newspapers of the day. One reported that he was every bit as good between the sticks as Thépot. Despite playing 67 minutes with ten men, France still romped to a 4-1 victory.

Who was sent off?

The draw determined that Peru made its debut against Romania on July 14. Romania opened the scoring at 95 seconds with a goal by Adalbert Desu, scorer of the tournament's fastest goal. After that, the match turned harsh: Adalbert Steiner suffered a fracture after a collision with Mariano de las Casas and had to leave his team with ten members, as substitutions were not allowed. After a while, Peru also lost a player: according to the official FIFA report, Plácido Galindo was sent off by Chilean referee Alberto Warnken. The sent-off took place in the middle of a mess in which several players exchanged slaps. Some versions assert that the one who was thrown out was

Mario de las Casas. With no numbers on the jerseys back then, and no penalty cards, confusion reigned.

A rule in the championship regulations said: "When a player is expelled from the field during the development of an international match, he will not be able to represent his country again in the next international match." Both Galindo and De las Casas were present against Uruguay in the second Peruvian match, but not Domingo García or Alberto Soria. Could one of them have been the punished one? If the referee Warnken expelled Galindo or De las Casas, the sanctioned player evidently evaded the suspension dictated by the regulations. The only certainty is that, ten to ten, Peru equalized the match thanks to a goal from Luis de Souza, but in the last minutes Romania sealed their victory with goals from Constantin Stanciu and Nicolae Kovacs. Then, at the Centenario Stadium, the white-and-red South American team lost again to Uruguay, although by a smaller margin, of only 1 to 0.

The whistle-stopper

One of the goals at the Parque Central stadium backed onto a railway. Nacional fans claimed it was cursed and that, if the train-driver blew his whistle when a locomotive went past, the ball would immediately end up in the accursed net. Argentina made their debut at the stadium on July 15 against France, whose goalkeeper Alex Thépot had made a miraculous recovery. In spite of having been carried off against Mexico only two days earlier, the French goalkeeper was almost unbeatable that afternoon. The Argentine forwards could not understand how Thépot, who had almost lost his life, could move with such catlike agility to deny the strikers with his hands, legs, elbows and even his chest. With just ten minutes left on the clock, and the game seemingly heading for a goalless draw, the Argentine forward Juan Evaristo was hacked down by Agustin

Chantrel 40 yards from the French goal and the Brazilian referee Almeida Rego awarded a free-kick. With the ball on the right wing at a tight angle to the goal, there seemed little danger of a direct shot. Thépot nevertheless ordered Chantrel, Marcelle Capelle and Etienne Mattler into a wall at the regulation ten yards, and positioned himself in the middle of the goal, where he had a favorable angle. The Argentine forwards, who appeared to have given up on beating the indomitable Thépot, left the free-kick to midfielder Luis 'King Size' Monti, who had a powerful shot. As the San Lorenzo player took his run-up, a train passed behind the French goal and the driver, seeing the stadium was full, sounded the whistle. Monti drove a powerful shot through a gap in the wall and into the top corner of the goal before Thépot could react. All the Argentine players piled on top of the goal scorer, although some wanted to run and hug the train driver.

Aggression

The match between Argentina and France was played amid great hostility towards the Argentine team. Newspapers of the time report that the Uruguayan fans spent the 90 minutes hurling abuse and projectiles at the Argentine players. The daily *La Argentina* reported on July 16th, the day after the match, that Boca Juniors forward Roberto Cherro had "an attack of nerves shortly before the match ended, two minutes exactly" which caused "a fainting fit" and "some teammates helped him off the field."

On leaving the stadium, the Argentine coach was surrounded by angry local fans. *La Nación* mentioned that "as the Argentine players boarded the bus . . . a group of youths and a handful of hotheads surrounded them and proffered certain undesirable phrases to the occupants. One of them threw a stone at the vehicle and broke a window."

On hearing of the incident in Buenos Aires, hundreds of people headed for the headquarters of the Argentine Amateur Football Association to request that the squad withdraw and return to Argentina. Uruguayan football directors and even the Uruguayan president, Juan Campisteguy, had to intervene to reassure the Argentine players. On July 17, *La Prensa* reported that the head of the Uruguayan FA "went to the Argentine base to repudiate and condemn the acts of uncouthness committed by a group of irresponsible people. He reiterated the feelings of brotherhood and affection that unite the Uruguayan FA with its sister association, the Argentine Amateur Association for historic reasons and for their support during the presentation of the World Cup"—a reference to the 1929 Barcelona Congress where Uruguay was elected to host the tournament. On July 18, *La Razón* wrote that "the Uruguayan President, Juan Campisteguy, received the president of the Argentine Amateur Football Association, Juan Pignier, at his private residence" to assure him that "the Argentine players would have the most secure of guarantees at future matches." Campisteguy "asked the Argentine director not to spread the news about the shameful attack to which his compatriots had been subjected by a group of hotheads" and, according to the newspaper, the president told Pignier that "all educated people in Uruguay feel very strongly about what has happened."

The local press also condemned the violence. The *Del Plata* newspaper denounced "such an undignified attitude in our culture, as it exceeds the bounds of what is tolerable. Expressions on the field of play, whether favourable or adverse, but which are expressed in a context of composure, which avoid offence or violence, seem to us to be heard and even justifiable in certain circumstances. But there is an enormous difference between that and insolence, or lack of personal consideration. The people of Montevideo cannot be held responsible for the outrages of four disorderly people, whose unforgiveable attitudes only provoke the protests of more sensitive souls." *El País,* meanwhile, wrote that "the indissoluble ties of friendship between our people and our neighbours across the River Plate cannot determine the conduct of the public, which turns selfish when it forgets the brotherly sentiments and sporting stimuli that no one may bargain with. This public, which yesterday expressed its sympathies with the French team, was inconsistent and even unfair with the players who represent a country to whom we owe the hosting of this great party in our own home." The Argentine players accepted the apologies and continued in the Cup. The only player to object was Cherro, who stayed in Uruguay but refused to play in the tournament any more.

Friends Day

USA coach Robert Millar blasted his players after his country's first match against Belgium, at Parque Central on July 13. After the final whistle, the coach locked his players in the dressing room and, waving his hands about angrily, screamed: "This is a disaster! I am so mad at you guys, you never played this horrible! If you repeat this performance, I will withdraw my friendship from you!" The odd thing about his criticism was that USA had just trounced their European rivals 3-0.

To the other side, manito . . .

On July 16, Chile was beating Mexico 1-0 and demonstrating a superiority that had not yet been registered on the scoreboard. Six minutes into the second half, the South American forward Guillermo Subiabre sent a low and very powerful center cross towards Carlos Vidal, who had scored the first goal. But before the ball reached the scorer, a leg of defender Manuel Rosas Sánchez—a boy who worked as a baker— got in his way and diverted the trajectory towards the bottom of the net. It was the first own goal in the history of the World Cup.

Backfiring Bolivians

Minutes before taking to the field against Yugoslavia on July 17 at Parque Central, the Bolivian team pulled white shirts over their green jerseys, with a giant letter daubed on each. The Bolivians had been rehearsing a special routine to win over the locals. As they lined up facing the grandstand, four of them were supposed to form the word 'Viva' and the other seven 'Uruguay.' But what Man proposes, God disposes, and God decided one of the Bolivians should be struck down by a bout of diarrhoea as he was about to leave the dressing room. The other ten, who hadn't noticed his absence, lined up as rehearsed and spelt out 'Viva Urugay'—doing little to win over the Uruguayan crowd.

Penalties

We have already said a lot about the excellent French goalkeeper Alex Thépot, but there's more: he was the first to save a penalty at a World Cup. On July 19, at the Estadio Centenario, France and Chile, who had both dispatched Mexico, met to decide who would vie with Argentina for top spot in the group. Eighteen minutes into the first half, a Chilean player went down in the French penalty area and the referee blew for the World Cup's first ever penalty. Carlos Vidal stepped up to take the kick, straight into the hands of the agile Thépot, though Chile would go on to win the match 1-0 with a 65th-minute goal from Guillermo Subiabre. Following this match, Argentina played Mexico in the same stadium. In the 23rd minute of the first half the Mexican goalkeeper Oscar Bonfiglio saved another penalty from Fernando Paternoster. Some sources suggest that Paternoster disagreed with the penalty decision by the Bolivian referee—and Bolivian team coach—Ulises Saucedo, and made a gentlemanly gesture of fair play in dispatching a soft shot to Bonfiglio to make up for the referee's supposed error. By then, Argentina were already 3-0 up and cruising towards a 6-3 win. Curiously, the Argentine goalkeeper Ángel Bossio also stopped a penalty in the 65th minute, saving Manuel Rosas' spot-kick. Rosas had already scored from the penalty spot in the 42nd minute to go down in history as the first player to score a World Cup penalty. Saucedo also passed into the record books: his three penalty awards in a single game have yet to be surpassed in World Cup history.

The Collaborator

French captain Alexandre Villaplane led something of a checkered life. He proudly represented his country at the first World Cup, but twelve years later, during the Second World War, he collaborated with the Nazis in occupied France. After the German troops had been driven out, Villaplane was executed by firing squad by a platoon of the French Résistance on December 26, 1944.

Sleepy Manager

During the semi-final between Argentina and USA on July 26, the U.S. forward James Brown went down injured. Manager Bob Millar, who was also in charge of his players' physical training and medical attention, ran onto the pitch with a suitcase full of oils, ointments and remedies to tend to the player. As he kneeled down to examine Brown, Millar's case fell open and his bottles and boxes were strewn across the pitch. A bottle of chloroform lost its cork and its contents spilled out. When the coach attempted to pick up the bottle, he got too close to the liquid, inhaled and passed out. Millar had to be carried off the pitch and laid out on the touchline by his own players. Brown recovered without needing treatment and went on playing.

An excess of distrust

Hours before the final between Argentina and Uruguay, the Argentine forward Francisco Varallo told the team managers he was in no fit state for the big match. 'The Little Cannon' had taken a heavy blow to his right knee against Chile and the injury had prevented him from playing against the USA. The Argentine delegation were so unprepared for such an eventuality that a doctor had not been included in the group, so the services of Dr. Julio Campisteguy, the son of the Uruguayan president, were sought out. Campisteguy examined Varallo and recommended that he not join the team, as he wasn't fully fit. However, believing the Uruguayan's diagnosis to be biased, the managers ignored Campisteguy's advice and included the forward in the starting line-up in place of Alejandro Scopelli, who was fully fit and had scored in the semi-final. The directors then made their own examination of Varallo's injuries, using the unorthodox method of having him kick a wall as hard as he could. By the time he took to the pitch, his thigh futilely bandaged for support, poor Varallo had given up the ghost. "I couldn't even move," the striker admitted, and went off in the second half overwhelmed by the pain, reducing Argentina to ten men. The Uruguayan doctor's diagnosis turned out to have been honest and correct.

Life Insurance Coverage

The Belgian Jan Langenus refereed more matches than anyone else at the Uruguay World Cup, with four games including the final. But Langenus had also travelled to Montevideo with the intention of moonlighting as a journalist. According to *Goles* magazine, "after every

Referee John Langenus knew he would be
putting his life at risk in Uruguay.

match, still wearing his shorts (with shirt, jacket and tie—an outfit unheard-of in this day and age), he phoned in his reports to the German weekly *Kicker*." To referee the clásico (derby) between Uruguay and Argentina, Langenus demanded that the organizers provide life insurance coverage, fearful of a tragedy befalling him at the Centenario. But nothing happened, and at the final whistle the Belgian raced off to the port of Montevideo to set sail for home.

The Battle of the River Plate

Although the wounds from the abuse suffered by the Argentine team during and after their match against France appeared to have healed after three consecutive resounding victories, spirits at the hotel in La Barra de Santa Lucía were not at their highest for the final against the tournament hosts. Roberto Cherro had ruled himself out. Adolfo Zulemzú said he couldn't play because of an injury, which a doctor's examination confirmed. Francisco 'The Little Cannon' Varallo didn't want to play either, as his right knee was injured. "They ended up playing me," said Varallo in an interview many years later, "because the older players, like 'Nolo' Ferreira, Monti and [Carlos] Spadaro, who made the team selection, realized that [Alejandro] Scopelli, who was the first-choice inside right, was a bit stage-struck with the atmosphere in Montevideo."

El Gráfico magazine reported that "in the Argentine camp there were far-fetched rumours about reprisals in the event of them winning." One of the targets was Monti himself, who in the hours before the final received innumerable anonymous threats against himself and his family. "They sent me messages and kept me up all night so I didn't sleep before the match," he said in a report years later. Varallo believes that "Monti should never have played in the final; you could tell he was intimidated, like he was afraid of playing." One version of events is that the Italian mafia was behind the threats levelled at the San Lorenzo midfielder. Their plan was that with the defeat of the Argentines, Monti would become the scapegoat of the fans, and, disgruntled at his own people, he would accept a transfer to Juventus and at the same time take up the reins as Gli Azzurri's manager. It is true that when he returned to Buenos Aires, Monti met with two representatives from the 'Vecchia Signora' and agreed on a move to Turin. "The Argentines all made me feel like trash, a worm, calling me a coward and putting all the blame on me for the defeat in the final against Uruguay. Then I suddenly found myself with two people who'd come from abroad to offer me a fortune to play football," Monti later admitted.

Another player who wasn't convinced about playing in the final was Ferreira. He was at loggerheads with various teammates, who begrudged him the fact that, in spite of not having played against Mexico when he went back to Buenos Aires to sit for an exam, 'Nolo' then found himself back in the first team for the semi-final against the USA. The players complained to the Argentine directors and coach Juan José Tramutola, but Ferreira was persuaded by the directors and the coach to join the squad.

On the pitch of the Centenario, with a capacity crowd and the matter of the match balls settled, the game kicked off and was soon marred by niggling fouls and hard tackles. The Argentine media accused the Uruguayans of sneakily kicking out at their rivals, while the Belgian referee turned a blind eye. The visiting goalkeeper, Juan Botasso, told *La Cancha* magazine that he was knocked about "left, right and centre, right from the off." Botasso remarked that Héctor

Uruguay scores on Argentina in the 1930 World Cup.

Castro dished out the worst treatment, a dig in the kidneys and another in his thigh that left him with a dead leg. Castro, who at the age of thirteen had lost his right forearm in an altercation with an electric saw, even rammed his stump into the goaltender's manhood. Monti remarked that "I was very afraid during that match because they threatened to kill me and my mother. I was so terrified I didn't even think about the match I was playing, and that jeopardized my teammates' efforts."

Nonetheless, Argentina went in 2-1 up at half-time: Pablo Dorado had opened the scoring for the home side, but the visitors came from behind with goals from Carlos Peucelle and Guillermo Stábile, top scorer at the World Cup with eight goals. Some journalists reported that the Argentine team was threatened by armed fans in the dressing room, but this has never been officially confirmed by any of those involved. Monti did claim that "when we went back on for the second half, there were about three hundred soldiers with fixed bayonets" standing along the touchline. "They weren't there to

27

defend us. I realized that if I touched anyone, the fuse would be lit. I said to my teammates, 'I'm a marked man, you lot press on because I can't.' After all, what did they want me to be, a footballing martyr?"

Cheered on by the home support in the second half, Uruguay came out in search of glory. Reports from the period agreed that most of the Argentina players didn't seem capable of reacting, captive as they were to a kind of stupefying tameness. "The Uruguayan team" reported *El Gráfico,* "gave 100%, whereas in the Argentine team Monti chose not to play, Juan Evaristo and Botasso were injured in the first half, and Varallo limped around in pain from previous injuries." With the physical advantage, the Uruguayan team overturned their deficit with three goals from Pedro Cea, Victoriano Santos Iriarte and Castro himself. The hosts, organizers of the first World Cup, lifted the little golden statuette of the Goddess of Victory for the first time. Years later, Varallo and Ferreira played down Argentine journalists' reports accusing the Uruguayans of winning by trickery.

'Nolo', meanwhile, went on record as saying that "the Uruguayans didn't kick us about that much, they played hard the way they've always done," although he reasoned that both the pressure and the threats "did have an impact on the Argentines and considerably reduced the team's performance." Uruguayan captain Nasazzi categorically maintained that "We won the Cup because we put more blood and guts into it."

Italy 1934

The first European World Cup could not detach itself from the political and social tensions that enveloped the Old Continent. The despotic regime of Benito Mussolini first put pressure on FIFA to have Italy designated as the host, and then used shady methods to prevent the team (reinforced with four Argentine players and one Brazilian) from stumbling on their way to the world title, which they achieved thanks to a 2-1 victory over Czechoslovakia in the deciding game. The Italian victory served the fascist cause that glorified nationalism. Local footballers were threatened with death to motivate them and were forced to join the National Fascist Party. An additional trophy was offered—the "Coppa del Duce," for the winning squad. Reliable testimony, including from several players, held that Mussolini bribed the referees to ensure local success.

Political pressure did not reach only Italian athletes. Soccer history books published in South America refer to the "Nazi" or "Fascist" greetings made by the German and Italian teams while their anthems played before matches. The truth is that all the teams performed the "Roman salute"—stretching an arm forward—that Adolf Hitler and Mussolini had adopted. For example, before meeting on May 27 in Bologna, the Argentine and Swedish squads greeted the official box with their arms extended. The Buenos Aires newspaper *La Nación* reported that "when the Argentine delegation disembarked" in the port of Naples "it sent a telegram greeting the head of the Government, Mr. Benito Mussolini." That same day, the paper noted, the players and delegation leaders "went to Forli to lay flowers on the grave of the Duce's parents."

As sixteen teams met for the second edition of the World Cup, Jules Rimet, father of the competition, lamented two notable absences: Uruguay and England. Uruguay's absence was payback for Italy's inconsiderate desertion of the first tournament, and an objection to Mussolini's dictatorship. In addition, the Uruguayan footballers who had recently managed to turn the sport professional preferred to stay home to play in profitable local matches, and not for the honor of wearing the lightblue jersey. England, meanwhile, would continue to turn its back on the ecumenical championship until 1950. Rimet added his own grain of sand to Mussolini's ambitions by stating, on May 13, that "the World Cup will be a success, largely because of the contributions of the Organizing Committee, which displays an activity difficult to match".

This time, the World Cup was a simple elimination tournament starting from the round of 16, so eight of the sixteen participating nations were eliminated at the end of their first match. It was also the first Cup to feature qualifying matches. The first was played by Sweden and Estonia on June 11, 1933: the Scandinavian team won 6-2. In this match, the first player substitutions took place in an official match organized by FIFA: Arnold Laasner replaced Friedrich Karm on the losing side. Although such changes were not allowed in official tournaments, for this first qualifying edition the Federation accepted that, for each game, the managers of the two teams would agree on the possibility of replacing the goalkeeper in case he was injured, as well as one or two of the field players.

The first game of the tournament itself, a 3-2 victory by Austria over France, featured yet another novelty—the first overtime to be played in a World Cup. Jean Nicolas opened the scoring for the bleu squad at 18 minutes but the Austrians equalized the count thanks to the famous Matthias Sindelar. The scoreboard was not changed in the second half, so Dutch referee Johannes van Moorsel add two periods of fifteen minutes. In that extra time, goals from Toni Schall and Josef Bican would cement the Austrian victory. Days later, Italy and Czechoslovakia would play the first overtime in a final.

Boats

Just as playing in Uruguay meant a very long sea journey for the European teams, reaching Italy was not easy for the American teams. Brazil and Argentina, for example, took almost two weeks to reach the World Cup host country, and in barely two or three days were eliminated, thanks to the new competition system. The Brazilian squad, coincidentally, had shared part of the route on the ship "Conté Biancamano" with the Spanish squad, which had boarded in Barcelona. The red squad was precisely the one that eliminated Brazil on May 31 in Genoa, 3-1. Worse was the odyssey of Mexico and the United States. The two teams made the very long journey to Rome together on the same ship, and on May 24 they played . . . the qualifying match! Why did two North American teams meet in a European preliminary duel? The answer deserves its own story.

The Talented Mr. Pozzo

After a low number of national teams had played in 1930, 33 countries were registered for the 1934 World Cup in Italy, forcing FIFA to inaugurate a qualifying system. (In the years since, almost every nation on the planet has participated.) The World Cup itself, designed for sixteen teams and a direct elimination from the round of 16, reserved a single place for the Caribbean, Central and North

American countries, which was decided in the host nation's capital three days before the formal start of the contest. How did this strange circumstance come about? One version assures holds that, initially, only three signed up from that portion of the American continent: Haiti, Cuba and Mexico. The Cuban squad defeated the Haitian first, in a three game set—another oddity—played over a week in Port-au-Prince. Then, the Mexicans crushed the Caribbean squad in the three duels in the Mexican capital.

And then the contoversy begins: some journalists and soccer historians hold that the United States then decided to sign up at the last minute. In that version of the story, FIFA and the Italian Federation obsequiously accepted the Americans in part to ingratiate themselves with that powerful nation and in part because of the great Italian community settled in that country. Other versions state that the U.S. entry was not last minute, and that Canada's dropping out allowed them to advance to a denouement with their southern neighbor.

The truth was that Mexico and the United States simply could not agree on a venue for their showdown. According to a story in the May 12, 1934 edition of the Turin newspaper *La Stampa*, written by Italy's coach Vittorio Pozzo—who also worked as a journalist—"the arrangement was not possible. All the diplomatic work carried out by the organizing committee was shipwrecked in the face of the rigid attitude assumed by the two interested sides. Neither of them wanted to take risks at the other's home field". Pozzo emphasised that thanks "to the patience and the Solomonic spirit of the organizers and the Italian Federation, the controversy was brought to a good end. The two contestants decided to come and play their card in Rome". The sly manager "forgot" to add in his writing that he himself had pushed to have the game played in Italy.

Amid strong pressure from Mussolini for the host nation to win the tournament—including death threats to the players and the coach—Pozzo confessed to the organizers his preference for starting the contest against a weak rival, or, at least, a weaker team than Austria, Spain or Hungary. The manager would have convinced the Federation leaders to invite Mexico and the United States to play in Rome, and then manipulate the draw so that Italy would debut against the winner, allowing Pozzo an early look at his first opponent.

On May 24, the teams from Mexico and the United States appeared on the immaculate grass of the National Fascist Party stadium in Rome to face off in front of some 10,000 spectators, the shrewd Pozzo included. The Mexican team scored two goals, but succumbed to the devastating power of the American Aldo Buff Donelli —a striker born in Pennsylvania, the son of Neapolitans and future star of another football, the American style—who scored a poker, or four goals. The United States celebrated, although not as much as the Italian coach.

In an interview several years later, one player on the Italian side recalled a detailed scouting report Pozzo gave him the day before their match with the United States: "Tomorrow (Ed) Czerkiewicz will mark you. He doesn't know anything, don't worry. The business is to threaten outside and go inside. Then, you have to throw the ball to Schiavio's head and he will kill them with headers". On May 27, Italy crushed the United States seven to one. Angelo Schiavio scored three goals, all with headers, all after connecting passes from Orsi, who had two goals of his own.

Frustrated Scorer

Irish striker Patrick Moore was actually the first player to score four goals in a single World Cup match, although it happened during the qualifying round against Belgium. The most striking thing is that, after such a remarkable performance, Moore would not taste victory. The game ended even, and Ireland then lost to the Netherlands and never got to Italy.

Cheating Qualifying

Italy was the only Cup organizing country that had to participate in a qualifying series to play its own World Cup. On March 25, 1934, two months before the start of the competition, the Italian national team had to face Greece in Milan. They won handily 4-0. The victory was a fraudulent, however, since the Italian side had three players who should not have been eligible. At that time, if a player wished to join the national squad of another country, a minimum of three years' residence in his new homeland was required, and a similar period since having played for his previous national team for the last time. Neither the Argentines Luis Monti and Enrique Guaita, nor the Brazilian Amphiloquio Marques (registered as Anfilogino Guarisi, the surname of his mother Wanda, who was born in Italy) met the requirements. Monti had played for Argentina on July 4, 1931, against Paraguay; Guaita, meanwhile, had performed against Uruguay on February 5, 1933, just one year before the duel with the Greeks. Marques-Guarisi, for his part, had emigrated to Italy in July 1931. (FIFA did not bend the rules for Romanian Iuliu Baratki. In April 1934, it issued a statement in which it decreed that Baratki "may be a Romanian subject according to the Treaty of Trianon (the peace agreement that, at the end of the First World War, divided up the Austro-Hungarian Empire), but having played in the Hungarian national team in 1932, he cannot appear in another national team for three years." Baratki was only able to represent Romania in a World Cup in France 1938.)

But these were not the only scams committed by the tournament organizers: the rematch game with Greece, which should have been played in Athens, never materialized. At that time, it was argued that the Hellenes, overwhelmed by the wide score of the first clash, were not willing to endure a second humiliation, especially on their home turf. Sixty years after the suspension of the meeting, it turned out that the then impoverished Greek federation accepted an offer from the Italians to buy it two-storey house in Athens, in exchange for canceling the match and giving up their participation.

No Rematch

Six of the thirteen participants of the first Uruguay 1930 World Cup traveled to Italy for the second tournament. Curiously, they all fell in the first round: Belgium lost to Germany 5-2; France fell to Austria 3-2; Romania, to Czechoslovakia 2-1; United States, with the local team, 7-1; Argentina, with Sweden 3-2; and Brazil, with Spain, 3-1.

Privileges? For No One!

When Benito Mussolini arrived at the "Nazionale" stadium in Rome to witness the clash between Italy and the United States on May 27, a horde of obsequious officials invited him to a privileged spot in the box of honor filled with grandiose flourishes. But Mussolini refused to enter to the coliseum without his corresponding ticket. The "Duce" ordered that there were no privileges "for anyone", and he himself went to one of the ticket offices to buy three admissions, for himself and two of his five children who accompanied him that day.

Hero with Glasses

The Swiss Leopold Kielholz did not look like a soccer player: he was only 5' 6" and wore thick glasses thanks to severe myopia. However, on the field, Kielholz—like Clark Kent, although without abandoning his glasses—was transformed into an indomitable forward. On May 27, at the San Siro stadium in Milan, the fierce striker scored two of the goals with which his team defeated the Netherlands 3-2. Four days later, in Turin, Kielholz again registered his name on the scoreboard against Czechoslovakia, but his national team finally fell by 3 to 2 against the squad that would later be runner-up. Four years later, the striker traveled to France, but did not participate in any of the three games played by the Swiss team.

Three Games in Four Days

Italy is the only country in World Cup history to have played three games in four days. The first took place on May 31 in Florence, where the local team drew 1-1 with Spain after 120 minutes, the first World Cup draw. As indicated by the regulations at the time, the two squads again faced each other on the same field the following day to break the parity. In their rematch, Italy won 1-0 with a goal from Giuseppe Meazza. Two days later, on June 3, Italy traveled to Milan to defeat Austria 1-0, thanks to a goal scored by Argentina's Enrique Orsi.

Defeated, but Medalists

The Spaniards left Italy convinced that they had won a moral victory in their duel with the home team. Iberian players, leaders and newspapers literally described the first match played in Florence on May 31 as "a robbery". Goalkeeper Ricardo Zamora had finished the game with two ribs fractured by a blow from center-forward Angelo Schiavo on the play in which Giovanni Ferrari scored in the 44th minute of the first half. Belgian referee Louis Baert annulled a Spaniard goal for an off-side that, in their opinion, had not existed. "They have stolen the game from us. The most outrageous of all have been the two goals that have decided the game: the one that (the referee) has given to them and the one that he has disallowed us," Zamora said after the match. "To tie they fouled me, which the judge was the first to warn: Schiavo gave me two superb punches that sent me to sit at the back of the net, and so Ferrari could shoot at will. The referee was going to annul it when the Italians brought in the linesmen, and they convinced him to give validity to such a goal."

The Spanish newspapers also complained that in the second game, which took place 24 hours later, the Swiss referee, René Mercet, let the locals hit with total freedom. The Iberians played almost the entire second half with ten men, due to Crisanto Bosch's injury, and also with their substitute goalkeeper Juan Nogués injured. Although eliminated—Italy won 1-0 on June 1 with a goal from Giuseppe Meazza—the Spanish returned home as true winners. In addition to the various banquets and parties in honor of the players, the Madrid newspaper *La Voz* started a national subscription to award a sum of money and gold medals to the team members. According to the journal, "the Italians won by their rough play, and the purpose of the collection is to show that the brave struggle of the Spanish is respected and admired." The first to deposit their contributions were the mayor of Madrid, the members of the Council and all the community officials.

Scolding

After Italy beat Austria 1-0 in Milan, visiting coach Hugo Meisl was in a rage: "We should have won, because on the field it has been shown that our technique is far superior to that of the Italians. My front line has failed. My attackers have lacked energy. At the time to shoot, they have been completely stupid," the coach told a journalist. In addition to recognizing the failings of his men, Meisl attributed the Italian victory to the Swede referee Ivan Eklind's partiality, and to the extra soccer pressures of fascism. "It is impossible to win in the environment they (for the Italians) have prepared. You have to resign yourself and let the blues take the title. But this will not prevent us from declaring that their football is not the best, and that the title of world champions will not be achieved with Justice". The manager was resolute: "They are unacceptable brutes and, if they are not corrected, they will disturb the real sport."

A Complex Oath

Enrique Guaita revealed several years after the final against Czechoslovakia that "if we had had to face Argentina, we would not play" for Italy. "Luis Monti, Raimundo Orsi, Atilio de María and I swore to it" before the start of the tournament, Guaita assured. Thanks to the quick defeat of the South American squad, the four Italian-Argentines did not need to resign from the team. It was fortunate, if you consider the reprisals that fascism used to take against those it considered traitors . . .

Enrique Guaita scores on Austria in the 1934 World Cup

The Nazi, the Wedding, and the Jerseys

On May 31, when he returned to his hotel in Milan after Germany's 2-1 victory over Sweden, midfielder Rudolf Gramlich received bad news: the shoe factory he worked for in Frankfurt, with Jewish owners, had been confiscated by the Nazi authorities. Gramlich, a professional tanner, had to put aside his passion for soccer and return home to try to help his employers and save his only source of income. Back in Frankfurt, Gramlich's reputation as a member of the German national team could do nothing to change the sad fate of his employers. As a German of Aryan stock, he didn't suffer the same fate. The blood of his bosses had put him out of work, but his own found him another position, a few hours later, in the ranks of the military corps of the German National Socialist Party—"Schutz-Staffel", better known as the dreaded "SS". Thus, the midfielder went from victim to victimizer.

Meanwhile, in Rome, without the presence of Gramlich, the German team lost the semi-final to Czechoslovakia, 3-1, and was relegated to play for third place with Austria. For this match, scheduled for June 7 in Naples, coach Otto Nerz was in trouble: Between defections and injuries, only 10 of the 18 players he had taken to Italy were available. Nerz sent an urgent telegram to the center half and star of Alemannia Aachen FC, Reinhold Münzenberg, who had already worn the national team's shirt four times. After receiving the cable, Münzenberg called the hotel where the delegation was staying and explained to Nerz's assistant, Josef Herberger, that he could not travel there because on the day of the game he had to participate in a very important event: his own wedding. Undaunted, Herberger appealed with a phrase that convinced the footballer to join the German team: "A wedding date can be delayed, but a World Cup cannot". With Münzenberg as the mainstay of the defense, Germany beat Austria 3-2 and won the bronze medal.

But this match had yet another curious story. When the two squads came out onto the pitch of the Neapolitan stadium, both were wearing their traditional uniforms: white shirt and black pants. The only difference was in the stockings, also dark: the Germans had a wider white stripe. Italian referee Albino Carraro summoned captains Fritz Szepan (Germany) and Josef Smistik (Austria) and conducted a draw to determine which team should exchange their jersey for a light blue one from the local team Napoli. Some sources say that in fact the match began with the two squads in white, and that a few minutes later, amid prevailing confusion and objections from the crowd—who couldn't tell the players apart—Carraro stopped the action and ordered the change of clothing. For the first time at the World Cup, a national squad wore the jersey of a local club. The Germans, finally, prevailed by three to two.

A Matter of State

Days before the start of the tournament, Mussolini met with the Italian coach, Vittorio Pozzo, to warn him: "You are solely responsible for the success, but God help you if you fail." The threat of "Il Duce" was also extended to Italian players. "You win or shhhh," he cautioned them by running his index finger across his throat during a supposedly "friendly" banquet. For Mussolini, the Cup was not a simple sports competition, but the ideal occasion to show the world fascist power. In this World Cup, as in the next one –France 1938—the Italian team wore embroidered, together with its federation shield, the fasces–or fascio littorio, a bundle of thirty rods with a small ax that the Etruscan kings and the high magistrates of the Roman Empire had used as a scepter. It was the emblem of the Italian fascist—hence the name of the political party. The stadiums were conveniently renamed: the one in Rome, today the "Olympic Stadium," was called the "Stadium of the National Fascist Party."

Faced with such a thick climate of political violence, Argentine transplant Luis Monti noted years later: "In Montevideo they killed me if I won, in Rome they killed me if I lost." He was lucky: both times the result kept him safe.

Mussolini's Reprimand

Had the referees really been paid off by the fascist regime? Luis Monti—many years later, when he was back in Argentina—told a story that left no doubt. According to the midfielder, when the Swedish referee Ivan Eklind, who had dinner with Mussolini the night before of the decisive match, whistled the end of the first half of the final between Italy and Czechoslovakia, with the scoreboard blank, the Duce jumped from his chair and ran to the home team's locker room. There, the dictator faced Monti himself and lectured him for the large number of turnovers he'd committed. Mussolini pointed out that when Monti, with a bold kick, had knocked down the Czechoslovakian Oldrich Nejedly inside the Italian area, the Italian squad had not suffered a penalty thanks to the benevolent Eklind. He was "collaborating" with the cause of the Azzurri (as the Italian team is known, for their Savoy blue jerseys.) However, the Duce warned the player that, if a situation of this nature were to recur, Eklind would have no choice but to penalize the action. The dictator asked the Argentine to help the judge and not complicate his "work" with acts so difficult to cover up. Mussolini returned to his seat to enjoy not only Italy's 2-1 victory, but also the exemplary behavior that the sweetened Monti displayed in the second half.

A Coach with Two Jobs

The Italian victory was celebrated in a very particular way in the local press. "The Azzurri conquer the World Championship in the presence of Mussolini", said *La Gazzetta dello Sport* on its cover. "Italian footballers in the presence of the Duce conquer the world championship", stated *La Stampa*. Obviously, the government's pressure on the press made it possible for Mussolini to appear as the hero of the Cup, much more than the authors of the goals that made the victory, Raimundo Orsi and Angelo Schiavio.

Meanwhile, it is striking that Pozzo, after the final match, had the necessary poise to write an article in *La Stampa*. "There is nothing in the world that exceeds the satisfaction of the duty fulfilled conscientiously, with truth, tenacity, with study, with prudence. It is a satisfaction that compensates everything," the manager-journalist stressed. In that text, more a chronicle of experiences than a detailed analysis of the game, Pozzo wrote "the world championship could not have had a more worthy epilogue" than the Italian triumph, in "a kind of apotheosis of soccer." The coach said "the varied tactics, the techniques and the quick flashes (of his men) that also shone with beauty," drew "tears of joy to the crazy crowd and to the Duce, who had his face and voice full of satisfaction." A moving ode to journalistic objectivity.

Not Even Similar

The day after the great triumph against Czechoslovakia, the Italian-Argentine Raimundo Orsi, author of one of the winning goals, agreed to do a photo session for the local newspapers. The reporters took Orsi to the National Stadium of the Roman National Fascist Party, where the decisive match was played, placed their cameras behind the goal in which the conquest had been marked, and asked the "hero" to repeat the formidable shot that had defeated the famous goalkeeper Frantisek Planicka. Due to the limits of photography back then, no one managed to portray Orsi at the time of the conquest. The Argentine—who had dressed for the occasion with the colors Azzurri to give more realism to the images—tried one, two, three . . . twenty times, but the ball never passed, not even close, through the spot next to the post where it had gone the previous afternoon. The sun set, shadows covered the grass, and photographers, who had spent their film in vain, had to return to their newsrooms without the signature image of the Cup.

France 1938

If the 1934 World Cup in Italy took place in the midst of incipient political conflict, France 1938 took place in a world headed for war, one bubbling with hatred and resentment. Adolf Hitler had decided that the German borders were not far enough from Berlin and in March 1938, he annexed Austria. This had the immediate effect of leaving Austria, who qualified after beating Latvia in the preliminary round, out of the competition. (Of course, the elimination of a team from a soccer tournament is little compared to the chilling conflict that was to come.) Austria was not replaced by another team and Sweden, who had been drawn as their rival, went directly to the quarter-finals. In a laconic statement, tournament organizers said only that "Sweden was going to the next turn for no-show from Austria," without saying anything of the drama that the Tyrolean nation was going through.

The German team, in fact, included seven Austrian football-ers in its ranks: Josef Stroh, Rudolf Raftl (they had been on the Austrian squad in Italy 1934, although they did not play), Wilhelm Hahnemann, Leopold Neumer, Johann Pesser, Willibald Schmaus, and Stefan Skoumal. At the sporting level, these incorporations were of little use: Germany—with the swastika embroidered on the

44

chest and also carved on the sides of the players' shoes—was eliminated in the first round by Switzerland. The German coach had also requested the services of Walter Nausch, captain of the Swiss squad at that time, but the Nazi regime had forced him to divorce his Jewish wife, and so Nausch preferred to flee to Switzerland with his spouse.

The best Austrian footballer of the time, Matthias Sindelar—known as "the Mozart of Soccer," he'd been a star in 1934— also refused to play for Germany. Born in 1903 in Kozlov (Moravia, present-day Czech Republic), Sindelar—called "the paper man" because of his height, thinness and apparent fragility—refused to serve the Hitler regime, even if it was only a matter of playing soccer, his great passion. Some historians say he refused because of his supposed Jewish origin, but in fact the forward was from a Catholic family. In addition, months before the 1936 Berlin Olympic Games, the Nazi government had passed laws that banned Jewish athletes from all sports competition. The most wonderful thing about Matthias's gesture against Nazism was that he made it out of generosity and without qualms, and vehemently opposed the sinister mandate of Adolf Hitler despite the risk it represented for himself. Sindelar protected numerous Jewish friends and even bought a bar from one to prevent the Germans from confiscating it. "The paper man" died on January 22, 1939, under strange circumstances. According to the official version, he died with his Italian lover Camilla Castagnola

Matthias Sindelar:
a spectacular career;
a mysterious death.

as a result of an accidental gas leak that occurred in the apartment they shared in Vienna. Some believe it was a suicide pact by the couple who were being persecuted by the SS. About 20,000 people attended his funeral in the Viennese cemetery of Zentralfriedhof. As his remains were entombed, the Austrian postal headquarters collapsed, some say from the volume of condolence telegrams arriving from all over Europe.

Austria was not the only country driven out of the tournament by serious political problems: since July 1936, Spain was submerged in a bloody civil war that would end with Francisco Franco's victory in 1939. Despite this, two delegates came to Paris from the Iberian Peninsula to witness the Cup and participate in a FIFA Congress, one for each side in the fight.

On the regulatory front, at that conclave, a motion was approved that "no replacement of players in organized championship matches is allowed by FIFA." It would only be permissible in friendly matches between national teams, if both captains agreed, that the goalkeepers could be replaced in case of injury. The tournament format was the same as in Italy four years earlier: direct elimination from the round of 16. For this edition, it was also established that the previous World Cup champion would not play a qualifying round, nor would the organizing country, and if a game were till tied after 90 minutes of play and 30 minutes of extension, both teams were to be declared "champions of equal merit." Another curiosity: each team had to present two photographs and a brief biographical summary of each player at the request of the FIFA observers.

The final of the championship—played on June 19 in Colombes, a suburb of Paris—was won by Italy, who prevailed 4-2 over Hungary. For the first time, an organizing country did not become a champion. For the first time, a country repeated the feat of raising the Cup.

Brazil and Cuba: The "Traitors"

The host country had been decided during the Berlin Olympics, when the FIFA Committee met at the Kroll Opera in the German capital. Argentina, the only candidate from the Americas, hoped the championship would swing back to the New World. The votes, however, mostly European, leaned towards another candidate: France. The decision was partly political—it was argued, among other things, that it would be a tribute to Jules Rimet, president of FIFA—and partly due to the enormous distances that Europeans had to travel to get to Buenos Aires. As a result of the decision, Argentina dropped out of the tournament and tried to convince the rest of the American nations to do the same. Uruguay, the United States, Mexico, El Salvador, Colombia, Costa Rica and Suriname all withdrew and joined the protest. But the continental boycott was not entirely successful because two countries, Brazil and Cuba, rejected the Argentine demands and sent their respective delegations to Paris.

The Salute

FIFA had received many complaints over teams having to perform the "Roman salute," used by the fascists and Nazis, in 1934 during the anthems prior to each match. For the World Cup in France, FIFA allowed each team to choose how best to acknowledge attending officials and the crowd "in order to avoid incidents that could hurt the sensitivity or national pride" of each squad. FIFA said "each team may salute or stand firm" during the ceremony. On June 4, before the opening game in Paris between Germany and Switzerland, the two teams formed up in front of the box of honor: the Germans made the Nazi salute, while the Swiss stood firm with their arms by their sides.

The Italians, meanwhile, also raised their arms before almost all of their matches. Roland Mesmeur, a French journalist who was at the Vélodrome stadium in Marseille for Italy's opening match against Norway, on June 5, 1938, said the salute irritated the hundreds of Italian exiles who had attended the match. In fact, an estimated 3,000 opponents of fascism had showed up at the train station to hurl insults as the team arrived in Marseille. "Those who had to leave their homeland for political reasons found in sport the best way to express their grudges," wrote Mesmeur.

The fascist salute was repeated in the next two games, against France and Brazil, but not in the final against Hungary: the players knew that among the 45,000 spectators that would fill the stands of the Colombes Olympic stadium, close to Paris, would be thousands of Italian expatriates, and that thousands of French also detested Mussolini, so avoided the gesture so as not to provoke the public and avoid riots.

Fans

Before the start of the tournament, the French soccer federation had asked the Ministry of Foreign Affairs to intercede with the German government to allow the fans of that country to travel to Paris for the opener against Switzerland. With war drums beating, a decree by Adolf Hitler prohibited groups of "more than thirty Germans from covering a distance greater than two hundred kilometers from the German borders." The German government remained firm and the squad played without fan support—some 10,000 Germans had to cancel their reserved seats because they couldn't leave their country.

Ejected, Even at Home!

During that opening match between Switzerland and Germany—which ended level at one and forced a tiebreaker five days later—Belgian referee Jan Langenus sent off Austrian Johann Pesser, who was a member of the German team, for having applied a violent kick to the Helvetian Severino Minelli. Pesser's action was so egregious that the German Soccer Federation itself sanctioned the player for "unsportsmanlike behavior." Pesser was suspended for six months from performing for his club, Rapid Wien, and for one year from the national squad.

The Miracle Bandage

The victory against Germany in the first round was a true Swiss miracle. At the replay match five days later, the Helvetic team was losing 2-0 in the 41st minute, due to a goal from Wilhelm Hahnemann, and Ernst Loertscher's own goal. At 42 minutes, Switzerland's Eugen Wallaschek scored, but two minutes later this team lost a player; the talented forward Georges Aeby hit his head against a post and had to be carried off unconscious on a stretcher. The Alpine squad went out to play the second half with one player less, but 13 minutes later Aeby returned to the pitch with his head wrapped in bandages. One newspaper noted that "his return seemed to give new breath to the entire Swiss team, which began to play brilliantly." So it was: the forward made three assists to Fredy Bickel and Andre Abegglen (on two occasions), turned the score around and sealed the Swiss victory by 4 to 2. The very strong contusion did not allow Aeby to join the team three days later, in Lille against Hungary. Without the "bandage-man" on the field, the Magyar squad easily won 2-0.

Expensive, and the Worst!

As the organizing country was responsible for the costs of travel, accommodation and food for all teams, several local newspapers complained about the invitation extended to the Dutch East Indies (now Indonesia), the first Asian nation to participate in the World Cup. According to the newspapers, "its participation cost the French Federation the sum of 400 thousand francs," a small fortune at the time. When the team was beaten 6-0 by Hungary and eliminated in the first match, played in Reims, one of the journals noted that "each of the ninety minutes of play of the Asian team represented for the organizing committee of the World Cup the 'trifle' of 4,500 francs." (This for a tournament whose trophy, produced by Abel Lafleur in 18 karat gold on a base of semi-precious stones, had cost 50 thousand francs.) Including the Russia 2018 edition, the Dutch East Indies/Indonesia is the only nation that has played just one single match in the history of the World Cup.

There was more to György Sárosi than brilliance on the pitch.

Lawyer

The Hungarian center forward György Sárosi was working for a important law firm in Budapest. In May, just weeks before the start of World Cup, he was asked to handle a crucial case which would bring in a lot of money and, if he won it, enormous legal prestige. So Sárosi informed his colleagues that he would not travel to France. But the players and the coach, Alfred Schaffer, convinced him to participate: he was the captain of the team, and the only one, due to his versatility, capable of playing

50

positions both in midfield and defense. In this edition of the Cup, Sárosi was the great star of Hungary and its top gunner: he scored two goals against the Dutch East Indies, on June 5 in Reims; one on Switzerland, on June 12 in Lille; one versus Sweden, in the semi-final in Paris; and another to Italy, in the final. His love of soccer not only made him abandon that court case, but his legal career altogether. Until his retirement in 1948, Sárosi won five leagues and four national cups, all with Ferencvaros of Budapest. He then moved to Italy, where he coached numerous teams, including Juventus and AS Roma.

Why Didn't You Stay in the Press Box?

In its first round match on June 5, Cuba drew 3-3 with Romania after the initial 90 minutes and the extra time of half an hour. This was the game in which Cuba's José Magriña scored the first "Olympic goal" in the history of the World Cup, beating goalkeeper Dumitru Pavlovici with a direct shot from a corner kick.

As France 1938 was a tournament with direct elimination, the two teams—as the regulations prescribed at that time—met again four days later on the same stage to settle the duel. Upon arriving at the Chapou stadium in Toulouse, Cuban coach José Tapia ordered the same eleven players who had performed in the debut to take to the field. But starting goalkeeper Benito Carvajales requested that his place be taken by his substitute, Juan Ayra, so that he could serve as a commentator for a Cuban radio station. With Ayra in goal and Carvajales in the press box, Cuba beat their European rival 2-1. After the victory, the squad traveled to Antibes to face Sweden in the quarter-finals. That day, June 12, there was no radio broadcast, so Carvajales asked to take back his spot. The manager agreed, though he later cursed the lack of radio transmission. The "commentator" gave up eight goals and Cuba was eliminated from the championship.

A Double Win

After Italy defeated Norway 2-1 in overtime on June 5, Italian captain Giuseppe Meazza, said his coach, Vittorio Pozzo, gave the squad a few hours of "rest" after so many weeks of rigorous preparation. Pozzo, softened by the victory of the debut, allowed his boys to go out for a walk until the evening, at which time they had to return to their hotel. Meazza, however, didn't reappear until the following morning after spending the night with "two beautiful young French ladies," as the captain himself admitted. The debauchery did not surprise anyone. Meazza, who had a reputation as a Casanova, used to "rest" the night before Italian league games . . . in a brothel in Milan!

Thank God they were sick . . .

The day before its clash with Brazil, the best player of the Polish national team, Ernest Wilimowski, remained in bed due to a dental condition. Because the striker did not want to miss the match, he asked the French dentist who treated him not to extract the tooth—removal would have forced him to stay out two or three days over risk of bleeding. That same day, a doctor was called to the Brazilian camp: the great scorer Leônidas da Silva was suffering from a severe ear infection. The specialist recommended he stay in bed until game time. On June 5, in Strasbourg, Wilimowski and Leônidas forgot their conditions and staged one of the most intense clashes in the history of the World Cup: the Pole scored four goals (a world record at that time), and the Brazilian, three, in an electrifying duel that the South Americans won 6 to 5.

Wilimowski left the stadium disconsolate that his team lost despite his four markers. One of Leônidas's goals, meanwhile, remained in the gallery World Cup memories for having been scored "barefoot." The game was played in the middle of a strong storm that turned the playing field into a quagmire. In the middle of an attack, Leônidas lost his boot in the mud but he continued the play and ended up sending the ball into the net with his foot barely covered by a sock. This goal should have been annulled by the Swedish referee Ivan Eklind, but he did not realize the irregularity because the scorer's white sock was completely dark, stained with mud.

The injuries continued for Leônidas. In that tough match, he suffered a severe blow to the head when he collided with a goal post, and also suffered an eye infection caused by the lime used to mark the pitch. But nothing could stop the indomitable Leônidas, who scored a goal against Czechoslovakia in a 1-1 draw on June 12 in Bordeaux, and another on June 14, on the same stage, in the tie-breaker that the Brazilians won 2-1.

In Black

As already noted, Italy did not enjoy the sympathy of the fans, not least from Italian expats who had fled fascim. When Vittorio Pozzo's team faced France in the quarter-finals on June 12 in Paris, hundreds of Italians came to the stadium to support the local national team! The two squads had both wanted to take the field dressed in blue, their traditional color. The day before, Belgian referee Louis Baert summoned the two captains, Etienne Mattler and Giuseppe Meazza, to carry out the draw to decide which outfit would retain its tonality. Mattler won and Italy had to resort to an alternate jersey. They had two: a white one, which Italy would normally wear in these circumstances, and a black one, which had never been used. Before the jerseys were distributed, a team official made a call to Rome to consult Mussolini himself. The answer was conclusive: The Duce ordered the team to wear a black garment–evocative of the Camicie Nere militia, the violent arm of the Fascist Party. For the Italian dictator, France was a rival in sports but more so in politics. Dressed in black for the only time in its history, the Italian team won 3-1 and went on to the semi-finals.

You Can Break, but Never Give Up

Each Cup had its major battle, and 1938 was no exception. The quarter-final match between Brazil and Czechoslovakia was the most balanced of the contest. It was resolved after two games, the first of which was truly bloody. The Hungarian referee Pal Von Hertzka, in charge of that game at the Parc Lescure de Bordeaux, on June 12, had to send off three players—two South Americans and one European—something that had not happened so far in a World Cup. Zezé Procopio had to leave the field after kicking two rivals; Machado and Jan Riha, and later, after exchanging punches. Although their rival had suffered more expulsions, Czechoslovakia ended up with one less player, as their star forward Oldrich Nejedly—who scored a goal from the penalty spot that day—had to retire with a broken foot, while Josef Kostalek left the field after taking a strong blow to the abdomen.

One who remained strong despite everything was the great goal-keeper Frantisek Planicka, the best in the history of his country, who had suffered a fracture. Some versions of the story claim the radius bone of one of his forearms had been broken; others, a collarbone. Planicka was injured during the first ninety minutes and but stayed in during the half hour of extra time. The tie was not broken, despite the advantage of an extra man that Brazil had in overtime.

Two days later, at the same stadium but with refereeing by France's George Capdeville, the teams met again, with many sub-stitutes—Planicka, for example, was replaced by Karel Burket. This time, however, the twenty-two protagonists carried on with absolute sportsmanship. The Europeans opened the score through Vlastimil Kopeky, but the Brazilians recovered and finally won with a goal by Leônidas and another by Roberto.

Useless Health Concerns

It's not quite true, as a previous story said, that "nothing could stop" Leônidas. To be clear, that only referred to injuries. At the end of the tiebreaker with Czechoslovakia, Brazilian coach Ademar Pimenta decided not to include the magnificent striker for the semi-final against Italy, scheduled for the 16th in Marseille. "Leônidas is too tired. I'm saving him for the next Sunday, when we will play the final in Paris," the confident coach told to the reporters. Pimenta added that "it would be ridiculous not to admit that the game (against Italy) will be tough, but I have absolute faith in our triumph." The Brazilians took their victory over Italy for granted, to the point of booking air tickets to arrive the night of the semi-final to Paris so they could rest three days before the final on Sunday the 20th.

But without their great player, Brazil lost 2-1 and would be relegated to playing Sweden for third place. When the game ended, the euphoric Italian coach Vittorio Pozzo approached the box where the Brazilian delegates were, and fired: "I hope you do not cancel the trip and take advantage of the plane tickets to attend our final with the Hungarians." Pozzo almost started a new pitched battle!

Leônidas returned to the field on the 19th in Paris and scored another two goals against Sweden in a 4-2 victory. With eight goals, he was the top scorer in the third edition of the Cup.

Bad Elastic

In the 60th minute of the tough semi-final, with Italy winning 1-0 against Brazil, Swiss referee Hans Wuethrich whistled a penalty on the defending champions for a foul on Silvio Piola. The Azzurri captain, Giuseppe Meazza, stepped up for the shot, although his uniform was not in condition: the elastic that held his pants had broken in a struggle with an opponent. Without removing his left hand from the waist, to prevent his shorts from falling, Meazza adjusted the ball, took a run and launched a shot that slipped into the net, despite the effort of the Brazilian goalkeeper Walter. Elated by the goal, which left his team with one foot in the final, Meazza ran to the stand where the Italian fans were and, raising both hands to celebrate, was left in his boxer shorts. The captain was surrounded by his teammates until an assistant of coach Pozzo handed him another pair of pants, with which he continued playing until the end.

The Prize

Shortly before leaving Rio de Janeiro for Europe, a group of fans, convinced that their team would be champions, promised goalkeepers Algisto Lorenzato Domingos, nicknamed "Batatais", and Walter de Souza Goulart, "Walter", a generous cash award for each game that they recorded a shutout. For the debut match, in Strasbourg against Poland, coach Ademar Pimenta appointed Batatais. But after he conceded five goals—some of which seemed weak—for the second match, against Czechoslovakia, the coach decided to change the goalkeeper. On June 12, in Bordeaux, Walter had a brilliant performance, but could not keep his net clean: at 67 minutes, Oldrich Nejedly scored the draw that forced a tiebreaker and then an extra game. From there, always with Walter as the starter, Brazil defeated the Czechoslovakian squad 2 to 1, fell to Italy by the same score in the semi-final, and beat Sweden 4-2, for third place. Back home, Walter met with the fans and demanded the promised money, arguing that Nejedly's goal should not be taken into account, because it had been scored on a penalty kick. But the supporters, miffed that their team had returned without the cup, rejected the goalkeeper's argument, ingenious as it was.

A Distracted President

French President Albert Lebrun went to the Colombes Olympic Stadium outside Paris to witness the final between Italy and Hungary, although he knew nothing about soccer. Minutes before the game, FIFA President Jules Rimet invited Lebrun to do the honorary kick off. The premier accepted, but his ignorance of this sport, which he had never played, showed: Lebrun carefully aimed at the ball, but hit the ground instead, causing guffaws from the stands. The President repeated the movement with more care and this second time the ball did move, toward Italian Silvio Piola's feet. Soon after, taking his place in the box of honor, Lebrun realized that his national team was not on the field. "Where are the French?," he asked Rimet. Embarrassed, the FIFA leader pointed his index finger at referee George Capdeville. "There you have it," he said, "the referee is French."

A Celebrated Defeat

The Duce couldn't help meddling in this third edition of the World Cup. On the one hand, he contributed with state resources, such as a plane that flew the team three times between Marseille and Paris for games, so the footballers were more rested. On the other, Mussolini threatened, once again, the Italian players. Several historians claim that hours before the final match against Hungary, a telegram reached the Paris hotel where the team was resting. The message had 23 recipients (the 22 players and coach Pozzo) and, according to those chroniclers, only three words: "Vincere o morire," win or die. Thus, like four years earlier, the Azzurri squad would have played with death threats. As in Rome, it was crowned champion again, defeating its Magyar opponent 4-2.

Others question whether the Duce actually sent such an intimidation. Interviewed by *The Guardian*, defender Pietro Rava, who

The victorious Italians in 1938

played in the final in Paris, rejected the notion that they played in fear of eventual punishment: "No, no, no, that's not true. He sent a telegram wishing us success but never that." One version specified that the phrase "win or die" might have been in the message, not as a threat but because it was one of the many slogans of the National Fascist Party. But the Hungarian goalkeeper, Antal Szabo, insisted coercion was definitely at play. Evidently, Szabo had heard comments in the locker room or on the pitch. He told an interviewer years later: "Never in my life have I felt so happy after a defeat. I may have let in four goals, but at least I saved the lives of eleven men."

Violent Times

The Italian brilliance was reflected in *La Gazzetta dello Sport* as "the apotheosis of fascist sport in this victory of the race." According to Uruguayan writer Eduardo Galeano, the semi-final against Brazil awoke a much darker sentiment in the servile press: "We salute the triumph of Italian intelligence against the brute force of blacks."

On its return from France, the team, decked out in military garb, visited Mussolini at the Roman Palazzo Venezia, headquarters of the fascist government. Each player received a bonus of eight thousand lire (equivalent to about three months of salary) and a gold medal. After the meeting, the Duce and the footballers left through the main door towards Piazza Venezia, where they were celebrated by thousands of fans. In that same place, but a month earlier, another crowd had also cheered for Mussolini and a special guest from Berlin: Adolf Hitler. A year later, Germany would invade Poland and touch off the Second World War, with Italy as its main political and military partner. The World Cup, meanwhile, would be postponed for twelve years until the cannons cooled down and the smoke from the bombs dissipated.

Brazil 1950

"Those outside (the pitch) are made of wood." Never has this sentence meant so much value as in the final of Brazil 1950: two hundred thousand people overflowed the Maracanã stadium in Rio de Janeiro to witness the last game of the fourth World Cup, two hundred thousand souls who generated a climate never seen before (or after) to cheer for the home team. Brazil reached the culminating match with tremendous defeats over Spain and Sweden—6-1 and 7-1, respectively—while its opponent, Uruguay, had tied Spain and had achieved a meager 3-2 win over the Scandinavians. The strange system of the championship, with a final quadrangular tournament, gave many advantages to the home side: they would get all the glory with just a draw. As if all this were not enough, Brazil had in its ranks the great scorer of the tournament, Ademir, owner of eight goals in five matches.

On July 16, 1950, however, what would become known throughout the world as the "Charrúa courage" emerged stronger than ever. (The Charrua were the indigenous nomads who lived in what is now Uruguay.) The extraordinary Uruguayan victory, 2-1, is possibly the biggest upset that the final of a World Cup has brought about. And it opened the door so that in other editions—such as the next one, or the one in 1974—it would be proven again that the favorite is not always the one who lifts the trophy, and that the match is not decided until the 90th minute.

The fourth World Cup should have been held in 1942, in Germany, but the Second World War forced an interruption. With the return of peace, FIFA held its first congress on July 25, 1946 in Luxembourg. There, none of the delegates from European nations, in full reconstruction, offered to host the next championship, which had been set for 1949. Brazil, which before the pause had demanded that the tournament return to America, was acclaimed the winning host, and even granted a one-year extension to refurbish its existing stadiums and build a new one: the now historic Maracanã. The congress also bestowed a grand honour on the father of the World Cup, who had led FIFA for a quarter of a century: the gold trophy was renamed the "Jules Rimet Cup".

Requests for participation from Germany and Japan were rejected; however, at meetings before the start of the tournament, FIFA announced the two countries could play matches again with any entity of the international federation.

As for other colorful details, numbers appeared on players' shirts, anthems were only performed in the final round and the coach was allowed to be accompanied by a doctor and a masseur on the side of the playing field. Initially, FIFA decided English referees should receive the assistance of an interpreter, but this measure was reversed, according to FIFA, "so that (the referees) can continue their tasks clearly and without obstacles with explanations".

The Swiss Fredy Bickel and the Swedish Erik Nilsson, who had participated in the World Cup in France 1938, were the only players who returned after the war. Two other Swedes, Karl-Erik Palmer and Lennart Skoglund, were able to travel thanks to the fact that King Gustav V granted them licenses to fulfill compulsory military service. Alcides Ghiggia was the ace up the Uruguayan sleeve: He was the first footballer to score goals in all the matches his team played, including the final.

Maracanã

The Maracanã stadium in Rio de Janeiro is an architectural gem whose construction took almost two years, the labor of eleven thousand workers, half a million bags of cement and ten million kilograms of iron. The gigantic coliseum, which owes its name to the narrow stream that runs along one of its flanks, has fully covered stands and a playing field that boasts the maximum measurements allowed by FIFA: 110 meters by 75. The Maracanã was built especially for this World Cup (it was restored and modernized for the 2014 Brazil edition) and its inauguration came barely six days before the start of the competition. Eight of the tournament's 22 matches were played there, including the historic last game on July

The famed Maracanã stadium held astonishingly large crowds

16, which saw the largest number of tickets in World Cup history sold—175,000, according to the official record. It's estimated another 25,000 people—gatecrashers and guests—came to that game. Five days before the tournament kick-off, the Maracanã hosted its first game, a friendly between the teams of São Paulo and Rio de Janeiro. Admission was free and people were allowed to enter until it as full. The architects wanted to check, in this way, if the materials had set well. Fortunately, everything was in order.

Desertions

Three teams that had qualified for the Cup did not appear in Brazil. Scotland, second in the "British" group behind England, decided not to go. Portugal—a team that had lost to Spain in the qualifying series but was invited anyway—argued "technical problems" and also withdrew from the competition. The absence of India, who initially had to play with Sweden, Paraguay and Italy in Group 3, was much more original: The Asian team refused to attend because their players were forbidden to play with bare feet, as was the custom on the fields of Bombay and New Delhi. FIFA remained firm in its position, although some Indians did not wear footwear when they participated in the 1948 London Olympic Games. India played a single match in that event: on July 31, losing 2-1 to France.

The French initially had accepted an invitation–they had fallen to Yugoslavia in the European qualifying round—to take up an empty space. But their managers complained because in their assigned group—Group 4, with Uruguay, Bolivia and, initially, Portugal—they had to play a game on June 25 in Porto Alegre, in the south of the country, and another on June 29 in Recife, to the north. French delegates said it was unfair that their team had to cover 3,900 kilometers between the two matches, while other teams did not change venues or only moved a few kilometers. When the organizing committee refused to change the fixture, France said "au revoir." Despite the defections, the structure of the championship was not modified, so that Group 4 was left with only two contenders: Uruguay and Bolivia.

Paella

When Spain's coach, Guillermo Eizaguirre, summoned players to travel to South America, all accepted but one—Valencia CF midfielder Antonio Puchades Casanova. He imposed a *sine qua non* to getting on the plane: transporting his own food. What kind of food? Canned paella. "I ate paella every day. If one day I did not do it, my gut would get disorganized. So I argued a lot with the doctor, but he swallowed his pride. Because if not, I would not have been able to go," he said, years later. So it was: Puchades loaded dozens of cans of the traditional Valencian dish to see him through his stay. His gut well organized, he started in all six games played by Spain.

On Ship, not Planes

One of the great tragedies in soccer history took place on May 4, 1949. The plane carrying the players and the technical staff of the Italian club Torino crashed into a basilica in the town of Superga shortly before reaching the Piedmontese capital. The squad was returning from Lisbon, Portugal, where they had faced Benfica in a friendly match. The tragedy also hit the Italian national team hard: ten of their eleven starters played for the Turin team, which had won the last four leagues in a row.

To travel to Brazil to defend the 1938 title, coach Ferruccio Novo faced two problems: one, to assemble a new team practically from zero; another, the trip to South America, since, after what happened, the players had no intention of getting on a plane. Novo determined the Azzurri squad would travel by ship, the only delegation that arrived by that means in Brazil. Once at sea, the coach ran into another problem: In the first training session, all the balls ended up in the sea. Upon arriving several days later in Santos, the port-town of São Paulo, the Italian players were poorly trained and slightly overweight. In their debut, on June 25, Italy lost to Sweden 3-2 and were eliminated four days later when the Scandinavian team drew with Paraguay. Italy became the first defending champion to fail to clear the first round of the following competition.

Upon his return to Rome, Novo stoically accepted the harsh criticism that inevitably followed: "I am ready to respond about the process in the World Cup. I swear to tell the truth and nothing but the truth, I place myself in the hands of public opinion, let them judge me. It is true that I was wrong, but many others who are not infallible have also been wrong. I can only be attributed one error: that of not having insisted on taking the players by plane."

10-1

For the first time, England agreed to play a World Cup and travelled to Brazil with all of its great stars, including Alf Ramsey and Stanley Matthews. The English squad was led by the famous coach Walter Winterbottom, the first to be hired to lead an English national team— before that, a committee of the Football Association had determined the team and summoned the players by telegram. Until Brazil 1950, the inventors of soccer had only officially competed with Scotland, Wales and Ireland for the British championship, and played friendly games against other countries, almost always at their Empire Stadium in the London borough of Wembley.

In their debut, on June 25 at Maracanã, the English easily defeated Chile 2-0. Up against a weak team from the United States in Belo Horizonte, on June 29, Winterbottom reserved Matthews for the decisive clash with Spain still to come. The coach believed he had won the match before starting and his optimism seemed logical: the Americans had arrived in Brazil after losing two friendlies (5-0 to Turkey's Besiktas and 1-0 to an amateur team from, paradoxically, England) and in their debut they had fallen 3-1 with Spain. In the London betting houses, an American victory was paying 500 to one.

But that afternoon the English played badly. At 38 minutes, a 25-meter ball from Walter Bahr found the head of Joseph Edouard Gaetjens±—a Haitian who was not even a U.S. citizen—and the ball went past the outstretched English goalkeeper Bert Williams. Trailing, the English threw countless crosses into the rival area, but all were rejected by the strong American defense, or strong that day in any case. The minutes evaporated, until one of the greatest upsets in the history of world soccer crystallized. After the game was over, Italian referee Generoso Dattilo told a journalist that "if I hadn't refereed it myself, I would never have believed it." *The Times* of London said that "probably never before has an English team played so badly." A worthy representative of British cold blood, Winterbottom took the embarrassing fall calmly, at least in front of the international press: "The defeat, even if this is an incredible defeat, is a normal accident in any sporting contest."

The 0-1 score received via telex from the Reuters news agency surprised British newspapers: many asked for confirmation of the result, but others, pressed for the closure and almost hanged by the time difference, thought it was a typographic mistake, something quite common in those days, and they headlined, proudly, "England 10-United States 1."

Meanwhile, the sports editor of *The New York Times* chose not to publish the news and make a ball of paper with the cable: he thought it was a joke.

A Manager Under Siege

On June 25, the day after Brazil's debut at Maracanã (a 4-0 win over Mexico), the Brazilian coach, Flavio Costa, traveled to Belo Horizonte to see Yugoslavia-Switzerland, future opponents of his team. When the spectators noticed his presence in the stadium, they gave him a long whistle in protest for not having included a single player from the state of Minas Gerais on the national team. Three days later, in São Paulo, Costa was confronted by local supporters after the draw with Switzerland, 2-2, at the Pacaembú stadium. A group of fans approached him at the field's exit when he was getting ready to board the team bus. Several policemen intervened to prevent Costa from being beaten. In addition to the disappointing result, people in São Paulo had no love for Costa because he had played and coached in Rio de Janeiro.

The Papers

England had to beat Spain by at least two goals to qualify for the final round. The English squad had beaten Chile 2-0, but had been defeated by the United States 1-0, while the Iberian team had won their two games: 3-1 against the U.S. and 2-0 against the South Americans. To prepare, the English coach Walter Winterbottom gave each of his men a paper with complex instructions. And to make sure the players studied his written orders, he forced them to repeat them out loud in front of him and sign a document declaring that they had read them. It didn't work: on July 2, in Maracanã, Spain won by 1-0 on a goal Telmo Zarraonandía, a Basque known as "Zarra." The English had to return home humiliated in their first World Cup appearance.

Poison

The Yugoslav team had shown an excellent level of play in its first two appearances, beating Switzerland 3-0 and Mexico 4-1. Upon arriving in Rio de Janeiro for the defining match of Group 1 against Brazil, the Balkan delegation decided not to eat at the hotel but at the Yugoslav embassy. The Europeans feared that, as the local squad desperately needed a win to qualify for the final group—Brazil had beaten Mexico but tied with Switzerland—they suffer food poisoning from their hotel kitchen.

After so much nutritional care, Yugoslavia faced Brazil on July 1. As the teams prepared to take to the Maracanã playing field, Balkan player Zeljko Cajkovaski slipped on his boots and hit his head against the iron frame of one of the tunnel's sliding doors. The blow gave Cajkovaski sent blood gushing from a deep cut on the forehead, and he had to return to the locker room to have four stitches applied. As the rules did not yet allow for changes and the official form was already signed with the wounded player among the eleven starters, Yugoslavia had to begin with ten men. Welsh referee Benjamin Griffiths refused to postpone the start because, according to the tournament regulations, "any team that delays the start of matches by more than one minute will be disqualified." At 15 minutes into the first half, Cajkovaski joined his team with his head bandaged. But Brazil had already used that quarter of an hour to its advantage, with a goal from Ademir after four minutes. Even with eleven, Yugoslavia could not equalize the score: at 65 minutes in, Brazil sealed its victory with a goal from Zizinho after a sudden counterattack from a Yugoslav squad fighting for the tie.

Do you think you invented that?

On the afternoon of Saturday, July 1, the Bolivian players held a light practice at the Parque Independencia stadium in Belo Horizonte, where the next day they would face the Uruguayans. The Andean footballers practiced crosses, corners and all kinds of shots on goal, with great precision and good control of the ball. Around four in the afternoon, the Uruguayan delegation arrived to survey the pitch and get their muscles moving. Noticing the presence of their rivals, the Bolivians purposely began to miss their passes and deliberately deflect their shots, faking a lower level of ability. Perhaps they believed themselves to be very original in this kind of ruse; they were surely unaware that their future adversaries had been the first to use it in the 1924 Olympic Games, before their opening match against Yugoslavia, which they won 7-0. But, unlike what happened in France twenty-six years earlier, it didn't work for the Bolivians. Uruguay had no difficulty, or mercy, and prevailed by 8-0.

Mexico from Porto Alegre

On July 2, when the national teams of Mexico and Switzerland came out onto the pitch at Estádio dos Eucaliptos—the former home of Sport Club Internacional, the popular Inter de Porto Alegre—Swedish referee Ivan Eklind thought something was wrong. In his opinion, the uniforms of the two teams were very similar: one dark red, the other cherry or maroon. Eklind summoned the captains, Horacio Casarín and Roger Bocquet, and asked for their help to solve the problem. The footballers could do little, because neither of the two squads had an alternative set of shirts to resolve the color problem. The referee then called a FIFA delegate who had the idea to borrow jerseys from a leader of the local club Esporte Clube Cruzeiro, who had just played a friendly match with another "red" team: Internacional. With the problem solved, the Swedish judge flipped a coin to determine which of the two would change their outfit. Mexico won the toss, but the chivalrous Casarín offered his Swiss colleague to choose whether he preferred to keep his uniform or wear blue and white. Noticing that the loaner clothes were soaked with sweat, Bocquet chose to keep the red shirt and ran to tell his colleagues that he had just saved them from an unpleasant incident. The Mexicans, on the other hand, stoically donned their dirty shirts—more than one with a muttered insult to their gracious captain. Although luck was again with the Swiss, who won 2-1, the gentle Casarín had his prize: he scored the goal of honor in the 89th minute.

Fireworks

The use of fireworks was a novelty at this World Cup. Foreign players and journalists were left speechless every time the local team took to the field: thousands of powerful firecrackers, bright flares and sparkling flying canes soared through the sky. It lent color to the spectacle, but also injured a lot of people in the stands. The Rio newspaper *A Noite* noted that "the explosions occur on the playing field at the most unexpected moment. There were many injuries and burns, some serious, during the opening match" between Brazil and Mexico. The players weren't safe either. On July 13, when striker Chico came out onto the Maracanã grass with his teammates to face Spain, a firecracker exploded a few inches from one of his legs. He had to be treated for several minutes before the start of the match. Fortunately for him, not only did the burn not impede his performance, it even seemed to give him a bit a spark Chico scored two of the six goals for his team and was one of the great heroes of the afternoon.

Oranges

For the final round matches, the management of the Maracanã Municipal Stadium made a "special" request to the Rio de Janeiro police: to prohibit the sale of oranges inside and around the coliseum. Newspapers reported the request was due to the complaints of several teams that were victims of "bombings, which in past matches were sometimes violent." A Uruguayan newspaper noted that the 1,400 agents in charge of maintaining order and security during the meetings were entrusted with exercising "special vigilance" to prevent the marketing of "dangerous" citrus fruits.

Whisky

On the night of Uruguay's triumph over Sweden, on July 13 at the Pacaembú in San Pablo, the winners were invited to a farewell party organized by local officials. As soon as the players arrived, an army of waiters entered the room with trays loaded with glasses of whisky, the Scottish tipple highly appreciated in the Uruguayan nation. Seeing the waiters come and go so often, and his teammates raising their elbows more than necessary, Captain Obdulio Varela quickly sniffed out the real goal of such generosity: Weaken the footballers, who a couple of days later had to play the final in Rio de Janeiro. Varela, smart and quick, stood in the middle of the room and, with his eyes fixed on the hosts, yelled: "Gentlemen: either the whisky is finished, or we will return to Montevideo." The party continued very well watered, but with sweet sodas and tasty fruit juices.

Maracanazo

Uruguay had to win to take the title—a draw would give it to Brazil—and things did not look good. Brazil had a dizzying scoring rhythm—they'd thumped Spain 6-1 and Sweden 7-1—and shortly before the Cup began they'd beaten Uruguay 3-2 in a preparatory friendly also played in Rio, on the Vasco da Gama field. While the Uruguayans were changing in the Maracaná locker room, a team official approached, brought them together and said: "Boys, don't make too much trouble. Just try not to recieve six goals. With four we are fulfilled." These defeatist words spurred the visitors' spirits and aroused a voracious appetite for triumph, both against the rival on the pitch and against internal enemies. In the tunnel, Captain Obdulio Varela gathered his companions and with his booming voice harangued them: "Those people outside are made of wood. We'll only be fulfilled if we are champions." The cunning Varela sent his team out onto the field at the same time as Brazil did, to prevent his teammates from feeling intimidated by what would have been a thunderous whistle. Some Uruguayan media, to emphasise the tranquility of their men in the face of the important duel, highlighted that defender Schubert Gambetta took a nap in the changing room of the gigantic stadium minuts before the final.

After a goalless first half, the local team opened the scoring two minutes into the second half through Albino Friaça Cardoso. Uruguay was not daunted and, with good play and better self-esteem, they turned the score around with Juan Schiaffino, at 66 minutes, and Alcides Ghiggia, at 79. The second Charrúa goal silenced Maracanã. Two hundred thousand "statues" could not believe what they saw. "It was the first time in my life that I heard something that was not noise. I felt the silence," Schiaffino later described. Mortally wounded, the Brazilian players tried by all means to approach goalkeeper Roque Máspoli, but the Uruguayan firmness caused their ideas to be diluted with every minute that passed, until the final whistle from English referee George Reader. The only sound in the stands were tears hitting the ground.

Back in Montevideo, the Uruguayan leaders sent silver medals to be given to the soccer players and gold for themselves. This distinction made the heroes nauseous. "If we had known, we were losing on purpose," said Varela. "I threw it out," added the scorer Ghiggia.

Rimet

When Jules Rimet left his seat in the official box to head down to the field for the closing ceremony, the game was not yet over: it was tied at one. So convinced Brazil would be champion, Rimet had practiced the final speech in only one language: Portuguese. By the time he reach the edge of the pitch, things had changed. Uruguay had won again. Among the celebrating players, Rimet discovered the Uruguayan captain Obdulio Varela and presented him with the trophy. Not a word came out: he just shook his hand.

A Heart Attack Match

The outcome between Brazil and Uruguay was literally a "heart attack match." In Uruguay, eight people died from heart attacks caused by the high intensity of the game: five during the match and three after the final whistle. Meanwhile, the doctors at the Maracanã stadium reported that 169 people with coronary problems, blood pressure, outbreaks of hysteria and fainting had to be treated. Six were referred to a nearby hospital in serious condition. That sad night, according to the police chronicles, there were a hundred suicides throughout the country. One who was on the verge of taking his life was the Brazilian forward Danilo, overwhelmed by defeat.

Never to Return

The talented musician Ary Barroso had been hired by a radio station in Rio de Janeiro to broadcast Brazil's World Cup matches. On July 16, with Maracanã bursting, Barroso got ready to lend the final the brilliance of his voice and his talent for improvisation. When the Brazilian Friaça scored the opening goal, the announcer exploded into shouts of joy. Uruguayan Juan Schiaffino lowered the decibels

Uruguay shocked Brazil in the 1950 final

with a tying goal, and when Alcides Ghiggia scored the winner, silence took hold. Barroso got up and with a laconic "I'm going to have a coffee" left the press box . . . and never returned. "It was so much disappointment that I could not continue," he said years later. So traumatized was the musician that he never called a soccer match again.

Woman

After the loss, the Brazilian players took refuge in the dressing room, and later left amid tight security. The team's coach, Flavio Costa, was left in the dressing room, convinced that he would be killed as soon as he set foot outside Maracanã. Costa was locked in for two days and only agreed to leave the coliseum when a relative gave him a very particular costume. Almost 48 hours after the final whistle, the losing manager escaped from captivity dressed as a woman.

Bad Luck

Goalkeeper Moacir Barbosa, who wore number one, never managed to overcome the "Maracanazo." Once an idol, he became the most hated man in the country. Although he continued his career until 1962, winning two local championships with Vasco da Gama, he ended his days abandoned in a miserable boarding house. In the 1980s, when the Maracanã was remodeled, the new administration gave Barbosa the old wooden goal where he had received the two fatal Uruguayan hits. The keeper cut the posts and lit a fire with them and prepared a sumptuous barbecue to invite the few friends he had left. When, in 1993, he tried to visit the players preparing for the United States World Cup, a director of the Brazilian confederation ordered the guards: "Take this man away, he only brings bad luck." He even spent some years in exile. Until the day of his death, April 8, 2000, Barbosa tirelessly repeated: "In my country, the highest penalty for committing a crime is 30 years. I have paid for a crime that I did not commit for 50 years."

The national jersey carried the stigma of defeat as well. Since 1919, the Brazilian squad had been dressed entirely in white, sometimes with bright blue colors on the cuffs and neck. After the "Maracanazo," the federation decided to change the colors of the team to attract luck and twist fate. It held a contest in 1953, with the only stipulation that the new look must include the four colors of the national flag: yellow, green, blue and white. Three hundred proposals were sent in, among which was the winner, that of Aldyr García Schlee, a 19-year-old boy who worked as a journalist for a newspaper in the state of Rio Grande do Sul, bordering Uruguay. The young man confessed the contest was not easy: "Up to three colors, all good, but with four it became really difficult, because the four colors of the flag together do not combine. I did more than a hundred designs, but nothing worked, until I came to the conclusion that the shirt had to be all yellow, with bright green" on the neck and sleeves, he explained years later. García Schlee added blue pants and white socks, and the new uniform was unveiled on March 14, 1954 at Maracanã, with a 1-0 Brazil victory over Chile. Although Brazil did not achieve the success it longed for in the following World Cup, Switzerland '54, the "verdeamarela" jersey remains the most famous in the world (and the term is a common moniker for the team).

Several years later, in an interview, the successful designer surprised everyone. Having grown up a few meters from the southern border of his country, he said, he was a fan of Uruguay, and had celebrated the "Maracanazo" after listening to the final on the radio. The beloved standard of Brazil turned out to be the product of the "Charrúa courage."

Switzerland 1954

Switzerland 1954 was the World Cup in which a legend began. Until then, the German team—which was barred from Brazil in the wake of the Second World War—had always been second-rate in Europe. For the sixth edition of the Cup, it was not even considered as a seed (or head) in the group draw, but would go on to win the final against Hungary, the best squad of that time and one to whom they had fallen 8- 3 in the first phase.

There were some who distrusted the German uprising and suspected the use of stimulants. It is said that hours after the final, the players developed strange spots and welts which were officially attributed to a spoiled meal served at the hotel. In any case, Germany—*West* Germany at the time—started a prestigious soccer campaign in Switzerland and has participated in every World Cup since, with four titles and four second-place finishes.

The final match against Hungary was a true milestone: if Uruguay surprised the world with the "Maracanazo," Germany impressed the world by defeating the Helsinki 1952 Olympic champions, owner of an unbeaten streak of 31 games: 27 won and four tied. In addition, the Magyars, led by the great Ferenc Puskás—who had changed his original surname, Purcsfeld, to Puskás, which means "rifleman"—had recently embarrassed England twice—6 to 3 at Wembley and 7 to 1 in Budapest—and reached the defining match with the chilling mark of 25 goals in four games played in the tournament. A curiosity: The Hungarian team had a 2-0 lead in every match they played, including the final they lost. The German team showed that you can never give up until the referee whistles the end of the game. In Switzerland, the best was not the best. It would not be the last time.

For this fifth tournament, FIFA determined that four zones of four teams would be set up and that the two top seeds of each one would face the other two teams in the group, but not each other, so that the supposedly stronger countries would only cross in the quarter-finals. The strange system provided more problems than solutions: several tiebreakers had to be played and three of the eight seeded teams were out in the first round.

A ridiculous detail had to do with the match for third place: if Uruguay and Austria had equalized, the two would have both been considered third. Another inconsistency: In the first round, if a match ended evenly, thirty minutes of overtime had to be played. But if the score remained balanced at the end of overtime, it was considered tied. One of those who complained loudly was organization the president of the Scottish club Celtic, Bob Kelly, who upon returning to his country said that "the organization was chaotic and the behavior of the players, hopeless." Kelly said that he would not allow his club's players to play in a Cup again. Scotland had lost 1-0 to Austria and 7-1 to Uruguay.

This World Cup was one of the highest scoring in history, with 5.38 goals per game, and also featured the match with the most goals: Austria 7-Switzerland 5.

The Germany/Hungary final was the first brothers would lift the Cup together: the Germans Fritz and Ottmar Walter (they would later be equaled by Bobby and Jack Charlton in 1966). Fritz Walter's participation may well be considered miraculous. The forward, captain of the victorious German squad, had been a soldier during World War II. Captured by Soviet forces, he was sent to a concentration camp near the Romanian city of Sighetu Marmației. There, despite contracting malaria, he participated in impromptu soccer matches alongside Hungarian and Slovak guards. When the Soviet army ordered captive enemies to be transferred to a forced labor camp in Siberia, Walter was saved by a sentry who had recognized him for having watched him play in a friendly match between Hungary and Germany. The guardian lied to his superiors that Walter was Austrian, which allowed the footballer to be saved from deportation and an almost certain death from disease, hunger, and cold.

Switzerland 1954 also marked the birth of a relationship that has strengthened every day since then: soccer and television. A broadcaster operating in eight European countries agreed with FIFA to televise nine games, including the opening match and the final. It was a relatively small step for the Cup organizers, but a giant leap for their future business endeavors.

Itlay played Egypt in a World Cup qualifying match.

Germany vs Germany

In the qualifying round, Germany had to face Germany. Rather, the Federal Republic of Germany (FRG), established at the end of World War II, fought against Saar, a Germanic region neighboring France, which the French controlled at the request of the United Nations until 1957. The FRG won both qualifying games easily: 3-0 at home and 3-1 away. In that group, there was another team: Norway. What a mess it would have been if, instead of the Scandinavian nation, the "third" Germany, the German Democratic Republic, had been designated for that qualifying group stage!

By the Hand of a Child

During the European qualifying stage for the World Cup, Spain and Turkey faced each other, which on paper suggested a simple victory for Spain. In the first leg, played in Madrid, the locals won 4 to 1 with a brilliant performance by the Hungarian László Kubala, who had been nationalized and was wearing the Iberian uniform at the time. But in the rematch, held in Istanbul, an indifferent performance by the referee helped the Turks to a 1-0 win. A tiebreaker was scheduled at the Olympic stadium in Rome. It seemed that, in neutral territory, the Spaniards would end the nightmare. However, a few minutes before the start of the third match, a telegram signed by FIFA arrived to prohibit the inclusion of the Magyar footballer on the field, since his signing had not been processed in a regular way. Kubala was already changed and about to go out with his teammates. The Spanish played under protest and, despite dominating the action, were tied at two as regulation time expired.

With the score unchanged after an additional thirty minutes, a hand-picked draw was used, as per the regulation at the time, to decide which of the two teams qualified for the tournament.

Two slips with the names of the two nations were placed in a hat and a boy named Franco Gemma was asked to take one. He drew out Turkey, so Spain was left out despite being the superior team. Amazed by the stroke of luck, the Turks invited young Franco to travel to Switzerland as their charm, but the boy's aura was not enough to prevent elimination in the first round.

Black Showers

Days before the opening of the Cup, FIFA drew up a list of directives that it delivered to all the referees. Compliance was mandatory. The six provisions were as follows:

1) Take a cold shower in the morning, before anything else when you get up, and another before going to bed.
2) Do the jumping rope exercise for fifteen minutes daily.
3) Do not drink alcoholic beverages of any kind on the day of a match under your charge, whether you are participating as a linesman.
4) Run two thousand meters every other day, and take a cold shower after that exercise.
5) Go to bed early on the eve of a match under your charge.
6) In the event of the death of the referee during the course of a match, it will be immediately terminated.

Some of these orders are merely curious, others outlandish. Fortunately, none of the referees was forced to comply with the last one.

Old Men

The average age of the Korean players was 31, one of the highest in the history of the Cup. This was due to Korean War—between 1950 and 1953, more than a million people died in the conflict and, at the time of the World Cup, the majority of young people between 21 and 23 years old were fulfilling their compulsory military service. As well, there was a great need for manpower across the country to repair or replace destroyed buildings. The twenty footballers who traveled to Switzerland were military personnel or civilian employees of the armed forces. Goalkeeper Hong Duk Yung was 33 years old; defender Min Byung Dae, 38; midfielder Chung Nam Sick, 37; former prisoner of war forward Choi Jung Mih, 32. Goalkeeper Yung was particularly outmatched: he gave up 16 goals in just two games, something never surpassed in a World Cup. On June 17, in Zurich, Korea lost 9-0 to Hungary, and three days later, in Geneva, 7-0 to Turkey.

A hot mess

Scotland's World Cup debut was a disaster. While this team has never made it past the first round in any of its eight World Cups appearances, the performance in Switzerland was hot, and not in any fashionable sense of the word. Due to ineptitude or ignorance, the Scottish Football Association sent its players in long-sleeved shirts made of thick wool to play games in a Swiss summer that had temperatures of almost 40 degrees Celsius. Warmly bundled up, they fell 1-0 to Austria on June 16, and three days later, when the mercury reaching 37 degrees Celsius at the Saint Jakob Stadium in Basel, they were crushed 7-0 by Uruguay. Defender Tommy Docherty was cutting when he explained the shameful defeat: "The Scottish Federation assumed that Switzerland is always cold because there are mountains. I think they thought we were going on an expedition to Antarctica". The South American team, which that day wore light short-sleeved T-shirts with a "v" neckline, scored two goals in the first half and another five in the second, when their rivals had already melted.

Reversed Decision

Italy and Switzerland starred in a very heated duel in Lausanne, on June 17, at the opening of Group 4 that they shared with England and Belgium. Shortly into the second half, with the score tied at one, visiting striker Benito Lorenzi—nicknamed "Poison" for his bad character—hit the Swiss defender Roger Bocquet violently. Brazilian referee Mario Viana ordered Lorenzi off the pitch. But the angry forward, instead of leaving the field of play, began to demand the referee to reverse the measure, and in a very bad way. Soon, Lorenzi was joined by several of his companions, who surrounded Viana. With slaps, shoves and threats, the Italians managed to get the Brazilian to cancel the punishment.

The game continued eleven against eleven and at 78 minutes the Swiss managed to break through with a goal from Sepp Huegi. At the final whistle, the Italians again besieged the referee, whom they accused of having favored the Swiss. Lorenzi, disconcerted, kicked the judge in the buttocks. Viana was finally rescued by the police, but he never reported the aggression of the Azzurri forward. FIFA did not act ex officio either, despite the fact that the attack was seen from the stands and on television. Lorenzi was not suspended and was a member of the Italian team that, in its next game, defeated Belgium 4-1. As Switzerland and Italy finished the round with the same number of points, they had to face each other again, in Basel, to decide which squad would go to the quarter-finals. Even with Lorenzi back on the field, the Swiss prevailed 4-1.

Sorry, Rimet, you're not allowed

The receptionist at the Hardturm Stadium in Zurich cared little what the old man with the white mustache said: he did not have any credentials to prove that he was Jules Rimet. The honorary president of FIFA, father of the competition and namesake of the trophy, tried to explain to the blonde girl that his documents had been left at the hotel. But the young woman stood firm: "Nein". Rimet waited patiently until a manager from the local organization recognized him and granted him access to the stands to watch the game between Germany and Turkey.

Fair Play

The Hungarian players were very concerned about having to face South Korea on June 17 in Zurich. It was not about sports, but politics. The Magyars believed the Koreans would act rudely and set out to injure them for belonging to a communist country (Hungary was then behind the Iron Curtain). But the game, which Hungary won 9-0, was one of the cleanest in history: only five fouls were blown by the referee's whistle.

Bicycle

A German woman pedaled her bicycle the 300 kilometers from her home to Basel to witness the clash against Hungary on June 20. Upon reaching the stadium, the woman took one of the seats, but fainted seconds before kickoff due to exertion. Upon regaining consciousness, the exhausted cyclist refused to go to a hospital and remained in the stands until the end. She might have received better treatment from the doctors than her compatriots got from the Hungarian players, who showed no mercy in beating the Germany 8-3.

84

A Great Game

On June 26, in Lausanne, Austria and Switzerland staged, in the quarter-finals, one of the best matches in the history of the World Cup, and the one with the most goals. Just 19 minutes in, the local squad was already 3-0 up, thanks to a goal from Robert Ballaman and two from Sepp Huegi. Austria stormed back with five consecutive goals but before the first half was over, Ballaman scored again to narrow the lead. Although it was intensely hot, the action did not decline in the second half. Austria's Theodor Wagner struck again to make 6-4, and five minutes later Huegi reduced the gap again. Finally, Erich Probst, at 76 minutes, scored the last away goal. The high temperature and the intensity of the action led the Austrian goalkeeper, Kurt Schmied, to cling to one of the goalposts so he wouldn't collapse. Scottish referee Charles Faultless was beaten by an angry young fan as he was leaving the stadium, despite a performance that was worthy of his name. Swiss spectators accused him of having favored the Austrians, but the referee was rescued from the fans by two Swiss soccer delegates, who accompanied him to his hotel.

Masterstroke

During the electrifying duel between Switzerland and Austria, the Swiss team captain, defender Roger Bocquet, received an elbow to the head that knocked him out for a few minutes. Bocquet came to his senses and continued playing, although he was said to be very dizzy and even speaking incoherently to his teammates. After the game, Bocquet was checked by a doctor who carried out some tests and discovered that the defender had a brain tumor that, if not removed immediately, could cause death in a few months. The soccer player underwent a successful operation and, although he did not wear the Swiss jersey again, he lived forty more years: he died in 1994, at the age of 73.

Roger Bocquet leads the Swiss team onto the pitch.

Pitched Battle

On June 27, Hungary and Brazil played a match so violent it was baptized "the Battle of Bern". The Hungarians, even without the great Ferenc Puskás, who injured a tendon in the first round clash with Germany, prevailed 4-2 in a match that had fragments of good soccer, but also of strong leg. English referee Arthur Ellis sent off Brazilian Nilton Santos and Hungarian József Bozsik in the 71st minute for hitting each other. Five minutes later, Ellis also sent South American striker Humberto to the locker room, for delivering a punch to rival defender Gyula Lóránt. At the end of the match, the Brazilians surrounded the referee to vehemently claim that in the penalty Mihály Lantos had converted there had been no previous foul, and that the fourth Hungarian goal had been offside.

Meanwhile, Mauro Rafael, nicknamed "Maurinho", approached Zoltán Czibor and extended his hand as a sign of friendship. When Czibor shook his right hand, Maurinho hit his jaw with a punch with his left. That unleashed a full-on brawl, in which players, substitutes and coaching staff from both teams participated. In the midst of flying kicks and punches, Puskás came onto the field and threw a bottle that hit the face of midfielder Joao Baptista Pinheiro. The Brazilian, with his face covered in blood, was helped away by a teammate. Two policemen who tried to separate the contestants were also injured. On the other side of the lime line, Brazil coach Zezé Moreira threw a boot at his Magyar colleague Gustáv Sebes. The shoe cut through Sebes' forehead; he would need stitches.

Once calm returned, FIFA analyzed what happened and decided that there would be no suspensions for anyone, despite having admonished the two delegations for their "unsportsmanlike behavior". The expelled Bozsik would have had a one game of suspension, at least, according to the regulations of the time, and Puskás would have faced even greater punishment. But, according to the organizers, tougher sanctions for all those expelled and for all participants of the brawl "would only harm Hungary for its meeting with Uruguay," in the semi-finals. Brazil was already eliminated. FIFA, like the Roman governor Pontius Pilate in biblical times, washed its hands of the matter, and left the punishments "in charge of the two national associations, with the order to inform the world federation as soon as possible about the measures adopted." Of course, neither Hungary nor Brazil raised a finger against their players.

The case unleashed the anger of the Uruguayans, Hungary's next opponent, who launched a complaint to FIFA over a ruling it said demonstrated "an attitude completely at odds with the standards of sport." The organization rejected the protest and Bozsik faced the Uruguayans. With this advantage, Hungary won 4-2.

The End of an Undefeated Series

Hungary's victory over Uruguay in the June 30 semi-final in Lausanne snapped an impressive 21-game unbeaten streak for the South American team in international tournaments. It had begun at the 1924 Olympic Games in Paris, where Uruguay won all their games. Four years later, at the Olympic Games in Amsterdam 1928, they tied in the first final against Argentina, and won the tiebreaker 2-1. In the first World Cup, held at home in 1930, Uruguay beat Peru 1-0, Romania 4-0, Yugoslavia 6-1 and Argentina 4-2. As it did not play in either Italy 1934 or France 1938, the next stop was Brazil 1950 where they again won all their games. In Switzerland, Uruguay started 2-0 against Czechoslovakia, followed by Scotland 7-0 and England 4-2. Hungary finally ended the streak, but it was a close-run thing, since the game was tied at two after ninety minutes. In extra time, two goals by Sándor Kocsis rounded off the Magyar victory and ended the remarkable Uruguayan run.

Can Dead Men Score Goals?

Something extraordinary happened in the semi-final in Lausanne: the Uruguayan Juan Hohberg went into cardiac arrest. Hohberg, who was born in Argentina and started his playing career as a goalkeeper, was making his debut for Uruguay that day, and scored twice to draw Uruguay level with Hungary. When the striker bagged his second, his teammates piled on top of him and in the excitement of the celebrations, he suffered a heart attack. He was brought round by physiologist Carlos Abate, who administered Coramine, a respiratory stimulant. He was still receiving treatment when extra-time started, but shortly returned to the field and played out the rest of the match.

A Champion Shoemaker

Adolf "Adi" Dassler worked hard for the German team. Dassler was a shoemaker who together with his brother Rudolf had opened a sports shoe workshop in the 1920s in the Bavarian city of Herzogenaurach. After the Second World War, the brothers separated: Adi founded Adidas; Rudi, Puma. For Switzerland in 1954, Adolf, who supplied footwear to the German national team, prepared an innovative design with a sole that allowed the cleats to be exchanged, attentive to the heavy rains that usually accompany the Helvetic summer. The final of the championship, played on July 4 in Bern, started with a light drizzle. With the fast pitch, the Hungarians went 2-0 in just eight minutes, but Germany did not give up, and managed to draw even before the end of the first half. At halftime, torrential rain turned the field at Wankdorf Stadium into a swamp. German coach Sepp Herberger ordered his men to change out their cleats for longer ones. With the help of Adi's innovation, the German squad scored the third goal at 84 minutes, after the Hungarian goalkeeper, Gyula Grosics, slipped on the wet grass. Germany defeated the invincible Hungary and won their first Cup, and Adi Dassler proved that the shoemaker plays too.

Goalscorer Telegram

Despite their victorious 4-1 debut against Turkey on June 17, German coach Sepp Herberger felt dissatisfied with his team's offense. Herberger believed he should add power to the attack, so he sent a telegram to Helmut Rahn, an effective gunner for the Rot-Weiss Essen club who, at the time, was in Montevideo, in the middle of a tour of South America. "Report urgently to Switzerland on the first plane," said the urgent message. Rahn got on a plane for Europe, via Brazil, and arrived in Basel after a two-day trip with numerous stops. Despite the exhausting journey, the player took to the field for the second game, against the powerful Hungarian squad. The clash was catastrophic for the Germans—they lost 8-3—the coach was very satisfied with Rahn's performance. He scored that day and again in the quarter-finals, against Yugoslavia. In the final, the great rematch against Hungary, Rahn scored twice, giving Germany the victory and catapulting him into the ranks of national heroes.

Celebrations

The World Cup victory caused great euphoria throughout Germany. When the train that transported the champion team from Bern to Munich crossed the Swiss-German border, 6,000 fans overflowed the railway station at Jestetten, the first town on the German side.

West Germany (white) outduels Hungary in the high-scoring 1954 World Cup

The fervent fans—who with singular decency had paid for tickets to access the platform—threw themselves onto the tracks to stop the train and greet their heroes. In Munich, on July 6, the champions were received in the main square by more than half a million people. For that day, on the recommendation of the local mayor, a general holiday was decreed in factories, banks and government offices. There were also no classes in schools or colleges. The team drove through the city streets in fifteen cars. The authorities assured the press that "the enthusiasm that reigns today far exceeds that of the concentrations of the time of (Adolf) Hitler, when Munich was the capital of the Nazi party."

Among the Hungarian players, frustration reigned. The socialist government in Budapest had promised an all-expenses paid holiday in Switzerland for the footballers and their wives if they won. In fact, the spouses and girlfriends had already packed their bags and were preparing to travel to join their partners. The thump fell like a bucket of cold water. The "holidays" came two years later, when the 1956 rebellion and the consequent Soviet repression took place: All the members of that wonderful Hungarian team went into exile in Spain, Germany and other countries far from the communist regime.

Sweden 1958

Sweden 1958 was most notable as the first time Brazil won the World Cup. Eight years after the humiliating "Maracanazo," the South American squad began to weave its history as the best team on the planet. Twelve years later, they become the first three-time champion. The just and deserved victory of Brazil in Europe was an extraordinary success for its time, and until the end of the Russian 2018 tournament, the squad was the only one to have lifted the Cup twice outside its region. This argument was used numerous times by the South American Football Confederation (CONMEBOL) when defending the (current) four and a half places given to a continent with only ten competing countries. Is it a fair assignment? If you look at the statistics, probably. Until the 2006 edition inclusive, South America had won nine championships (five from Brazil, two from Uruguay and two from Argentina) against nine from countries on the other side of the Atlantic (four from Italy, three from Germany, one from England and France). European teams were always the majority to the detriment of the representatives from other parts of the world, especially Africa and Asia.

Currently the distribution has been balanced somewhat, although the teams of the "Old Continent" still take possession of no less than

The teenaged Pelé in action against Sweden.

13 of the 32 World Cup seats. Europe has also had another advantage: of the first twenty-one World Cups, eleven were played in its domains, against only eight in the Americas. Another detail: in Brazil 2014, the Cup returned to South America after 36 years!

Joining the gallery of legends in Sweden was a 17-year-old who, for many people, was the greatest footballer of all time: Edson Arantes do Nascimento, the "King Pelé." In addition to his talent and exquisite flair, Pelé is remembered for two World Cup records: he is the only player to win three Cups and he is the youngest ever to score. He was 17 years and 239 days old on June 19, 1958, when he destroyed the Welsh net.

In this edition, gloves became popular among goalkeepers, led by the hands of the Soviet star Lev Yashin, known as "the black spider" (or "the black panther") for always wearing black jerseys, pants and socks. On June 11, Brazil and England played in the first match without goals, in the sixth edition of the Cup and after 115 games. FIFA also implemented a new competition system, the fifth: Four zones of four teams each, in which the first two qualified for the quarter-finals. From there, a direct elimination table was followed.

Another great achievement was French striker Just Fontaine scoring 13 goals in a single tournament, a record that was not equaled until the end of the 2018 World Cup in Russia. Fontaine—who had traveled as a substitute and joined the team because of a severe sprain suffered by the starting center-forward, Raymond Blair—inscribed his name on the score sheets of the six games played by the French team—including a four-goal performance against Germany. At the end of the championship, a Swedish newspaper gave Fontaine a rifle as a reward for being the top "gunner".

British Poker

Sweden 1958 was the only time the four British associations— England, Scotland, Wales and Northern Ireland—qualified to play the Cup. Three of them (England, Scotland and Northern Ireland) did so after winning their respective European groups. The Welsh needed to add a dose of luck to their soccer. It happened that in the qualifying zone for Asia and Africa (Turkey and Cyprus had joined), Israel went through rounds without playing because different rivals refused to face it on political grounds: first Turkey, then Indonesia and finally Sudan. Because the rules stated that, except for the host nation and the last champion, no team could qualify without having played at least one game prior to the tournament, FIFA determined that the Israelis would face a European squad, selected by a draw. Fate favoured Wales, who arrived in Stockholm thanks to two wins over Israel: on January 15, 1958, in Tel Aviv, and then, on February 5, in Cardiff.

Nebulous Failure

Only three times did Italy not compete in the final phase of the World Cup: in Uruguay 1930, the team decided to not travel to South America; the second occasion was Sweden 1958, because for the first time in its history Italy stumbled in the qualifying round (the same would happen for Russia 2018). The Azzurri squad shared their zone with Northern Ireland and Portugal and reached the last game, scheduled for December 4, 1957 in Belfast. They only needed a draw—and they got one, 2-2, no ticket to the World Cup. Why? Due to heavy fog in London, which forced the airports to close, the referee appointed for that game, the Hungarian István Zsolt, was unable to make his stopover and arrive in time for the match.

The mishap caught the two teams off guard; they only learned of the mishap at the last minute, as they were already preparing in a Windsor Park full of fans. The coaches and players agreed to play, but in a friendly match and under the arbitration of local referee Thomas Mitchell.

More than a month later, on January 15, 1958, Zsolt did make it to the official match that would determine which country would move on for the World Cup. In the same packed stadium, Northern Ireland took the lead in the first half with goals from Jimmy McIlroy and Wilbur Cush. The visiting team scored in the second half, a goal by Dino da Costa, a Brazilian born nationalized player. But they were shattered when Uruguayan Alcides Gigghia—the hero of Maracanazo, who had also become a naturalized Italian—was sent off, and could not draw equal. Italy was eliminated and Northern Ireland got its first ticket to the World Cup.

The Munich Air Disaster

England easily qualified. The English team thrashed Denmark twice (5-2 at Wolverhampton, 4-1 at Copenhagen), and also easily outscored the Republic of Ireland: 5-1 in London and a 1-1 draw in Dublin. The big star of this preliminary round was Thomas "Tommy" Taylor, an extraordinary Manchester United striker who scored eight goals in his team's first three games.

On February 6, 1958, a chartered airplane was bringing Manchester United back to England after qualifying matches for the European Cup, now the Champions League. The aircraft had to make a stopover in Munich, Germany, to refuel in the middle of a heavy snowstorm. To plane tried to take off twice but the wheels skidded on the icy runway. One version of events claims the control tower suggested the pilot postpone the return flight, but he tried again. The plane was barely able to rise off the runway, rammed the perimeter fence and crashed into a nearby house: 23 of the 44 passengers died, including eight players. Four of the fatalities were starters for England: Roger Byrne, David Pegg, the exquisite mid-fielder Duncan Edwards and the efficient striker Tommy Taylor.

Four months after the fatal crash, England struggled at the World Cup: they tied all three matches in the group stage and were eliminated after losing a tiebreaker against the Soviet Union, 1-0. Fans of "three lions" stoically accepted their fate. The dream of the Cup had died in Munich.

Short Cut

In a relaxing moment between training sessions leading up to the start of the Cup, German striker Helmut Rahn bet defender Erich Juskowiak 50 Krona (then about 9 American dollars) that he would cut his long, wavy hair short. Rahn walked into a local hairdresser's one afternoon with Juskowiak and other teammates and, without hesitation, put his head at the stylist's disposal. Rahn liked winning a bet more than playing soccer. The attacker's hair made the news again a few days later, when a hairdresser from the German town of

Bückeburg announced to the press that Rahn could get free styling at his premises for life, as a reward for scoring two goals against Argentina. The stylist also sent a telegram to the German club in Sweden, telling the player of his "generous" reward.

On the home team, goalkeeper Karl Svensson and defender Nils Liedholm bet with some teammates that they would *not* reach the final. They lost and played against Brazil with shaved heads.

The Professional Singer

Just as in 1930 when the Argentine team enjoyed the visits of the legendary Carlos Gardel, in Sweden the South American squad had its own singer: Julio Elías Mussimesi. The substitute goalkeeper had a second career as a tango singer and had even recorded several albums. In his luggage, Mussimesi took along with his cap and gloves several of his LPs, so as not to end up exhausted by the double duty of training with, and singing for, the team. But, as he deftly admitted to a journalist, it was mainly because "I don't like to spend time singing without getting paid." A total professional.

Crusaders

Shortly before the tournament opened, the Northern Ireland Football Association made a strange request to FIFA: to not play on Sundays. It was based on the fact that six of the members of the team—Billy Simpson, Sammy Mc Grory, Bobby Rea, Sammy Chapman, Tommy Hamill and Bobby Trainor—were devout Christians who took the biblical seventh day rest very seriously. The six players had warned that two of the three matches of the first phase—against Germany and Czechoslovakia—had been scheduled for a Sunday. FIFA rejected the request and Northern Ireland traveled to Sweden with a reduced squad of 16 players: the other six preferred stayed home.

Perhaps it was by diving intervention then that Northern Ireland lost neither of those two Sunday games: on June 8 they beat the Czechs 1-0, and on June 15 they drew 2-2 with Germany. God may have been too busy though to follow their matches on Wednesday June 11, when they lost 3-1 against Argentina, and on Thursday June 19, when they were eliminated by France, 4-0.

Garrincha's Radio

Few know that the fantastic Brazilian forward Manoel "Mané" Francisco Dos Santos, popularly known as "Garrincha", came quite close to missing Sweden 1958. Among the innovations that Brazilians dreamed up was the hiring of a psychologist, Joao Carvalhais. After interviewing and studying the player, Carvalhais said Garrincha should be expelled from the team for his extremely low IQ. He warned coach Vicente Feola that the Botafogo FC striker had "bottles instead of brains." Upon hearing of the report, Nilton Santos and Didí, also Botafogo players and leaders within the national team, met with the psychologist and convinced him not to insist on Mané's removal: "Doctor, Garrincha knows how to play soccer," they told him. Despite his poor intellectual capacity, and his feet turned inwards (one leg was six centimeters shorter than the other, and his spine was twisted), Mané played 60 games with the national team: he won 52, drew seven and lost only one.

His detractors, however, tell a tale that could be meant to justify the psychologist's recommendation. During the tournament, the forward bought an expensive transistor radio from a local shop. When he returned to the hotel, Garrincha proudly showed off his purchase to his teammates, who, amazed, congratulated him on his good taste. But Americo, the club's famous masseur, scoffed and told him he'd made a bad deal. "This device is not going to work for you in Brazil," he said, "because it only transmits in Swedish." Garrincha turned on the radio and verified that, indeed, on all stations, the announcers spoke only the Scandinavian language. He cursed the seller who had deceived him. The masseur suggested he'd be willing to take it off his hands at a low price. Mané, relieved, agreed.

The Golf Tournament

The German players discovered there was a miniature golf course in their hotel, which soon began to liven up their leisure time. They quickly went from simple bets to organizing a tournament with a grand prize of an all-expenses-paid trip for two to Italy. Coach Sepp Herberger found out and ordered the cancellation of the competition. "It would be inappropriate for my boys to worry more about a miniature golf tournament, with such an attractive prize, than about the Cup," he said, justifying his decision to journalists who followed the team.

The Packages

Every day, a huge bag of parcels sent by mail from Paris arrived at the French hotel. And, every day, the French officials were embarrassed by the generosity of the tricolor fans. Bottles of wine, salami, cheeses, hams, chocolates and other delicacies travelled inside the packages so that the players felt at home. Apparently, the food went down very well—the French had their best World Cup performance so far, finishing third. And striker Just Fontaine, as mentioned, set the record for goals scored in a single tournament, at 13. Not bad for a team that had arrived in Sweden with just three sets of jerseys because their own officials thought they would not pass the first round.

Broken Shoes

Just Fontaine did not start the tournament on the right foot. In training before his debut against Paraguay on June 8, the forward broke one of his boots. "At that time there was no sponsor and I found myself without anything. Fortunately, Stéphane Bruey, one of my fellow substitutes, wore the same size as me and lent me his shoes," the striker confided. Six games later, Fontaine gave Bruey back the pair with which he scored twelve goals, seven with his right foot and five with his left. The thirteenth was scored by the hero's head.

The ever-dangerous French forward Just Fontaine.

Unfortunate Fortune

A lucky young Swede found a ticket for the final, the June 29 showdown between Sweden and Brazil, on the street in Stockholm. The honest boy, instead of keeping it for himself, instead turned it in at the police station. For his gesture, the young man received a reward of two and a half krona, ten percent of the official value of the ticket—which on the black market would fetch 500 krona. The police issued a statement in which it specified that "whoever makes the claim" to recover the ticket "must reliably prove to be its legitimate owner." The boy was told that if no one claimed it, he could demand the precious pass for himself but as local laws held, he must first wait to see that no one showed up for six months.

Excessive Complaint?

Before their match with Argentina, the Czechoslovakians demanded FIFA appoint another referee, feeling that the Englishman Arthur Ellis had hurt them against Germany. According to the complaint, Ellis had conceded a goal to the German squad, although the ball had not crossed the line. The Czechs were winning 2-0, and the match finally ended in a 2-2 draw. The petitioners even presented a film to support their claim, but FIFA, after analyzing the case, dismissed the complaint: "The referees will not be changed just because a team says it does not like the man in charge of the game," it said in a statement. The Czechoslovaks played "under protest", but then celebrated without reservation: They beat the Argentines 6-1.

A Rain of Coins

After the terrible performance of its team, and to avoid the worst of the fan reaction, the Argentine coaching staff headed by Guillermo Stábile decided the team should return to Buenos Aires in two groups—with them as part of the second group. The first batch arrived at the Ezeiza international airport on the cold morning of Sunday, June 22, and hundreds of fans were there to hurl insults and pelt coins from the public terrace into the plane detention area where passengers alighted directly from the aircraft. Once inside the main building, when passing through customs, the players received a second slap: they had to leave behind a radio, a Mauser rifle, five type-writers, a calculator and clothing because they didn't have enough money to pay import duties. Maybe, if they had taken the coins . . .

Too Yellow

When the two semi-final matches were over, the championship organizers noted that both finalist had yellow jerseys. A draw was called, Sweden won, and Brazil would have to wear an alternate colour. The Brazilian officials realized they did not have a spare set of soccer shirts, so they called the kit-man, gave him money and ordered him to buy a new uniform: in that time, they had no uniform sponsor. The only condition they set was that he not buy white jerseys, the colour used on the fateful afternoon of the "Maracanazo." The man walked the streets of Stockholm, until he found 20 blue polo shirts in a textile store. For two days, he worked "with four hands" to sew the numbers on the backs and the shields of the Brazilian Confederation on the chest. On the other side, the Swedish officials were delighted with keeping the yellow for the final. "It gives us a decisive advantage. There is a favorable psychological factor in being able to play with the colors of our national soccer squad, and there is always the possibility that a player from the opposing team makes the mistake of passing the ball to our guys," one of the managers told the press. But the Brazilian coach Feola was not concerned. "My players know the game well and they will not make such a mistake," he said. The 5-2 result his men achieved proved Feola right.

Nepalese Disinterest

The only person who turned down the invitation to watch the final match between Sweden and Brazil was King Mahendra of Nepal. The Nepalese royal couple had lunch on Sunday, June 29, with the Swedish

King Gustavo and Queen Louise. When the protocol department of the Foreign Ministry invited the visitor to go to the Rasunda Stadium honor box to accompany Gustavo, Mahendra replied that instead of watching soccer, he preferred to visit the tourist spots in Stockholm. It was not a good afternoon for the king: on top of the rudeness of his guest, he had to chew on his team's defeat.

Awards

After their brilliant triumph against the Soviet Union, all the Brazilian players received a bicycle from the Swedish company Monark as a gift. After winning the championship, a television factory in Rio de Janeiro delivered 23 sets free of charge, one for each athlete and one for coach Feola. Also, just 24 hours after winning the tournament, the *Gaceta Sportiva* of Rio de Janeiro collected some 500,000 cruzeiros from its readers to reward the champions. When the heroes got home, the number had reached a million. For his part, the Brazilian president, Juscelino Kubitschek de Oliveira, signed a decree to grant a pension to the players and their families, a prize that showed how much the world conquest meant to the country.

Chile 1962

It was not easy for Chile to organize the seventh edition of the World Cup. On June 10, 1956, when the FIFA Congress held in Lisbon awarded the event to the South American country, the President of the Organizing Committee, Carlos Dittborn, pronounced: "Because we have nothing, we will do it all." Chile began a spectacular building boom, which included stadiums, hotels and even the installation of the first television station. The fervent impulse could not be stopped, even by a horrific earthquake on May 22, 1960, which damaged the city of Concepción and left 125 dead and hundreds injured. With a lot of effort, Chile managed to organize a very good tournament. Unfortunately, Dittborn never saw his dream come true: He died a month before it started, at age 41, from cardiac arrest.

In this edition, Brazil achieved four interesting records: first, a second consecutive championship (as Italy had done in 1934 and 1938), this time against Czechoslovakia in the final. The second was the work of forward Edvaldo Isidio Neto, better known as "Vavá": he is the only player to have scored in two consecutive finals. Vavá, who had a goal against Sweden in 1958, scored his team's third goal against Czechoslovakia in 1962. The champion coach, Aymoré

Moreira, was the brother of Alfredo "Zezé" Moreira, coach of Brazil in Switzerland '54: they are the only pair of brothers who have managed the national team in different World Cups. The fourth achievement? Brazil used only twelve players. The only change came after the first round clash with Czechoslovakia—the teams played each other twice in this tournament, in the initial Group 2 and in the finals. Pelé had to leave the tournament due to an injury and for the next game, against Spain, Moreira included Amarildo. From there, Brazil always presented the same lineup.

As to the competition, FIFA determined that the system used in the last championship would be repeated, with zones of four teams and a draw starting from the quarter-finals. One novelty was that goal difference began to be used to define classifications for the second round, instead of resorting to a tiebreaker match. This variation favored England over Argentina, in Group 4: both teams had finished with three points, but the English team advanced to the quarter-finals thanks to their advantage in the score (+2 goals against -1 for the South Americans).

Finally, Czechoslovakia ended with the rather unhappy distinction of losing the first two World Cup finals it reached, despite having opened the scoring in both cases (Italy 1934 and Chile 1962).

More Languages than Years

One of the problems that most concerned the organizers in Chile was language. The date of the start of the contest was approaching and interpreters had only been obtained for the most traditional tongues, such as English, German, and French. When the situation grew alarming, a boy from the Temuco region appeared before the Information Subcommittee, dressed in the humble traditional clothes of the place. The young man, who identified himself as Segundo Sánchez, was looking for work for a small amount of money. "I speak eighteen languages, no more, sir," Sánchez warned the skeptical members of the commission, who decided to test him.

Asked about his command of English, the young man began to speak in the language of Shakespeare with the same ability as a native of Great Britain. They switched to French and Sánchez once again astonished his examiners: he was as fluent as if he had grown up in Paris. The surprising boy continued with the same brilliance with German, Italian, Latin, Greek and Hebrew, until he exceeded the capacity of the commissioners, who had to request help from several embassies to check all the languages that the unusual candidate spoke. "I actually speak up to twenty-five languages, not counting some dialects like Malay and Indonesian," said Sánchez, who explained that he had learned everything on his own through dictionaries, books and magazines. The boy was immediately hired and placed in charge of a staff made up of fifty bilingual guides (English-Spanish and French-Spanish), twenty-four German translators, fifteen trilingual operators and more than one hundred volunteers. Likewise, the polyglot was offered a salary that far exceeded the amount originally intended. After the competition, Sánchez continued his career in the Chilean Ministry of Foreign Affairs.

Salty Juices

Before traveling to Santiago, Argentine officials sent 1,340 cans of grapefruit and orange juice to the airport, along with clothing and other items which they believed were cheaper than those they would find in Chile. When passing through customs at their own airport, however, what was expected to be a smooth exit procedure turned into a very bad business: managers were forced to pay eight thousand pesos for export duties, which significantly increased the cost of the citrus lot. Cheap was expensive.

CCCP

Colombia's first World Cup appearance was not exactly successful: they fell to Uruguay 2-1 and Yugoslavia 5-0. However, the South American team got a fabulous draw against the Soviet Union, who finished first in the group and beat Uruguay and Yugoslavia. Why fabulous? Because the Soviets were winning 3-0 at eleven minutes of the first half, and 4-1 at eleven of the second. But the Colombians came back to tie 4-4, with the tying goal just four minutes from the final whistle. After the intense match, several Latin American newspapers joked about the CCCP acronym embroidered on the chest of the red Soviet shirt, stating that it meant "Con Colombia Casi Perdimos" (With Colombia We Almost Lost).

This meeting saw another rare event: the second Colombian goal, scored by Marcos Coll at 68 minutes, came directly from a corner kick. Until Russia 2018 inclusive, only Coll and Cuban José Magriña had scored an "Olympic goal" in a World Cup.

Finally, Mexico!

In this tournament, Mexico finally achieved its first World Cup victory. It came on June 7 at the Sausalito stadium in Viña del Mar, 3-1 victory against Czechoslovakia, no less, a team that would be runner-up in the final. The Mexican squad had participated without success in the Uruguay 1930, Brazil 1950, Switzerland 1954 and Sweden 1958, competitions in which they stacked up the worst historical run of defeats (9 in a row) and only achieved one draw: against Wales, 1- 1, in Sweden.

Glutton

A few hours after leaving for Chile, the Argentine defender Rubén Marino Navarro had to undergo a hepatogram—a medical imaging of the liver—to determine if his health was good enough to participate in the World Cup. Navarro—who was known as "brave ax" because of the roughness of his play—had suffered a terrible stomach troubles days before, for having eaten, by himself, a whole piglet.

The Battle of Santiago

Two Italian journalists—Corrado Pizzinelli, from the Florentine newspaper *La Nazione*, and Antonio Ghiselli from the Bolognese *Il Resto del Carlino*—put the World Championship on the brink of a diplomatic conflict with two articles in which they contemptuously described the Chilean nation and its inhabitants. According to one of the stories, Santiago was "the sad symbol of one of the underdeveloped countries of the world and afflicted by all possible evils: malnutrition, prostitution, illiteracy, alcoholism, misery." The

Bodies strewn everywhere as Chile and Italy compete.

stories, which were reproduced by Chilean newspapers, caused deep discomfort among local residents. The Chilean Foreign Ministry demanded a correction, which never came, and the two journalists had to leave.

The incident overheated the clash between Chile and Italy on June 2, for the second date of Group 2, which they shared with Germany and Switzerland. Some accounts say Enrique Omar Sívori, born in Argentina and nationalized Italian, refused to participate for fear of fthe difficult situation. The Italian footballers entered the field with bouquets of white carnations, which they threw to the almost 66,000 spectators in a vain attempt to calm the waters: the fans threw back the flowers as a symbol of rejection, along with a loud whistle. The game was characterized by rough play and had passages of extreme violence, with players exchanging kicks and punches. The locals won 2-0 on goals scored by Jaime Ramírez and Jorge Toro.

Italy played the second half with nine men, due to the send offs of Giorgio Ferrini and Mario David. English referee Ken Aston tossed Ferrini for hitting Honorino Landa. The Italian refused to leave the field of play, for which he was arrested by a group of "cabarineros," the local police, who took him out by force. A few minutes later, Landa himself committed a very strong foul, but continued playing thanks to the complacency of the referee, who seemed not to measure the actions with the same yardstick. Aston also did not penalize a punch from local striker Leonel Sánchez—son of a former boxing champion—to Mario David. But he did expel the Italian when, seconds later, he threw a "flying kick" at Sánchez in retaliation. This victory, which allowed Chile to qualify for the quarter-finals, exacerbated the nationalistic mood of the local public. Days later, when the South American team defeated the Soviet Union, titles such as "Red wine 2-Vodka 1" or "Underdeveloped 2-Europeans 1" were published in the local papers.

Once Again, the "Charrúa Courage"

On June 6, in Arica, the USSR defeated Uruguay 2-1 in a tough game, a result that allowed the Europeans to go to the quarter-finals and meant the elimination of the South Americans. Uruguay midfielder Eliseo Álvarez wrote one of the most heroic passages in the history of World Cup: He refused to leave the field despite having suffered a fibula fracture in his left leg. Some stories say Álvarez had suffered a "double fracture of the tibia and fibula," which was really very difficult to believe, since that type of injury would make it impossible to walk. The player's daughter, Analía Edith, assured the author of this book that it was only a fibula fracture and stressed that, due to poor healing and the enormous effort during that match, her father almost lost his leg. The footballer did not have a complete recovery and had to wait almost a year to step on a pitch again. But that afternoon in Arica, until the final whistle of the Italian referee Cesare Jonni sounded, Álvarez, audacious like few others, kept running as best he could, and showed—once again—that the "Charrúa courage" was not just a fantastical story.

The Puppy

During the quarter-final clash between Brazil and England on June 10, a dog entered to the field of play. The French referee Pierre Schwinte, upon noticing the intruder, stopped the action while several players and some policemen tried unsuccessfully to capture the meddling animal. English midfielder Jimmy Greaves got down on all fours and, slowly approaching, managed to capture the dog and hand it over to a policeman, amid the applause of the public. The hound couldn't escape from Greaves' iron arms, but it had enough time to obtain his revenge: it left a trail of urine on the player's chest. "I smelled very bad. It was horrible. But, at least, the stench kept the Brazilian defenders away from me," said the English attacker.

At the end of the meeting, with the Brazilian victory 3-1, Garrincha adopted the puppy and took him home. He was baptized "Bi" for the two World Cups won, up to that moment, by the Verdeamarela squad.

An Unusual Celebration

On June 10 at the Carlos Dittborn stadium in Arica, a venue named after the late, great Conmebol president, Chile were tied 1-1 in their quarter-final with the favorites, the Soviet Union. In the 29th minute, the Chilean defensive midfielder Eladio Rojas, who had only broken into Fernando Riera's squad after an injury to Alfonso Sepúlveda, let fly a powerful 35-yard drive past the flailing Soviet keeper and into the back of the net. On seeing that his speculative strike had gone in, Rojas ran the thirty-five yards to the Soviet goal and hugged the keeper. Quizzed about this strange celebration after the match, Rojas explained that he had been overwhelmed with emotion after getting one over his idol, the 'unbeatable' Lev Yashin.

The Forgotten Whistle

Soviet referee Nikolaj Latychev was a busy man. He officiated Italy-Switzerland for Group 2, Argentina-England for Group 4, the quarter-finals between Czechoslovakia and Hungary, and the final between Brazil and Czechoslovakia. But more active was his arrival in Santiago. As soon as he set foot in the Chilean capital, Latychev had to run out to buy a whistle—his was inside the suitcase, with clothes and other personal effects, that he had lost at the airport.

Report Book

The legendary German coach Sepp Herberger—author of the 1954 triumph in Switzerland—implemented a report book for each player in 1962. In it he kept weekly scores for his men in a range of different categories: technique, tactics, performance, hygiene, neatness, health, speed, strength, obedience, athletics, discipline, intellectuality, public and private morality, punctuality, civility and education. Whatever their scores, the team's overall performance would not have pleased the coach. They were eliminated by Yugoslavia in the quarter-finals, 1-0.

Short of Light

During the tournament, Chile was going through moments of electricity rationing. The cuts were repeated every afternoon, but were suspended for June 13, on the occasion of the semi-final between the local team and Brazil. The General Directorate of Electrical Services agreed to postpone the interruption of the supply after receiving thousands of letters and calls from people affected by the rationing who wanted to follow the match on radio or television, because they had not obtained tickets. One of the neighborhoods that had been cut off was, in fact, the National Stadium, where the semi-final was played.

Encouragement?

Shortly before the end of the Cup, when the local team had already qualified to face Brazil in the semi-finals, the Chilean Football Association published a strange request in all the capital's newspapers. Entitled "To all Chileans" the article asked fans inside the stadium "not to shout too loud" because "they could upset our team emotionally." "The championship enters a phase in which the concentration of all physical forces is necessary to make a good presentation. We ask all of Chile, from the highest authorities to the closest relative, to keep the Chilean team within the structure of sports preparation and emotional peace in which it is located. Everyone must sacrifice the pleasure of entertaining our players and put aside the shouting and hugs until Chile has finished its performance in the contest." The silence of the stands did little to help the red squad, which lost to Brazil 4 to 2.

Indulgence

Seven minutes from the end of the clash between Chile and Brazil, local midfielder Eladio Rojas was struck down by a heavy blow from rival striker Garrincha. Mané had scored two of the four goals for his team, and had become the great target, receiving kicks and elbows from the "red" defenders, especially from Honorio Landa, who had been sent off a few minutes before. The Chilean players reported Garrincha's punch to the Peruvian referee Arturo Yamasaki, but he assured them that he had not noticed any irregularity. However, on the advice of one of his linesmen, who swore to have seen the blow, and possibly to "balance" the scale in the heated National Stadium of Santiago, Yamasaki ordered Mané to leave the field of play. As soon as the scorer crossed the lime boundary, Rojas, who until that moment was writhing in pain on the ground, recovered and continued to perform in perfect condition up to the end. After the game, Garrincha—who took a stone to the head from a fan while going to the dressing room—admitted to the journalists having attacked Rojas: "I deeply regret what happened, it was an involuntary reaction of my part, probably as a result of some blows that I had received in rough actions. I was provoked and they spat in my face, but this does not justify my reaction and I want to apologize to the Chilean public."

For the final against Czechoslovakia, Brazil was in serious troubles. It had to face the had managed to play it to a draw, in the first round, and without Pelé, injured in that same clash. They also

113

couldn't afford to face the decisive game without Garrincha. For this reason, a "diplomatic" campaign was launched with the help of the then prime minister, Tancredo Neves, who sent a private telegram to the president of FIFA, the Englishman Stanley Rous. In addition to praising the organization of the championship, and giving other warm congratulations, Neves said that "the Brazilian government hopes that the FIFA authorities will authorize the presence in the final of all the Brazilian stars and especially Garrincha, an extraordinary athlete whose discipline and clean play are known throughout the world. I ask this in the name of the joy of the Brazilian people." Three days before the final, FIFA issued a statement in which it reported that Mané was only being reprimanded for hitting Rojas, because "he always behaved well on the pitch."

Gastronomic Incentive

The Chilean coach, Fernando Riera, used gastronomy as an original way to concentrate and stimulate his players. Hours before the debut for Switzerland, on May 30, the coach made each of his men eat a piece of Gruyère cheese: The Andean team won 3-1. On June 2, the Chileans had pasta for lunch and, in the afternoon, they defeated Italy 2-0. The sausages with sauerkraut were not enough to avoid a 2-0 defeat against Germany, but the vodka, in the run-up to the quarter-final duel with the Soviet Union, did have an effect. They won 2 to 1. For the semi-final, the coffee didn't help: Chile fell 4-2 to Brazil. It was not revealed what Riera fed his boys for the 1-0 victory over Yugoslavia in the duel for third place.

Somewhat Distracted

On June 17, minutes before the decisive match against Czechoslovakia, Brazilian coach Aymoré Moreira gave a brief technical talk to his men in the dressing room of the National Stadium. Moreira trusted his players and did not bother to highlight the strengths or weaknesses of the rival team, which they already knew. "Guys, today is the final. You know everything, just play," he began, before being interrupted by Garrincha. "Today is the final?" he asked. "Yes, Mané", Moreira replied, surprised by the question, "today is the final." "Now I understand why there are so many people!" said the striker, who got up and walked to the pitch with a huge smile. Despite having the flu and a 39-Celsius degree fever, the great Garrincha masterfully led his team to their second Jules Rimet Cup in a row, with a 3-1 defeat of Czechoslovakia.

England 1966

The "inventors of soccer" finally got the pleasure of being the best in the world, officially, though they needed their own turf to do it. After having spent many isolated years convinced there were no worthy rivals on the planet, and after having failed consecutively from Brazil '50 to Chile '62, England managed to lift the Jules Rimet Cup in 1966.

For many people—not for the champions, of course—the victory was a bit cloudy and not a few facts threw a cloak of doubts over the legitimacy of the conquest. In the final against Germany, in fact, the Swiss referee Gottfried Dienst saw as a genuine "goal" a shot from local striker Geoff Hurst that bounced off the crossbar, dipped a few inches in front of the lime line and escaped from the German goal. This unique marker came at 101 minutes, during overtime (the first ninety minutes ended 2-2), and although Hurst scored again before the final whistle, that irregular goal opened the door for English success.

Another detail: England is the only world champion who played every game in the same stadium, Wembley, northwest of London, without having to move to another city. It is true that Uruguay was the same in 1930, but in that case the situation was even for everyone—all the matches were played in Montevideo. In 1966, the semi-final between England and Portugal had originally been scheduled in Liverpool, but it was changed to Wembley. FIFA Secretary Helmut Casser reported that the organizing committee "decided that the most attractive match would be held in the place where the largest number of spectators could attend". Another incident that provoked angry protests, especially in South America, came in the quarter-finals, with the curious appointment of a German judge for England-Argentina, Rudolf Kreitlein, and an English referee, James Finney, for Germany-Uruguay. The two European teams passed the round and the two defeated teams complained of having been victims of unfair arbitration. Kreitlein sent off Argentine Antonio Rattin in the 35th minute, when the score was blank, and Finney sent off two Uruguayans: Horacio Troche and Héctor Silva. The day after those two games, a German newspaper published a photo of defender Karl-Heinz Schnellinger committing a clear hand ball inside his defending area to stop a goal. It should have given Uruguay a penalty kick when they were tailing 1-0. Some media denounced a plot against the two South America squads, but nothing could be proven.

The Brazilians also complained about the refereeing by Englishman George McCabe, who allowed the great Pelé to be forced out by the Portuguese at Goodison Park in Liverpool. Mc Cabe did not admonish any of the ferocious Lusitanians who went after Pelé's legs—he had to retire to the locker room early. With this reprehensible strategy, Portugal eliminated the squad that had won the last two World Cups, something quite convenient for the aspirations of the locals.

In addition to these controversies, the championship left other pearls: in Uruguay's 2-1 victory over France on July 15, Pablo Forlán in the South American line-up and Jean Djorkaeff played for France; curiously, their sons Diego and Youri, respectively, were members of the Uruguayan and French teams which crossed paths again in Busan, South Korea, in World Cup 2002. (On this occasion, neither say action.) Another notable record was set by Mexican goalkeeper Antonio Carbajal, who played his fifth World Cup in England. Carbajal only played against Uruguay and managed to keep his goal empty.

Heads or Tails

For this World Cup, FIFA established that if the quarter-final and semi-final matches ended in a tie after ninety minutes and thirty minutes of extra time, a coin flip would decide the winner. For the final, however, it was determined that if the score continued even after 120 minutes, the game had to be played again two days later. On that second opportunity, if everything remained balanced after 120 minutes, the referee had to summon the two captains and toss the coin to see who was lucky enough to lift the Cup. Luck favored all participants, since there was no need to use this unfair tiebreaker system throughout the entire championship.

Food and Drink

To make their players feel at home, the Portuguese delegates asked the Wilmslow hotel in Chesire to provide a basement and kitchen space to store 600 bottles of Portuguese wine, several barrels of olive oil and large quantities of fish. The Hungarians banished beef from the diets of their players. Giorgy Honti, secretary of the Magyar association, said that "we consider meat as a second-rate food."

The members of the Chilean national team were perplexed when they received several liters of whisky upon arrival at their hotel in Gateshead, on the outskirts of Newcastle. A bottle "per capita" awaited the delegation as a welcome gift from the local neighborhood committee. For the German players, bread baked in their country arrived every morning by plane. Throughout the tournament, shipments totaled about 100 kilos. The Germans also packed dozens of kilos of bacon in their luggage.

The directors of the Alexandra National hotel in London imported several bottles of tequila to entertain the Mexican players who stayed there. But they got a nasty surprise. Upon arrival, coach Ignacio Trelles rejected them: "No alcoholic beverages for my boys," he ordered. Another curious demand from Trelles complicated the local cook for the Mexican delegation: he had to go all over the English capital to find goat's milk for the players.

The Uruguayan diet was based on spinach, famous in those years as the food that invigorated the Popeye comic book character: athletes ate spinach and egg cakes all day.

The French brought a thousand bottles of wine, far more than those imported by the Argentines and Spanish. The French team drew 1-1 with Mexico and fell to Uruguay (2-1) and England (2-0), which meant their elimination in the first round. The footballers returned home but the thousand empty bottles were left in London. Meanwhile, Spanish coach José Villalonga made his men sit four per table and sent a bottle to share equally. The Argentines were only allowed one glass per meal. The manager Juan Carlos Lorenzo stressed that even on July 9, the country's Independence Day, "that ration will not be modified." However, the night the team beat Switzerland and qualified for the quarter-finals, he was a little more generous: As a reward, he allowed the players to have two glasses of red wine.

On the day of the opening game between England and Uruguay, twenty thousand sandwiches, four thousand cans of beer, twenty thousand cups of tea and five hundred bottles of whisky were sold at Wembley Stadium. The total number of antacids and analgesics consumed in the stands was not reported.

No Saliva

A few days before the start of the Cup, a priest from the English town of Newmarket publicly asked that the footballers "not kiss when they celebrate goals." Vicar Thomas Edmondson wrote in his congregation's weekly bulletin that "this ridiculous madness must be removed from the playing fields." The plea did not meet with much success, since the "demonic" custom not only remains, but has multiplied on the fields around the world.

Can I see your papers?

The opening match between England and Uruguay, played on July 11 at Wembley, started several minutes late as seven of the English players had forgotten their identity documents at the hotel. To prevent the home team from have to change its line-up, a policeman was dispatched on a motorcycle to retrieve the IDs. The agent was able to overcome the complicated London traffic and arrived at the stadium in time for coach Alf Ramsey to present his starting team, which that day drew 0-0 against the tough South American opponent.

Pickles

Pickles, the black and white collie famous for finding the stolen Jules Rimet trophy back in 1938, attended Wembley Stadium to witness the opening match. Accompanied by his owner, the doggy sat in one of the most expensive boxes and behaved very well. It remained calm despite the noisy crowd of 150,000 people that overflowed the coliseum, and it left without leaving any "little gift" on the carpet.

Many Steps Taken, but No Goals Celebrated

A Swiss window cleaner named Emil Hollinger walked the 1,290 kilometers that separate Zurich and Sheffield—he only used the help of a ferry to cross the English Channel—to see his team against Germany. Hollinger wore out two pairs of shoes on his journey; a few miles from his goal, a generous English merchant gave him a new pair to complete the feat. The Swiss players were as not as generous. Not only could they not reward their selfless fan with a single goal, but they let the Germans send five balls into the Helvetic net.

The Korean Miracle

The participation of North Korea in 1966 caused astonishment—in part because of its performance, but also because of the astounding athletic state of its footballers. The team trained for two weeks at a sports school in Mecklenburg, East Germany, where they were devoted entirely to physical training and played no practice games. At the hotel where the players stayed in England, in the town of Arlington, employees were surprised to see the Koreans consume a kilo of pepper daily. Cigarettes and alcoholic beverages were strictly prohibited and the delegation—the largest at the Cup, made up of 75 people—included a person in charge of organizing and leading a claque of local fans to cheer at their games.

North Korea, which has only been back to the World Cup once (South Africa 2010), finished second in Group 4. It qualified for the quarter-finals thanks to a 1-1 draw with Chile and a triumph over Italy, 1-0, with a goal scored by Doo Ik Pak, an army dentist. The victory, which took place on July 19 at Ayresome Park in Middlesbrough, is regarded by many journalists as the biggest surprise in World Cup history. The Italians, with stars such as Sandro Mazzola, Gianni Rivera and Giacinto Facchetti, could not find a way to beat them, though they were playing down a man for more than half of the match due to an injury to Giacomo Bulgarelli. All the Italian attempts died at the hands of Li Chan Myong, the youngest goalkeeper in the history of the World Cup at 19.

Even the Koreans themselves were suprised at their qualification for the round of 16, and had to cancel their tickets to return home the night of the game with Italy. Their unforeseen success forced the delegation to move to Liverpool to face Portugal, and as there was no hotel available for all the athletes and coaching staff, the Koreans ended up staying in a Protestant church: most of the players slept the night before the game on the pews. On July 23, at Goodison Park, North Korea once again stupefied the world by scoring three goals in just 25 minutes. But the Portuguese recovered and, led by striker Eusebio, who scored four goals, finally prevailed 5-3.

Not too skilled with the ball, the Koreans had remarkable physical capacity that allowed them to run non-stop for ninety minutes. Perhaps out of envy, perhaps out of ignorance, a large number of journalists and other delegation members raised questions. Sporting success went hand in hand with a rumor, never proven, which suggested they changed out almost the entire team during halftime and no one noticed.

Tomato Storm

Upon arriving at the airport in Genoa in the early morning of July 23, after the embarrassing elimination at the hands of North Korea, some 700 angry fans riddled the players and the coaching staff of the Italian team with tomatoes. The "tifosi" had brought several crates of ripe tomatoes with them to use as projectiles. The angry fans called out insults and threats against the members of the delegation, and kicked at the cars that transported the players. Despite the violent welcome, the footballers left the air station, somehow grateful.

"Luckily, it was decided to go to Genoa at the last minute, so as not to land in Milan or Rome. There, they would surely have killed us," said one of the players.

Dog Day

The day before the England-Argentina quarter-final, the South American delegation wanted to go to Wembley Stadium to survey the pitch. England had played all their first-round matches there, but Argentina had faced Spain and Germany at Villa Park in Birmingham, and Switzerland at Hillsborough in Sheffield. As it happened, the South Americans could not walk on the "cathedral" grass, because the stadium was hosting greyhound races there that afternoon.

Germany playing Argentina (stripes) at the 1966 World Cup.

Cards

According to FIFA, it was the extremely tough quarter-final match between England and Argentina on July 23 that gave rise to the yellow and red cards used by referees to caution or send off a player. That clash, in which Argentina's Antonio Rattin was thrown out, was characterized by violent tackles and constant interruptions due to arguments between the players and the German referee Rudolf Kreitlein. The man in black later conceded that Rattin was sent off because "I didn't like the way he looked at me." The Argentine player left the pitch with gestures towards the public, which infuriated the local fans. The host squad won 1-0 with a header from Geoffrey Hurst in the 78th minute, and until the end of the game the kicks sought the opponents' bodies more than the ball. English coach Alf Ramsey fired at his South American rivals—shouting "animals"— and even struggled with his defender George Cohen so that he would not exchange his shirt with Argentine Oscar Mas.

The following day, the Disciplinary Committee suspended Rattin for four games, and Roberto Ferreiro and Ermindo Onega for three matches, the latter for "spitting in the face of a FIFA official." The body even suggested the organizing committee for the 1970 Cup "refuse to consider the Argentine registration, unless certain assurances are given about the conduct of the players and managers".

The peculiar game, made worse by misunderstandings due to language gaps, gave former FIFA referee and observer Ken Aston an idea. When he returned home from Wembley, he took the idea of using yellow and red cards from traffic lights, a color code known universally. Aston presented his idea to FIFA, which put it into practice at the 1968 Mexico Olympics. The result was so positive that the cards made their World Cup debut in Mexico in 1970.

Timeless Caution

When he retired after 500 games for Manchester United, and 106 for his country, Robert "Bobby" Charlton had only seen the yellow card once in his long career, and that due to a misunderstanding with a referee about the timing of a free kick in a league game. However, almost thirty years after his last official game, Charlton was reprimanded by FIFA for having participated in one of the many discussions that took place in the 1966 match against Argentina. During a conference on "fair play" held while World Cup France '98 was in progress, one of the speakers told Charlton that he had been warned by Rudolf Kreitlein, but the German referee had not been able to communicate it amid the confusion and chaos that afternoon. The talented English midfielder had never heard of the warning so he requested that the records be reviewed. As it was found that he had indeed been reprimanded by Kreitlein, a member of FIFA participating in the conference took the stage and, to the laughter of the audience, showed Charlton the yellow card to communicate his warning "officially."

Pay with Your Life

Months before the championship began, a Brazilian clairvoyant from Salvador de Bahia had taken bets and promised that if Brazil did not win the Cup for the third time in a row, he would kill himself. Minutes after Portugal beat the South American team 3-1 and eliminated them in the first round, the fortune teller disappeared so as not to keep his word . . . or return the money. His clients, furious at the defeat and feeling cheated, tried to locate the astrologer to force the issue, but he was gone.

The elimination in the first round caused numerous incidents in Brazil. One man committed suicide and several were injured while attempting to kill themselves. In addition, a Portuguese merchant was almost lynched for having celebrated this country's triumph, much as a Brazilian boy who had bet in favor of the Europeans and celebrated in an exaggerated way.

A Caviar Victory?

The controversial third English goal in the final, the winning marker in the 4-2 victory over Germany, has an unusual story behind it. It came on a shot by Geoff Hurst that bounced off the crossbar and dipped a few inches *in front* of the goal line, but was validated by Swiss referee Gottfried Dienst. The linesman who convinced Dienst it was in was Tofik Bakhramov, who came from the Soviet Union. Before dying in 1999, another Russian referee, Nikolai

Queen Elizabeth presents the 1966 World Cup trophy to England captain Bobby Moore.

Latyshev—who officiated the 1962 World Cup final between Brazil and Czechoslovakia and acted as an observer in England—revealed that two jars of excellent Russian caviar could have changed the history of the 1966 final. According to Latyshev, his compatriot was not in FIFA's plans for the final, but was appointed at the last minute after allegdly having a meeting with a Malayan delegate named Koe Ewe Teik. At that meeting, the Soviet seems to have offered the Malaysian two pots of sturgeon eggs in exchange for being chosen to accompany the Swiss Dienst. Apparently, Teik took the tasty bribe and convinced his fellow FIFA commissioners to put Bakhramov on the list. "As far as I can remember," Latyshev said in an interview, "two jars of Russian caviar did the trick."

MEXICO 1970

Forty years and nine World Cups were enough for the Jules Rimet trophy. Brazil, driven by the immense talent of Pelé, now took possession of the sculpture of the goddess Nike forever. In Mexico, as in Sweden and Chile, the Santos star was not alone: coach Mario "Lobo" Zagallo surrounded him with four other exceptional players: Gerson de Oliveira Nunes (known only as "Gerson"), Roberto Rivelino, Eduardo Gonçalves de Andrade (the famous Tostao, who also played as a center forward) and Jair Ventura Filho, known as Jairzinho, one of the great cannoneers of this Cup and the only one who sent the ball to the back of the net in all his matches. Jairzinho scored two on Czechoslovakia, one on England, Romania, Peru and Uruguay, and yet another in the final against Italy. Regarding Tostao, the former Argentine player and current coach César Luis Menotti, said that "if Pelé hadn't existed, Tostao would be Pelé".

Mexico 1970 was the first time the yellow and red cards were used in a World Cup, after the chaos of the England-Argentina match in the previous tournament. In fact, only the caution was used—the Soviet Evgeni Lovchev had the "honor" to debut the system in the opening match between his country and the host team—because there were no players sent off in thirty-two games.

Another innovation had to do with substitutions: each team was allowed to change two players per game. This regulation was also put into practice at the opening encounter: Soviet Anatoli Puzach replaced Viktor Serebrjanikov at halftime. The Mexican Ignacio Basaguren was the first substitute to score a goal. It happened on June 7 at the Azteca stadium in the Federal District, against El Salvador. Basaguren had replaced Jaime López in the 76th minute, and in the 83rd minute he got the fourth and last host goal.

Another peculiarity of this contest—which would be repeated in 1986, again in Mexico—was that, despite the fact that the games were scheduled between noon and early afternoon, in the intense heat of the summer, the level of play was extraordinary. All the quarter-finals, the semi-finals and the final featured electrifying passages. The semi-final between Italy and Germany, won 4-3 by the Azzuri squad in overtime, was described as "the match of the century".

The Swedes brought their own chef, Peter Olander, who worked in the palace of King Gustaf Adolf to Mexico. They would do so again in the next World Cup, and this role became so important that FIFA determined that the chefs of the champion, runner-up and third-place teams should receive a medal. As FIFA spokesperson Keith Cooper once pointed out, the chef "is as important as the captain".

Finally, in this edition an already legendary dynasty began: the official Adidas ball. In Mexico, the ball was called Telstar, grandfather of the now famous Tango, Azteca, Etrusco and Jabulani, among others.

Crowd

The match Brazil and Paraguay played on August 31, 1969 at the Maracaná stadium in Rio de Janeiro, part of the qualifying round for South America, had the highest attendance of paid ticketholders in all World Cup history. According to FIFA records, 183,341 people bought their ticket to witness the host side's victory that day, 1-0. But was it the biggest crowd ever? Officially, when the 1950 World Cup's last game was played in Maracanã, between Brazil and Uruguay, 174,000 tickets were sold. But that afternoon the audience climbed to 200,000 people, if gatecrashers are taken into account. These remarkable attendance records cannot be repeated, because the Maracanã's capacity was reduced to 120,000 places for security reasons. Nor is there another stadium in the world large enough to receive more than 150,000 spectators.

The Soccer War

In July 1969, soccer was, once again, used by political and military leaders for spurious purposes. Honduras and El Salvador had had a strained relationship for years, until a series of qualifying matches was the excuse that led to an armed conflict. The "Soccer War" began to unfold on June 8, when Honduras, in its capital, Tegucigalpa, won 1-0. A week later, El Salvador won 3-0 at home, balancing the series. In this meeting, there were serious incidents in the stands between the followers of both teams. The events were magnified by the Honduran media at the request of the dictator Oswaldo López Orellano, who took advantage of the situation to hit on the true cause of anger between both nations—the constant migration of Salvadorans, who were looking for work on the other side of the border.

López Orellano launched a strong nationalist campaign through the media, and when xenophobic hatred lit the fuse, he ordered the expropriation of the assets of Salvadorans residing in his country and the redistribution of their lands and properties among local peasants. The situation became increasingly strained, especially when El Salvador defeated its rival 3-2 in the playoff match played on June 27 in Mexico City. On July 14, the Salvadoran army crossed the border to defend its compatriots and arrived at the gates of Tegucigalpa. The rapid intervention of the Organization of American States (OAS) limited the war to five days, but it left four thousand dead. As always, the ball kept rolling, and between September and October of that year, El Salvador eliminated Haiti and qualified to play a World Cup for the first time.

Bobby Moore and the Last Emerald

On May 26, the captain of the England team, Robert Frederick Chelsea "Bobby" Moore, was detained by the police at the El Dorado airport in Bogotá, the Colombian capital, accused of having stolen a valued gold and emerald bracelet worth $1,500. He was on his way to Mexico along with the entire English delegation. The detention warrant had been issued by a criminal court, before which the owner of the "Fuego verde" jewelry store located inside the hotel where the team had stayed, blamed Moore for the disappearance of the jewel. The merchant claimed Moore took the opportunity to grab the bracelet while staff were overwhelmed by several players interested in acquiring a piece. The defender was taken to court, where he was accompanied by the British ambassador in Bogotá, Tom Rogers, and a local criminal lawyer employed by the embassy. Meanwhile, the rest of the English squad traveled ahead to the host country of the Cup.

From England, Moore's wife, Tina, assured everyone that the episode was "ridiculous", not only because the player was not "capable of such a thing" but because his salary was many times higher than the value of the bracelet. British newspapers also supported Moore's innocence. The *Daily Express*, for example, said on its front page that "Colombians are adept at self-theft." The soccer player was detained for three days at the house of an official with the Colombian federation and got up every morning at 6.30 to train at the Millonarios club facilities for two hours, assisted by two players from the club's lower divisions. During that time, the English captain was sprinting, practicing passes and doing gymnastic exercises.

Three days later, Moore was released and, although he continued to be processed for the theft, he was authorized to travel to Mexico and participate in the World Cup. "The accusation made against me was unfounded. I have a clear conscience, and that is enough for me. Now all I want is to forget the incident and go back to my job as a soccer player, and help England retain the Jules Rimet Cup. I am in very good physical condition, and I hope that my colleagues in Mexico are even in better shape and that this incident has not affected them," the defender told the press as he left for Mexico. Although he reached Guadalajara poorly trained, seven pounds lighter, and with just 72 hours to get ready, Moore started in the debut against Romania, which England won 1-0.

Things were very different for Clara Padilla, the saleswoman who accused the English soccer player. She lived for a long time in terror of a wave of threats that reached her by letter and by phone. The pressure was too much: she quit her job and requested police protection. "You should not live in this world. The best thing that can happen to her is to have her head cut off," one of the anonymous messages that came from London told her.

More Problems

When the plane flying the almost complete English squad to Mexico touched down, the journalists waiting to collect statements regarding the "Moore case" were surprised by the sinuous gait of forward Jeffrey Astle. "He was just dizzy from the ups and downs of the aircraft", said the delegation spokesman. However, an "unofficial" source revealed that the player had "an atrocious fear of flying" and that, every time he embarked, he drank "a few measures of whisky." Astle must have exhausted the stock of scotch during the four hours that the trip lasted. The English team suffered another setback upon their arrival. The local health authorities seized the 38 kilograms of butter they were carrying along with their boots, clothes and other food. "The confiscation was due to the fact that butter can be a vehicle for the transmission of foot-and-mouth disease, which in Great Britain has not been eradicated as in our country," explained a local government official.

Mexican Hat

For this tournament, the plan was that if the final ended tied, a second match would be played two days later. It was also determined that, in the event of a tie after 30 minutes of extra time in the quarter-finals or semi-finals, the games would be decided by a very particular lottery: with two papers with the names of the teams placed into the top of a Mexican hat. The curious resolution, according to the championship regulations, had to be carried out in the center of the field, in the presence of the captains of each team. With all the games resolved in 90 or 120 minutes (two went to extra time), the hats remained in storage.

Families

The World Cup continued to be a family affair. The Mexican José Vantolrá was the son of the Spaniard Martín Vantolrá, who played in Italy 1934. They are the only father and son to perform for different countries. The Romanian Nicolae Lupescu, the Belgian Jan Verheyen and the Uruguayan Julio Montero Castillo had children who would go on to play, respectively, in the 1990 and 1994, 1998 and 2002, and 2002 cups. Perhaps the most surprising case corresponds to that of the Mexican Mario Pérez, whose grandfather Luis Pérez had worn the Aztec jersey in Uruguay 1930.

The Berlin Wall

Referees Kurt Tschenscher (from the Federal Republic of Germany) and Rudolf Gloeckner (from the German Democratic Republic) did not speak to each other. The divisions caused by politics were so deep that, despite having refereed together on June 6 in Puebla, when Italy faced Uruguay, they did not speak or say hello. On that occasion, Gloeckner was the main referee and Tschenscher was the linesman. Rudolf was later appointed to lead the final between Brazil and Italy.

To War!

When the tournament was about to start, Israel's physical trainer, Amos Bar Hava, had to return home, the result of a military conflict with Lebanon. Bar Hava was an active colonel in the Israeli army, which had invaded Lebanon supported by airplanes and artillery. Despite the absence of the coach, the team had an acceptable performance: it lost 2-0 to Uruguay, but drew with Sweden (1-1) and drew scoreless with Italy, who would finish as runner-up.

I Tot I Taw a Puddy Tat

Upon arriving in the city of Puebla, the Belgian delegation received as a gift a five-month-old tiger, which had been baptized "Rajá." The feline delighted the footballers, who spent a large part of their rest hours playing with it in the gardens of the Mesón del Ángel hotel. But sometimes, while the athletes were training, the restless kitten got bored and went for a walk. One morning, the little tiger slipped down one of the hotel corridors and frightened several guests. That day the mischief was forgiven, but the next day Raja ran away again and this time he behaved very badly: he bit a woman and injured a photographer from the force of two claws and a nibble. Despite the pleas and tears of the Belgians, the tiger was locked up in the city's zoo. Overwhelmed by the loss of their mascot, the European team was eliminated in the first round.

The English, much more austere, had a dog named Winston. The organizing committee allowed the players to keep the animal next to the substitute bench, but he was well looked after—and perfectly secured.

Big Foot

One free afternoon, the Brazilian footballers took the opportunity to walk through the center of Guadalajara, the city where they stayed and played all their games, except the final. To cure their boredom, the boys visited various stores, including a shoe factory. The athletes were invited to tour the facilities and, at the end of the itinerary the owner gave a pair to each of his illustrious guests. The only one who left without a gift was substitute defender Joel Camargo: in the entire factory they found no shoes that would fit his huge feet.

Offended

The Mexican journalists took it as an insult that the Italian team did not drink the local water with their meals. When witnessing a lunch at their hotel, the scribes were horrified that the players drank only wine that they themselves had brought from their homeland. Several reported that of the Italians despised their water for fear that it would harm them or had been adulterated. The doctor of the team, surnamed Fini, put an end to the controversy with a touch of sarcasm: "None of us drink water at meals. From childhood we get used to wine. That does not mean that we do not have respect for water: it is very useful for bathing."

The Bulgarians and the English also carried their own drinks, especially mineral water. The Balkan squad arranged for a collaborator to closely monitor the cooks at the Hotel La Estancia, where they were staying. The imported water was used even to boil pasta.

Thirteen

According to the Agence France-Presse, FIFA considered allowing teams to use a shirt without a number for the player who was assigned 13, if he did not want to use it for fear of bad luck. The possibility of replacing the "tragic figure" with the 23 was also studied. Despite those alternatives, no changes were made. What's more: several footballers chose 13 because they supposed it was as a talisman to attract good fortune. One of them was the German striker Gerd Müller, who opted for that number because he wanted to equal the record of the France's Just Fontaine, the highest scorer of Sweden '58 with exactly 13 goals. Müller failed to catch up with Fontaine, but wearing the number 13 must have helped. He was the top scorer, with ten goals.

Argentine Help for the Finals

Brazilian goalkeeper Félix Miéli Venerando (known simply as "Félix") arrived in Mexico with the hope of finding gloves for his enormous hands to replace his old, worn-out pair. When Félix could not find an appropriate pair in local sporting goods stores either—they were not of adequate quality or flexibility—a delegate began an intensive search with the help of the Brazilian foreign relations service.

A few hours later, a saving telegram arrived from the Buenos Aires consulate: the former goalkeeper of River Plate and the Argentine national team, Amadeo Carrizo, had several pairs with the size and characteristics Félix required. An envoy from the Buenos Aires diplomatic headquarters bought four pairs and sent them to Mexico by air. Thus, Argentina, which for the first time had been left out of a Cup in the qualifier round, gave the world champions a "hand".

Amnesty

Defender Omar Caetano and forward Julio Cortés were two of Uruguay's prominent players with many epic victories to their credit. An anti-doping test of the two players, however, revealed "the existence of an unknown and rare substance." A researcher determined that it was "ibogaine," an alkaloid extracted from an African bush which Aboriginal hunters use in the jungle to prevent them from sleeping for three or four days. The commercial sale of the substance, also used as a hypnotic and aphrodisiac, is prohibited due to the serious consequences that can arise from its consumption. According to the newspapers of the time, the National Physical Education Commission of Uruguay recommended a six-month suspension for Caetano and Cortés, but a few weeks later, the president of Uruguay, Jorge Pacheco Areco, granted them both amnesty to attend the World Cup. The two players, who had vowed to shave their heads if they were finally allowed to travel, arrived in Mexico suitably shorn.

A Professional Staff

The Mexican team consisted of nine athletes who, in addition to playing soccer, had other professions. Among the twenty-two summoned by coach Raúl Cárdenas were a dentist, an economist, a lawyer, an architect, an expert in business administration, a chemical engineer, a seminarian, a philosopher and a ceramic artist. This did not prevent Mexico from reaching the quarter-finals, where they fell to runner-up Italy.

Security by Decree

According to a dispatch from the UPI agency, dated May 26, tourists "will be able to walk safely after ten o'clock at night" throughout Mexico during the World Cup. Why? The report claimed that "the police headquarters prohibited stealing after 10 PM". Was there "security" for only two hours a day? Or was it a ploy to get the Mexican thieves to bed early?

Not the Referee's Fault After All

The Mexicans did not like the appointment of Israeli Abraham Klein to referee their clash against Italy in the quarter-finals. They held him responsible for a defeat suffered against Japan two years earlier, a 2-0 loss in the bronze-medal match in the 1968 Olympic Games, which also took place in Mexico. The home side complained to FIFA and two days later, the referee mysteriously presented a medical certificate for an "indisposition" that did not allow him to assume his commitment. On June 14, Mexico and Italy took to the pitch of Luis Dosal stadium in Toluca with Switzerland's Ruedi Scheurer dressed in black. The change of referee did not change the fate of the Mexican squad, which was decisively beaten 4-1.

Watch Out for Tostao

Many analysts and fans agree that Pelé's true partner in this World Cup was Tostao, a left-footed midfielder with an exquisite punch. This player, whom the Brazilian "torcedores" called "the white Pelé," arrived in Mexico almost by miracle. The previous September, during a match between Cruzeiro, his club, and Corinthians, a powerful shot by rival defender Ditão had caused a detached retina in his left eye. To regain his vision, Tostao had to travel to Houston and undergo five risky operations. Aided by science and sustained by his enormous self-esteem, Tostao rehabilitated himself quickly to rejoin the national team. Years later, he revealed that he could not see Brazil's fourth goal in the final against Italy, scored by Carlos Alberto, not because of an eye problem, but a tear problem: "After Jairzinho's third goal, I knew we had won and I started to cry with joy. I played fifteen minutes with tears in my eyes." After the final, Tostao returned to Houston, but to present his gold medal to the surgeon who had rehabilitated him, in a profound gesture of gratitude. A few years later, Tostao again had problems with his injured eye, and had to leave soccer. Away from the ball, the "white Pelé " enrolled in university and in record time received a medical degree. His speciality? Ophthalmology.

Bad Calculation

On June 14, in the city of León, England was beating Germany 2-0, with goals from Alan Mullery at 31 minutes and Martin Peters at 49. Convinced that the victory of the 1966 final would be repeated, English coach Alf Ramsey sent substitute Colin Bell to warm up to replace Bobby Charlton, to preserve him for the semi-final with Italy three days hence. When Bell was at the lime line ready to go, Germany's Franz Beckenbauer shaved the lead. Still, Ramsey ordered the change to be made, confident that his men would maintain the advantage. But the Germans pulled equal in the 76th minute and won in the overtime on a goal from Gerd Müller. Ramsey paid dearly for his decision, and Germany had the pleasure of taking quick revenge for the controversial Wembley final.

An Untimely Knighthood

After his brilliant saves helped England to the 1966 World Cup, Gordon Banks was given a knighthood by Queen Elizabeth II. But

Banks was informed of the honor at an inconvenient moment, before the quarter-final against West Germany—a hard-fought repeat of the final in England four years earlier. Banks got the good news by telephone two days before the match and became so worked up that he went down with a serious case of stomach cramps. A weakened Banks, who had played in all three of England's first-round games, had to relinquish his place to Peter Bonetti and followed the match sitting on a toilet. Officially, to preserve the goalkeeper's honor perhaps, it was reported to the press that his indisposition was a bad case of food poisoning. Without Sir Gordon in goal, England lost 3-2. Although he was proud, Banks couldn't help but wonder why the news from Buckingham Palace couldn't have waited until he got home.

Medal Rankings

Following their elimination, the defending champions were deeply depressed. Upon returning to their hotel, the English received a medal that commemorated their passage through Mexico. Alan Ball—a champion four years before at only 21 years of age—took his and threw it through one of the hotel windows. "The only one that has value is the champion," said the midfielder, famous for his bad temper and his obsession with victory. Yet he was right: in 2005, at age 59, Ball presented his 1966 gold medal to the auction house Christie's, which managed to sell it for 164,800 pounds sterling to an enthusiast English fan. Asked by the press why he would sell his precious medal, Ball explained it was the best way to divide the award among his three children. "Winning the World Cup will always be in my memory, but it is time to look to the future, not to the past," he declared. He died two years later at his home in Southampton.

Small Trip

The Uruguayans angrily complained about what they considered an unfair and unforeseen change of scenery to face Brazil in the semi-final on June 17. According to their complaint, the South American clash was initially scheduled for the Azteca stadium in Mexico City where three days before Uruguay had beaten the Soviet Union 1-0. But then the organizers decided to move the match to Guadalajara, where Brazil had been lodged for two months and had played their four previous matches. The change was taken as a vile maneuver to favor the Verdeamarela squad. The Brazilian delegation was perfectly adapted to the hot Tapatio summer and had also won over the local fans; the Uruguayan team, meanwhile, had to travel by bus the 700 kilometers that separated the capital city from the new stage. "It seemed that (in Guadalajara) the Brazilians were in their country because everyone supported them. And we had to go from the height to the heat," recalled defender Juan Mujica. Rumor had it that the outraged president of Uruguay, Jorge Pacheco Areco, had asked the delegation to withdraw from the World Cup, but delegation officials in Mexico denied it. Team doctor Roberto Masliah had much to do to keep his athletes healthy. "Our players lost five kilos during the match with the Soviet Union," he said. "When we planned an intense physical recovery method with a studied program, FIFA surprised us with the resolution to make us travel to Guadalajara. That hurt us, because it altered our work." For the player Ildo Maneiro, the move was an outrage: "We came to a match with an extension, they woke us up at five in the morning because we had to have all our things ready, after two and a half months of touring. It was not just any little trip. There were many setbacks, which added to the team's performance." With these advantages in their favor, the relaxed Brazilean squad won 3 to 1 and reached the final. The Uruguayans, exhausted, fell again three days later to Germany in the Azteca for third place, after suffering another troublesome trip back to the Mexican capital.

Lunch Service

A tying goal by Karl-Heinz Schnellinger in the last minute of the other semi-final forced Germany and Italy to settle who would meet Brazil in the final in a half hour of extra time. The heat, the altitude and the exhausting 90 minutes already played did not seem to promise an epic outcome: But Gerd Müller put Germany ahead at 94 minutes; Tarcisio Burgnich and Gigi Riva turned the score around for Italy, at 98 minutes and then 104.

Pelé celebrating with his Brazil teammates.

Müller balanced things out again at 110 and a minute later Gianni Rivera sealed Italy's 4-3 win. Many of the astonished spectators wondered if such a wonderful soccer demonstration was related to a kind of "refreshment" that the players enjoyed before the extension began. A couple of waiters served the Italians some rolls on a tray, with a tablecloth in the style of a high-class restaurant. The Germans were offered crescent-shaped lemon candies, which they consumed with relish as Franz Beckenbauer's dislocated right shoulder, injured in a collision, was immobilized.

While the "game of the century" was being played, 23 prisoners from the Tixtla prison, a town near Acapulco, took advantage of the fact the guards had gone out to a bar to watch the game and escaped with their weapons.

West Germany 1974

The Netherlands surprised the world, and Germany surprised the Netherlands. As had happened in Switzerland in 1954, the soccer world surrendered to the feet of a team that displayed the most virtuous and effective game. The media covering the tenth World Cup, held in the Federal Republic of Germany—the western portion of a Germany divided after World War II—baptized the Dutch show as "total soccer," due to the mobility of its players and their ability to interchange functions and occupy all the spaces of the field. The brain of the team was Henrik Johanness Cruyff, a tall and elegant man who got tired of scoring goals and winning championships with Ajax in Amsterdam and Barcelona in Spain. The Dutch played like never before, thrashed several rivals and reached the final undefeated, having surrendered just one goal—an own-goal at that. But as had happened in Switzerland, the virtuosity of the orange squad was not enough to lift the Cup. In the final, the perseverance and confidence of West Germany were stronger, and the white team was champion, again without being the best of the tournament. The Germans had a very good team based on the saves of their remarkable goalkeeper, Sepp Maier, a defensive wall in which Franz Beckenbauer shone and the power of the "gunner," Gerd Müller, all mobilized by a heart of steel.

After four championships under the same competition system, in Germany a more tangled path was set. It consisted of a first round with four zones of four teams, with two classified in each group for a second round—two quadrangular semi-finals. At this stage, after playing "all against all," the first squad of each group went to the final, the second to the match for third place and the rest were eliminated.

The final, on July 7 at the Olympic stadium in Munich between Germany and the Netherlands, had several peculiarities. It was the first decisive match not played in the capital of the host country (at that time, Bonn), a circumstance that would be repeated later in other Cups. It started several minutes late because two flags were missing, one in a corner and the other at mid-field. And the Netherlands took the lead before a single German player touched the ball. The orange side served out of the middle and passed the ball fifteen times between them, until Johan Cruyff, who had left behind his personal pursuer Berti Vogts, was brought down inside the box by Uli Hoeness. Johan Neeskens took the penalty kick that put the Dutch ahead.

In this tournament, another "national" curiosity took place: the Federal Republic of Germany (FRG) faced on June 22, in Hamburg, the German Democratic Republic (GDR). Germany against Germany. The FRG, or West Germany, had already met Saar—a "third" Germany created after World War II—in the 1954 qualifiers, and now it would face its eastern brothers. The East Germans won by a score of 1-0, with a goal from Juergen Sparwasser.

A singular fact was that the value of the tickets included insurance for the spectators, a measure taken as a result of the murder of eleven Israeli athletes at the hands of an Islamic extremist group called "Black September" during the 1972 Munich Olympic Games.

The New World Cup

After Brazil won its third World Cup in 1970 and took permanent possession of the Jules Rimet trophy, FIFA organized a design competition for a new one. Out of 53 projects presented, the winner was by Italian sculptor Silvio Gazzaniga—it remains the World Cup trophy today. It's 75 percent 18-karat gold, with a base made from a decorative stone called green malachite. It weighs five kilograms and measures 36 centimeters high. FIFA paid $20,000 for its creation in 1974 and unlike the Jules Rimet trophy, the new cup can never be taken forever. The champion of each competition only gets a smaller replica, which its association keeps in perpetuity.

The Ghost Squad

In August 1973, a group of sixteen young people arrived in the city of Tilcara, in the Argentine province of Jujuy, to acclimatization to the altitude with a very important objective: a month later, dressed in light blue and white shirts, they'd play Bolivia in the city of La Paz, 3,600 meters above sea level, to qualify for the Germany 1974 World Cup. The group, named "the ghost squad" by a magazine, was led by the alternate coach of the national team, Miguel Ignomiriello, and included, among others, Ubaldo Fillol, Mario Kempes, Juan José López, Marcelo Trobbiani, Ricardo Bochini and Reinaldo Merlo. The idea was to play the Bolivians with a team consisting mainly of novice footballers acclimatized to the altitude (Tilcara is 2,500 meters above sea level) with a sprinkling of two or three of the most experienced players. The main coach, Enrique Omar Sívori, drew up his plan remembering that Argentina had lost in qualifying four years earlier when facing the same scenario. The stratagem was perfect: Argentina defeated its rival 1-0, with a goal scored by Omar Fornari on a header. Thanks to this victory and good results at home against Bolivia and Paraguay, Argentina got their passport to the World Cup.

Chile Versus Nobody

On November 21, 1973, the National Stadium in Santiago de Chile was the scene of one of the most ridiculous events in the history of soccer. There, the local team played a game against . . . nobody. How did it happen? For these qualifying rounds, it had been determined that the winner of Group 9 in Europe, consisting of only three teams, would participate of a playoff with the first of Group 3 in South America, also made up of three countries. First the draw and then the results set the clash between Chile and the Soviet Union. On September 26, the "first leg" match was held in Moscow, which ended tied at zero. The rematch was scheduled for November 21 in Santiago, but the USSR announced that it was withdrawing for political reasons.

It was the Cold War, and the Soviets opposed the overthrow of Chile's socialist president Salvador Allende—friend of the Kremlin government—at the hands of the fascist General Augusto Pinochet, a "partner" of the United States in the fight against communism and later of England during the Falklands War. From Moscow, it was announced that the Soviet team would not play at the National Stadium, for its having been the scene of torture and executions. The Chilean captain, Francisco Valdés, acknowledged years later that, upon his return from the game in Russia, he had to intercede with Pinochet himself to save the life of defender Hugo Lepe, the first president of the Professional Footballers Union, who had been detained in that place for being considered a "dangerous activist." Valdés saved Lepe's life, but could not prevent other players from being tormented or killed.

The USSR requested the game take place in a neutral setting and even mentioned Buenos Aires as a possible venue. FIFA declined to move it, and the Kremlin banned its team from traveling to South America. On the day of the match, in the absence of the Soviets, Austrian referee Eric Linemayr, appointed by FIFA, declared the match won for the locals, who thus obtained their passage to Germany. However, the Chileans mounted a parody as extravagant as it was regrettable: their principal eleven went out onto the playing field dressed in their official uniforms and with local referee Rafael Hormazábal officiating—Linemayr did not want to attend such a farce—an unusual game of a team against nobody began at the designated time. When Valdés sent the ball into the empty net, the 15,000 people in the stands cheered the outrageous goal. Without opposition, the red squad "won" the match. Once again, soccer was the loser.

Colors

The Netherlands' orange shirt drew as much admiration in this Cup as the team's performance. Many people wondered why the squad's jersey is a color that does not appear on their flag, which combines blue, white and red. Orange identifies the House of Orange, the Dutch royal family. It's the same with Italy, whose flag is green, white and red (a design contributed by Napoleon Bonaparte in November 1796 to a corps of Lombard volunteers who joined the French army), but its team wears blue. When Italy played its first international match, in 1910, the House of Savoy reigned in that country, whose characteristic color was precisely the "azzurri."

There are more countries wrapped in colors that do not represent their flag: the blue of Japan echoes the Japanese philosophy of worshipping the sky and the sea, but also hides the need to distinguish itself from the red of South Korea and China. The garnet of Venezuela, or "vinotinto," was adopted by chance in 1938, when a delegation of athletes from that country attended the Bolivarian

Games in Bogotá. The Venezuelans had worn a yellow uniform, reflecting their flag, which matched the jersey of the host nation, Colombia. The International Olympic Committee assigned the Venezuelans the intense garnet for their official uniform. Sportsmen and fans liked it so much that it was adopted forever.

The Uruguayan "sky blue" has already been commented upon, but not the golden yellow and green of Australia, which in Germany 1974 played its first Cup. The official flag is blue with six white stars, and a small Union Jack in the upper right corner, but the sports uniform was designed based on the national flower, the golden wattle, with dark green leaves that grows in forests and jungles in the south of the country.

The Two Stripe Brand

Johan Cruyff had threatened the Dutch federation that he would not go to the World Cup if he was forced to wear the official orange jersey. This was not based on simple whim, but on a controversial business dispute. In those years, Puma and Adidas were the strongest sportswear firms in the world and had divided the soccer planet. (They'd been born on opposite sides of the same street in the German city of Herzogenaurach, created by two rival brothers, Rudolf and Adolf Dassler, respectively.) Puma had hired Cruyff for a lot of money to be its main advertising face, and didn't want its star to appear before the eyes of the world with another symbol on his chest, shoulders and arms, much less that of its number one enemy. Cruyff proposed a Solomonic solution: Adidas would continue to dress the national squad, but he'd use an almost identical shirt with no logo on the chest and with only two of the traditional three Adidas stripes on the sleeves. According to a Puma spokesperson consulted for this book, it was Cruyff himself who tore off the badge and one of the stripes "as a sign of loyalty" to that company.

The skilled Johan Cruyff (centre) represented both the Dutch and Puma.

Australian Penalty

Australia's national team was reprimanded for wearing "anti-regulation clothing" against the German Democratic Republic. On June 14, in Hamburg, the team did not wear the dark green shirt that FIFA had indicated, but their traditional yellow. This, according to the organizers of the Cup, confused viewers around the world who mostly followed the action on black and white televisions—on which the yellow shirt and dark green shorts of the Australian uniform looked identical to the white jerseys and black shorts of the Germans.

Pricey Quote

Shortly before the game between Uruguay and the Netherlands, the opening of Group 3 in the first round, the South American defender

Juan Carlos Masnik put a price on his press availability: He charged $300 for spending three minutes before the cameras of Dutch television. Masnik collected a good amount, much greater than his reward for playing for Uruguay—the team was eliminated in the first round.

The First Doping Case

The Haitian Ernst Jean-Joseph found fame by becoming the first player to test positive in a World Cup after FIFA began anti-doping tests in 1966. In Jean-Joseph's urine sample—taken at the end of a 3-1 loss to Italy—traces of ephedrine were found and he was immediately expelled from the Cup. The next day, Jean-Joseph made headlines again for seeking asylum in Germany, fearful of reprisals when returning home. Despite this, and before his claim could be considered by the German government, he disappeared from his team's hotel. According to newspaper accounts, Jean-Joseph was kidnapped by members of the Haitian dictator Jean-Claude Duvalier's guard, and secretly taken back to Haiti. The soccer player would have been reprimanded and even beaten by Duvalier himself.

The Robbery

June 14 was not another day in the life of Doğan Babacan. That date, at the West Germany-Chile game at the Olympiastadion in Berlin, he became the first and only Turkish referee to work a World Cup match until Brazil 2014 (there, Cüneyt Çakir was the second). In the match, which the home team won 1-0, Babacan sent off Chile's Carlos Caszely in the 67th minute, the first player to see a red card in the history of the World Cup. The red and yellow acrylics had been released for the previous edition, Mexico 1970, but in that championship no ejections were recorded. Meanwhile, back in Turkey, while the referee's wife and daughter were at a neighbor's house to follow Babacan's performance on television, a group of criminals broke into their house and stole money and other valuables. News of the robbery made the Chilean fans feel a bit of vengeance—they felt the referee had favoured the local squad. Many of the red supporters repeated again and again that Babacan's thieves had also stolen their heart.

Witchcraft

A couple of days before the team from Zaire faced Yugoslavia for the second round of Group 2, some sorcerers from the African country arrived in Germany to exert their spiritual influence and help their inexperienced national soccer team. In their debut, the "Leopards" had fallen 2-0 to Scotland, and as their third game was against Brazil—the defending champions—they needed all the help they could get. But the sorcerers were not welcomed by Zaire's coach, Blagoiev Vidinic, himself of Yugoslav origin. The witches, gathered in front of the team's hotel, told the international press that the coach "rejects us because he fears that our fetishes will help the 'leopards' to win over his brothers." They accused the coach of "preparing the defeat of our team because he cannot betray his people." On June 18, in Gelsenkirchen, the Balkan squad crushed the Zairians, who without the help of rites and magical ceremonies were thrashed 9-0.

Just 22 minutes in, Yugoslavia was already leading by 4-0. Annoyed by the Balkan superiority, the Zairian defender Mulamba Ndaye approached the Colombian referee Omar Delgado to demand that he disallow the last goal because in the previous action there had been a foul committed. When the referee ignored his complaints, perhaps due to the language mismatch, the Zairean player used a universal gesture to express his discontent: he kicked the man in black in the backside. Ndaye was immediately sent off, and FIFA applied the maximum penalty: a one-year suspension from local and international matches. The game continued, as did the Yugoslav shots. With one less man, the Africans gave up five more goals.

A Negative Undefeated Campaign

Scotland became the first country to be eliminated from the World Cup without losing a single game. The Scots competed in a very complicated group with Brazil, Yugoslavia and the weak Zaire. They tied Brazil (0-0) and Yugoslavia (1-1) and beat Zaire 2-0. As Brazil and Yugoslavia also tied each other, and both teams beat Zaire, there was a triple tie with four points, and goal differential would make the difference. Yugoslavia had scored nine against Zaire, Brazil three and Scotland just two, which sent the unbeaten Scottish squad home.

Rematch

In its last match prior to the World Cup in Germany, the Argentine squad faced the Netherlands in Amsterdam. The Dutch, commanded by Johan Cruyff, crushed the South American team 4-1, although the beating could have been more thorough because of the quality and speed of the Europeans. "The result is a lie, I want revenge", demanded Víctor Rodríguez, one of Argentina's triumvirate of coaches. Fate granted the big-mouthed coach his second chance a month later, during the Cup: On June 26, in Gelsenkirchen, Argentina and the Netherlands opened the semi-final Group A. Rodríguez found out the result in Amsterdam had not been a "lie." The Netherlands won again easily, this time 4-0.

Perón

On July 1, the Argentine delegation asked FIFA to postpone the match against the Democratic Republic of Germany when the death of President Juan Perón was reported from Buenos Aires. Their officials argued that the government had decreed three days of mourning before the funeral, to which the soccer players wanted to adhere. Although both squads were in fact eliminated by then, FIFA determined the game would be played on the scheduled day and time. Organizers did authorize that honors be rendered to the deceased president, through a minute of silence, flags at half-mast and black armbands on the players. That day, Ubaldo Fillol, the third goalkeeper on the team, made his debut in the Argentine goal because Daniel Carnevali (the starter) and Miguel Santoro (his substitute) were fervent Peronists and refused to play.

All by Themselves

Until the final on July 7, the Netherlands had played six games without an opponent scoring. In the first round, they'd beaten Uruguay 2-0, drew goalless with Sweden and defeated Bulgaria 4-1. In the second, they won all three of their games: 4-0 over Argentina and 2-0 against East Germany and Brazil. The only goal, from Bulgaria, was also scored by a Dutchman: Ruud Krol, against his own net.

Stamps

Confidence in the orange team proved expensive for the Dutch government. Days before the final, a series of stamps was printed honoring the squad. But, the day after the West German victory, the postal administration had to destroy one hundred thousand stamps bearing the inscription "Netherlands World Soccer Champions."

Until Triumph Do Us Part

Forward Gerd Müller, who scored West Germany's winning goal in the final, resigned from the national team the night of the championship celebration because footballers' wives were not invited to the official gala dinner. The board of directors of the German federation had made the decision, and so while dinner was taking place in their hotel's banquet hall, the women, abandoned, had to await the completion of the gala in another sector of the building. After that night, Müller never wore the German national jersey again. His wife was very grateful.

Müller and teamate Wolfgang Overath (left) celebrate their 1974 victory.

Argentina 1978

As happened in Italy 1934 and France 1938, the eleventh edition of the World Cup could not be detached from dark politics. The Argentina 1978 tournament was held in a dictatorship that spared no blood or torture to fight the "communist guerrilla." One of the bloodiest clandestine detention centers was in the Escuela de Mecánica de la Armada (the Navy Mechanics School), a few meters from Monumental stadium of the River Plate Football Club, home to several games, including the final.

This scenario caused deep unease in a lot of European countries, which called for a boycott against the brutal dictatorship. In the Netherlands, the Labor Party congress asked that the national squad not participate in the tournament, but the Government considered that "a boycott will not change the violation of human rights in Argentina. We should take advantage of the World Championship to publicize what it happens in that country." Other leaders of human rights organizations demanded that the contest be moved to Brazil. Although the Dutch national team arrived to play their matches, they did so without some of their celebrities: Johan Cruyff, star of Barcelona, considered the best player in the world of the 1970s; Ruud Geels, Ajax striker and top scorer that year in Dutch league;

155

Eddy Treytel, the Feyenoord goalkeeper; and Jan Van Beveren and Willy Van der Kuylen, two brilliant PSV Eindhoven midfielders.

German goalkeeper Sepp Maier did travel to defend the 1974 title, but before embarking for Buenos Aires he signed an Amnesty International petition in favor of Argentine political prisoners. In France, the newspaper *Le Matin* assured that "the world of soccer would be honored if (the French team) refused to play in Argentina, between the concentration camps and the torture chambers. The Argentine Military Junta does not deserve the World championship." The socialist deputy Lionel Jospin (who years later would be Prime Minister) requested the transfer of the World Cup to another country or, otherwise, urged those involved to "take advantage of this event to denounce the violence of the Argentine military regime."

French anger at the Jorge Videla dictatorship even generated an attempted kidnapping of coach Michel Hidalgo. Four people who were part of an organization that defined itself as "humanitarian and non-violent" tried to capture Hidalgo when he was driving his car on the outskirts of Bordeaux, but the coach managed to escape unharmed. In a letter sent to the media, the failed kidnappers said their objective was to exchange Hidalgo for French citizens "disappeared" in Argentina by the military forces. They also highlighted that, at first, they had thought of hijacking one of the best players of the team, Michel Platini, but then they decided on Hidalgo "because this man describes himself as a humanist, is a trade unionist and, in effect, has intervened in demonstrations of humanitarian character." The Videla regime took note of these events and a few days later released one of the twenty-two French "disappeared" in an attempt to improve his image in the Old Continent.

The World Cup was played, as planned, regardless of what happened. Three weeks before the start of the competition, a car bomb exploded in the parking lot of the San Martin Municipal Theater, in the heart of Buenos Aires, where the press center had been set up. The attack caused alarm among journalists around the world who had to travel to Buenos Aires to cover the games. Finally, the guerrilla groups adopted a kind of "truce" during the month that the competition would last, although propaganda continued. The "Montoneros" organization, one of the main comando groups that fought against the military dictatorship, interfered several times with the broadcast of the matches to issue statements or speeches by its boss, Mario Firmenich, who was hiding in Europe.

The day after the final, won by Argentina against the Netherlands, 3-1, the Jorge Videla appeared at the press center to talk with the foreign correspondents. "After two and a half years in which the armed forces took over political power and received a prostrate country, we can show it standing in the eyes of the world with the effort of all Argentines and moving towards the achievement of the objectives end: a truly representative democracy." The only thing more pathetic than his words were the autograph requests that several journalists made to the nefarious dictator.

Despite the pools of blood, the ball rolled and left, again, hundreds of stories. Mario Kempes, the hero who allowed the blue and white to lift their first World Cup, became the first player to wear the "triple crown": he was champion, top scorer and chosen as the best in the tournament. (Brazilian Garrincha was nominated as the top star of the 1962 Chile edition, in which he was also a top scorer along with five others, although that came many years later when FIFA decided to honor the heroes of the Cups prior to 1978.)

The Netherlands' Dick Nanninga was the first substitute sent off in a World Cup. On June 18, at the Chateau Carreras stadium in Córdoba, Nanninga came into the pitch in the 79th minute for Pieter Wildschut while his team was even at two with Germany. In just nine minutes, the forward recieved two yellow cards from Uruguayan referee Ramón Barreto. France set a record, but an unsatisfactory one: coach Hidalgo used all 22 players he called up, including their three goalkeepers: Dominique Baratelli, Jean-Paul Bertrand-Demanes and Dominique Dropsy.

The competition system was identical to the terrifying scheme used in Germany. It would be the last time. Argentina, the Netherlands and Brazil—champions, second and third, respectively—had finished second in their groups during the first phase. The Brazilians had one more reason to return home without their traditional joy: they were the first team to finish the championship undefeated without being champion. They tied Spain and Sweden and beat Austria in the first round, and then beat Peru and Poland and tied Argentina, who qualified for the final by having a better goal differential. They then defeated Italy in the insipid duel for third place. This course of events, which occurred for the first time in Argentina '78, would be repeated several times throughout the history of the Cup.

With a penalty kick against Scotland, The Netherlands' Nicolaus Robert Rensenbrink scored the thousandth goal of the World Cup on June 11. His feat was well rewarded with gifts: watches, fine clothes, hams, and a week-long stay in a Buenos Aires ranch. The German coach Helmut Schoen, meanwhile, completed 25 World Cup matches (all with Germany, in the 1966, 1970, 1974 and 1978 editions), a record that has not yet been surpassed.

Bottle rain

After two absences in Mexico 1970 and in Germany 1974, Spain managed to return to the World Cup. The Iberian squad had to work very hard to get ahead of Romania and Yugoslavia to make it through. In the decisive qualifying match, on November 30, 1977 in Belgrade, Yugoslavia needed a decisive victory. With nothing to lose, the Balkan team bombarded the goal posts guarded by Miguel Ángel González, then Real Madrid goalkeeper, and also the legs of their opponents: captain José Martínez Sánchez, known sportingly as Pirri, had to leave the icy field after thirteen minutes, suffering a sprained ankle after a very hard kick from Miodrag Kustudic. Ironically, it was Argentine-born Rubén Cano who scored the late goal that would send Spain to Argentina 1978. A few more moments later, Juan *Juanito* Gómez was replaced by Daniel Ruiz-Bazán. As he left the pitch, the forward made a mocking gesture to the audience: he waved his right thumb down, signaling that Yugoslavia was eliminated. The answer was a shower of glass bottles, one of which exploded on *Juanito*'s head. Unconscious, he had to be removed on a stretcher. Back in Madrid, with his head bandaged, the controversial *Juanito* assured that returning home with his skull damaged by the bottle "was worth it, because we have played the bravest game in recent years. We were not daunted at any time and we have always faced the consequences." In his case, the face and also the head bore those consequences.

The coach who did not choose Maradona

"I have to give the three names that are not going to join us in the World Cup. I couldn't sleep all night because it is the most ungrateful moment in these three months that we have been together." The hoarse voice of César Menotti dominated the Salvatori Foundation training field, where the camp for the Argentine team that would play in the 1978 World Cup had been set up. That afternoon of May 19, 1978, twenty-five nervous young men awaited the final verdict of *El Flaco*. A World Cup roster could onliy list twenty-two players. Three would be left behind.

A little while before, Roberto Saporiti, the coach's assistant, questioned one of the surnames. "But did you see what today's practice was like? He made three goals!" he objected, confused. Menotti nodded his head. "Are you sure?" the assistant insisted. Menotti's answer was conclusive: "Yes, *Sapo*. Don't bust my balls anymore."

Sitting on a ball, the coach suddenly stopped his speech, took a deep breath and released the names of the three boys who would be disappointed: Humberto Bravo, Víctor Bottaniz and . . . Diego Maradona, a 17-year-old kid and author of the hat-trick in that morning training session. For a few seconds, only the wind chasing through the trees of the property was heard. *El Flaco* took a deep breath again and, by way of apology, invited the three excluded to continue training with the squad. Bravo and Maradona—distressed by the decision, overflowing with tears—chose to leave that same day. Bottaniz, on the other hand, preferred to remain with the twenty-two lucky ones. Diego reappeared, albeit on the phone, the night before the final match with The Netherlands: he called, spoke with Menotti, wished good luck and sent a hug to each of the players, convinced that his great moment would come another time.

Forty years after the thorny determination, the former coach acknowledged: "At one point you have to decide. I left Diego out in '78. If someone asked me now if I was wrong, I would say that it is probable, very probable," although he stressed that the fact was hidden behind the title of champion.

Mother's Day

Shortly before traveling to Argentina, Jan Zwartkruis—assistant to the Dutch coach, the Austrian Ernst Happel—summoned the players for a training session in Amsterdam. All those selected showed up, except for Dick Nanninga, forward of JC Roda. At the end of the session, Zwartkruis called Nanninga to ask for an explanation. "I apologize, but I was unable to attend because I could not leave my business alone," said the forward, who in addition to playing soccer, had a flower shop in the heart of the capital city. "Mother's Day is approaching and I have to take advantage, because many people buy flowers on that date. There will be time to train." With much sacrifice,

Nanninga recovered that lost practice with double training days. The striker scored his team's only goal in the final against Argentina, and it fored the game into overtime, although it was not enough to avoid a 3-1 defeat.

Loaned jerseys

On June 10, France and Hungary surprised everyone by going out on the field at the City of Mar del Plata stadium with identical, totally white uniforms—curiously the second or "away" colors of both teams. This was due to error in the official FIFA communication, which understood that the blue colors of the French team and red of the Magyar squad could be confused on the black and white televisions of the time. The real problem arose when Brazilian referee Arnaldo Coelho called the captains: neither team had a set of spare jerseys. An official with the local Kimberley Football Club offered to lend a complete set of shirts. The offer was quickly accepted, and forty minutes later France appeared on the pitch dressed in vertical green and white stripes. As the numbers on the jerseys were sequential from 2 to 16, Dominique Rocheteau and Olivier Rouyer performed with 7" and 11 on the back, and 18 and 20 on the shorts, respectively.

He's Positive

After Peru's 3-1 victory over Scotland on June 3 in Córdoba, the Scots caused a commotion, not because of their play but because one of their forwards, William McClure Johnston, tested positive for doping. Traces of a stimulant called fencamfamine were found in Johnston's urine, although the player denied ever using that substance. "I was in the best shape of my life and I didn't need any artificial stimulants. That game (against Peru) was the worst of my international career, so you can't say that (fencamfamine) improved my performance," he told the press. Johnston was expelled from the World Cup and never called up for the Scottish national team again. In the wake of the incident, Scottish Labor MP Dennis Canavan requested an official investigation into the use of drugs in sport. According to Canavan, the Johnston case served "to discredit the country's soccer even more than the unfortunate performance of the team in Argentina."

Johnston was notorious for his bad behavior on the field (he was sent off 22 times in about 400 official games) and for other unusual attitudes. Once, playing for the Vancouver Whitecaps of the Canadian league—he was effectively exiled there for two years after the World Cup scandal—he accepted a glass of beer from a fan as he approached the stands to throw a corner kick. After several refreshing sips, Johnston launched a precise ball that a teammate headed into the rival's goal.

Better alone than in bad company

Scotland's 1-1 draw against Iran on June 7 was seen as a humiliation by the country's press and fans. It also meant the premature elimination of the Scottish squad, which had already fallen 3-1 to Peru in the first match of Group 4, three days earlier. The morning after the duel with the Persian team, the Scottish coach, Ally MacLeod, faced the journalists from his home country at an informal press conference on the grounds of the team's hotel in Alta. Between questions and answers, a puppy passed through the garden and sat next to MacLeod. Noticing his presence, the depressed manager said: "Look at me now, without a single friend in this world, only with this little dog." Almost without letting him finish the sentence, the pup stood up, bit the hapless MacLeod and staggered away.

Boozers

The Polish players arrived in Buenos Aires with extra luggage: 380 bottles of vodka. Coach Jacek Gmoch allowed his boys to drink alcohol and smoke, "always within tolerable limits." As the Polish delegation was 35 strong, each player received just over ten bottles of vodka for his one-month stay in Argentina. Perhaps a questionable "tolerable limit" for a professional athlete.

The Scots had a high tolerance for the booze as well. The staff of the hotel in Alta Gracia, Córdoba, where the delegation stayed, had to work overtime to collect the large quantity of empty bottles of whiskey and other spirits left by the players when they abandoned the place.

Additional job

The many years spent at the Barcelona club in Spain forced Dutch midfielder Johannes Neeskens to assume, upon arriving in Argentina, an onerous additional task: to be the group's translator. Because he was fluent in Spanish, the journalists turned to him as well, even to interview his teammates—until poor Neeskens got fed up and stopped going to the long and exhausting press conferences. After all, he had earned the break: he didn't charge a penny for his interpreter's services.

Another player who took on extra work was the Austrian Hans Pirkner, who served as the altar boy in his delegation. Pirkner assisted the priest Frederic Petchel, who had traveled especially with the group, at each mass celebrated to provide spiritual help to the athletes.

In the air

When Welsh referee Clive Thomas whistled a corner kick for Brazil, there were just a few seconds left in the clash with Sweden, which opened Group 3 in Mar del Plata, on July 3. Thomas gave the order, José Dirceu sent in a cross and the talented midfielder Arthur Antunes Coimbra, known as "Zico," with a header, broke the draw by one.

All the Brazilians ran to hug Zico, but immediately noticed that the referee did not mark the center of the field, nor had he validated the goal. When Thomas was asked his ruling, the Welshman replied: the end of the game with the ball in the air. The South Americans protested, made a fuss, begged . . . but the referee remained firm: it was not a goal. The Brazilians left the pitch cursing and accusing the man in black of having favored the Swedes. To justify their complaint, they claimed that during the second half, Thomas had put his hands on his head in disappointment after a shot from Bo Larsson missed the net.

To be or not to be?

German referee Ferdinand Biwersi, who worked Spain's 1-0 victory over Sweden, was chosen in his country as "athlete of the 1977/78 season" by various associations and specialized media. Biwersi rejected the honor, however, saying that a referee "is not an athlete." "The work of a referee is not sports, since he is limited to directing a sports competition. For this reason, I see myself in the decision to renounce that title," Biwersi argued.

Firm hand

A few weeks before traveling to Buenos Aires, Brazilian coach Claudio Coutinho gathered his players at a Tersépolis training camp, about a hundred kilometers from Rio de Janeiro, and gave them a set of 19 rules they were to follow until the final of the Cup. Among them: no beards or long hair, no gambling, drinking alcohol or smoking "before or in the interval between matches." Coutinho also prohibited his men from criticizing teammates, using the hotels telephone for long-distance calls, appearing in commercial advertisements and, especially, complaining about any decision of the referees or the linesmen.

The tie

Germany had no mercy. In just 38 minutes, it was already leading Mexico 3-0 with goals from Dieter Mueller, Hans Mueller and Karl-Heinz Rummenigge. The German team was a nightmare for the Aztecs who, in addition, had lost their goalkeeper: before the third goal, the tank Rummenigge crushed the soft Pilar Reyes, who had to leave the field due to a strong blow that left Reyes needing sixteen stitches. His spot in goal was left to Pedro Soto. According to one story, he'd told coach José Antonio Roca that he preferred the comfort of his refuge on the bench to being torn to pieces by the Germans. This unleashed a new threat, this time from the coach to the goal-keeper. With the substitution made, the Germans refused to take their foot off the accelerator: Heinz Flohe welcomed Soto just five min-utes after he arrived with a long-range cannon shot that dug into the upper right corner. In the second half, the Europeans scored another two goals—again Rummenigge, again Flohe—to complete a 6-0 rout that, even today, is Mexico's worst defeat in World Cup history. After the final whistle from Syrian referee Farouk Bouzo, the overwhelmed Soto entered the dressing room and found Reyes and his bloody right leg. Amid the pain, the starting goalkeeper gathered the strength to ask how the match ended. Perhaps touched by the misfortune of his partner, Soto replied with a remarkable irony: "We tied, Pilar. They scored three goals on you, and they also scored three on me."

Phone

When Germany and Austria appeared for the closing game of semi-final Group A, only the German squad had a chance of reaching the final or, failing that, the match for third place. The game had been scheduled at the same time as the Netherlands-Italy match, and the Germans needed a victory and a draw in that game to play in the final and repeat as World Cup champions. On its own, a win over Austria—already eliminated—would ensure a fight for the bronze.

Germany took the lead in the 19th minute with a goal from Karl-Heinz Rummenigge and went into halftime in the lead. At that time, the Italians were leading 1-0, but the Germans were confident the Netherlands would come back. However, games must be played until minute 90 and, as the maxim says, "you must not sell the skin before killing the bear." Austria drew level at 59 minutes with a Berti Vogts's own-goal and then went ahead on the scoreboard thanks to its great star, Hans Krankl, at 66. The Germans pulled even at 72 minutes, but at 88, as they desperately fought for victory, a lethal counterattack from Krankl sealed the Austrian victory. The Germans were furious with their neighbors, who had "unnecessarily" left them empty-handed. In retaliation, a German newspaper published Krankl's home phone number alongside the game's report. The device did not stop ringing for several days, transmitting all kinds of insults and threats to the scorer and his family. The intimidation created the ideal environment so that, a few months later, the forward accepted an offer from Barcelona and moved with all his relatives to Spain.

Controversial match

There was no more controversial match in this World Cup than the one between Argentina and Peru in the second round. The local squad won by a huge margin, 6-0, and thanks to that enormous goal difference, it qualified for the final against the Netherlands and sent Brazil to play for third place with Italy. The remarkable performance of César Menotti's team and the poor showing of the men led by Marcos Calderón gave rise to well-founded suspicions.

For one thing, Brazil-Poland and Argentina-Peru did not play at the same time: the first match started at 4:45 pm in Mendoza, and the second at 7:15 pm in Rosario. Because of that, after Brazil's by 3 to 1 victory, given the tournament's goal differentials to that point, the Argentines knew that they needed a victory by four goals to make the final. Much has been said about alleged bribes paid by the Argentine military government to Peru to force its boys to tank the match. Supposedly, the regime sent two ships loaded with wheat to Lima as thanks, and Peru's goalkeeper, Ramón Quiroga, born in Argentina, is said to have been paid off. What these stories do not explain is why Quiroga continued his career in the national squad, including in the 1981 South American Qualifiers and the 1982 World Cup in Spain. Nor why visiting striker Juan José Muñante rang one off the goalpost when the score was 0-0. Nor was it widely known that there would also have been an enticement from the Brazilians to the Peruvians so that they would *not* fall by a landslide, an offer consisting of $5,000 per man and a trip for each player and his family to a luxury hotel on the island of Itaparica. This version of the story was acknowledged by two of the Peruvian protagonists, Héctor Chumpitaz and Rodolfo Manzo.

Cast

As he took to the pitch for the final, visiting midfielder René Van de Kerkhof wore a cast on his right wrist. Argentine captain Daniel Passarella warned Italian referee Sergio Gonella of the irregularity. "Until the cast is removed, the final will not begin," he said. And so it was: The Dutch doctor removed the plaster shell and placed on a

Argentine captain Daniel
Passarella hoists the World Cup

plastic one, much less dangerous in case of a blow or friction with an opponent. The start was delayed just eight minutes.

Celebration on the rocks

After the 3-1 victory over the Netherlands, the 22 Argentine players who won the 1978 World Cup showered, dressed in towels and robes and sat on lounge chairs in a covered space bordering the dressing room. They had time to relax before they needed to put on suits and leave for the gala dinner where the medals would be distributed and the prizes would be awarded to the top scorer and the best player of the contest. As the boys chatted, a club employee came up and asked the brand-new champions what they wanted to drink. Mario Kempes looked mischievously at his friend Héctor Baley: "Shall we have a whisky together?" he proposed in his booming Cordovan voice. The goal-keeper nodded. "Bring us a big whisky to share with the boys," El *Matador* requested. The man returned at once with a tall glass filled with Scotch with a big chunk of ice. Kempes took a sip and handed the chalice to Baley, who followed suit. Then, the glass passed from hand to hand and all the champions toasted the unprecedented feat of the Argentine national team.

Spain 1982

The 1938 World Cup had been played in France with the world on the brink of war, a conflict that would see the tournament suspended until 1950. In the 1940s, war beat soccer. But in 1982, soccer—or perhaps the business of sport—was stronger than war. And so Spain '82 featured something unprecedented: Never before had two nations participated, at the same time, in an armed conflict and a World Cup. On April 2, 1982, Argentina's military regime decided to invade the Malvinas/Falkland Islands, an archipelago located about 500 kilometers east of Patagonia that since the middle nineteenth-century had been British territory. Argentina claimed— and still does—the enclave as its own, considering it sits within the country's maritime territory. The United Kingdom did not sit idly by. It sent its military might to the South Atlantic to regain the Malvinas/Falklands. The confrontation, which caused more than 900 deaths and 2,000 injuries, lasted until June 14, a day after the opening match between Argentina and Belgium. That same day, the Argentine armed forces surrendered.

Many voices had been raised demanding both countries be excluded from the Cup—in fact, three teams from the United Kingdom had arrived in Spain: England, Scotland and Northern

Ireland. Former Argentine player and coach Alfredo Di Stéfano said from Madrid that "it is not logical that while some are risking their lives in Las Malvinas, others compete in the '82 World Cup to entertain people." The Argentine government disagreed. Two weeks before the start of the championship, the military junta assured that there was "no cause whatsoever to cancel the participation of the Argentine team." In London, a group of parliamentarians declared that "the British government should request the expulsion of the Argentine soccer team, defender world champion, from the final phase of the '82 World Cup."

In the event, Argentina, England, Scotland and Northern Ireland all participated in the Cup as if nothing had happened in the South Atlantic. Well, actually, almost, because the British government blocked the broadcast of the inaugural match between Argentina and Belgium. If they had known that the "red devils" would defeat the defending champions 1-0, they would surely have shown it. In Buenos Aires, channels 2 and 11, which had announced the broadcast of the game between England and France, showed Germany-Algeria instead.

Fortunately, Argentina did not meet any of the United Kingdom teams in the contest and the issue, in Spain, ended in peace. In September, two months after the end of the World Cup, the head of the English Football Association, Bert Millchip, promoted a friendly meeting with Argentina, arguing that "there should be no political interference in sport. We maintain sports ties with Argentina, since Ricardo Villa, who returned to Tottenham Hotspur, was well received and it is possible that Osvaldo Ardiles will also return [he did, although mourning the death of his cousin, José Ardiles, 32, an Argentine Air Force pilot who was killed in one of the battles in the archipelago]. I hope that by June of next year the waters will have returned to their course." Due to obvious political disagreements, however, Millchip's match was never played. (The great shock would only occur four years later, in Mexico, but that will be another story. A great story.)

Away from the diplomatic wrangling, some excellent soccer was played and Italy was a fair champion, even if an unlikely one at first. In the opening round, the Azzurri team did not win a game—it tied 0-0 with Poland and 1-1 with Peru and Cameroon—but in the second round it beat Argentina with authority, 2-1, and Brazil, in an exciting match, 3 to 2. It met Poland again in the semi-finals, and took the match 2-0. In the final, played against Germany at the Santiago Bernabeu stadium in Madrid, the squad had a tepid first half, but in the second it took an immense advantage thanks to the three goals scored by Paolo Rossi, Marco Tardelli and Alessandro Altobelli. Paul Breitner got one back at 83 minutes, when there was no way to change history.

The championship format presented two novelties: the number of participating teams was increased from 16 to 24 and the table system was modified once again: six groups of four squads were assembled, of which the first two qualified for the second stage. That round would be four zones of three teams, with the winner of each trio qualifying for the semi-final. At that point, and for the first time, the shootout by penalty kicks was incorporated to break the ties. Germany and France inaugurated this method of unlevelling following an electrifying 3-3 tie in 120 minutes. The Germans prevailed thanks to the saves of their goalkeeper, Harald Schumacher, and advanced to the final.

The overwhelming victory of Hungary over El Salvador, 10-1 was the biggest win in the history of the World Cup—although it did not surpass the Austria's 7-5 triumph over Switzerland in 1954 for the highest number of goals. Hungary's Laszlo Kiss, who entered to the pitch in the 55th minute for Andras Torocsik, became the first substitute player to score three goals in a single game. Incredibly, despite this achievement, the Hungary did not get past the first round: it lost against Argentina and drew with Belgium.

Forever young: Italian goalkeeper Dino Zoff established himself as the oldest world champion in history, aged forty years and four months on the day of the final, July 11. Northern Irishman Norman Whiteside, at the other end, became the youngest player to perform in a Cup, facing Yugoslavia at the age of 17 years 41 days on June 17.

The witch

For the 1982 World Cup qualifier in Spain, the Colombian federation hired Argentine coach Carlos Bilardo, who had done a good job as manager of the local club Deportivo Cali. In addition to preparing his men to face Uruguay and Peru in a three-team group, Bilardo hired a "witch" named Beatriz Becerra, a woman from Cali who was said to have supernatural powers, and took her to the "Nemesio Camacho" stadium minutes before the debut against the Peruvians. The woman entered the locker room and performed whatever incantations she thought would help the home team win. Becerra's alleged powers seemed to have been activated when Pedro Zape, at 40 minutes, stopped a penalty shot by Teófilo Cubillas. The magic worked again at 65 minutes, when Hernán Darío Herrera broke the zero. But four minutes from the end, Guillermo la Rosa scored the final goal for a 1-1 draw. The goal deprived Colombia of starting with a victory, and the witch Becerra of keeping her job: Bilardo fired her as soon as he returned to the dressing room.

The 10

At the 1978 World Cup, Argentina coach César Menotti decided that the numbers on his team should go in alphabetical order. Thus, it drew the attention of the footballing planet that Ubaldo Fillol played with jersey number 5, and that midfielder Osvaldo Ardiles performed with 1, a number generally reserved for goalkeepers.

Before the 1982 World Cup in Spain, Menotti decided to repeat the alphabetical classification. In this way, Diego Maradona received the 12. Dissatisfied, Maradona had his agent, Jorge Cyterszpiler, ask the coach for a license to wear the 10 on his back, the number that had been given to Patricio Hernández, coincidentally the Diego's roommate. Menotti replied that he was not opposed to changing the order of the list, but only if Patricio agreed. The next morning, in their room, Diego, shy, said that he had always worn 10 and that he would like to do so again at the Iberian World Cup. Before Maradona could finish his request, Patricio agreed: "Stay calm: it's yours." Joyful, Diego took a gold watch decorated with precious stones that he had kept on his nightstand and tried to give it to Hernández, but his teammate did not accept it. He explained that he had agreed because he believed that his friend had earned the right to wear the prestigious 10 jersey on the field.

Inaugural goal

When Argentina, the defending champions, and Belgium kicked off the tournament, it had been 20 years since a goal was scored in the opening match of a World Cup. After Chile's victory over Switzerland 3-1 in 1962, a blank score was repeated between England and Uruguay in 1966, Mexico and the Soviet Union in 1970, Brazil and Yugoslavia in 1974, and Germany and Poland in 1978. On June 13, at the Camp Nou in Barcelona, Belgian striker Erwin Vandenbergh cut the streak by beating Argentine goalkeeper Ubaldo Fillol at the 62 minutes mark. With that goal, the only one in the match, Argentina became the first champion to be defeated in their debut of the next edition since 1950, when Italy, winnner in 1938, lost to Sweden 3-2.

Clandestine casino

In order to entertain themselves during the long hours at the hotel, the Germans set up a kind of clandestine casino in one of the rooms. Every day, in their free time, Uwe Reinders, Karl-Heinz Rummenigge, Paul Breitner and Hansi Müller played long games of poker, in which other players occasionally participated. According to some journalists, the unluckiest player was Müller, who left Spain about $10,000 poorer. Breitner also apparently left $5,000 on the gaming table, making Uwe Reinders the great winner, though perhaps for the only time. The Werder Bremen striker was a compulsive gambler who had lost more than $100,000 on a casino roulette wheel the previous year. To cover the debt, his club deducted a large part of his salary each month, and deposited it in the bank accounts of his creditors.

Stop! Robbery!

The Chilean press reported that, when their national team arrived in Madrid, several members of the delegation had suffered the theft of money, clothing and other valuables. The newspaper *La Tercera* ran a front-page headline: "Film-like robbery to the Chilean team." The story said their flight had been so full the players had to send their hand luggage to the hold, along with the rest of the baggage. Upon arriving at the Barajas airport, the Chilean boys discovered to their surprise that cameras, razors, and other items were missing. Forward Juan Carlos Letelier reported the loss of $3,500. Team officials took great care not to make unfounded complaints, but it was striking that they constantly emphasized the flight between Santiago and Madrid had had a stopover: Buenos Aires.

The camel

The Kuwaiti players entered the José Zorrilla stadium in Valladolid in a very bad mood. It was June 17, and they were up against Czechoslovakia. The boys had intended to go out onto the pitch with their pet, but the organizers had flatly refused. "It stays out," was the blunt reply. The match ended in a tie, a good result for the Kuwaitis. Had they lost, they would surely have blamed those who forced their good luck charm, a huge camel, to stay out in the parking lot during the almost two hours of play. Accustomed to the desert heat, the hunchbacked animal stoically endured the hot sun until the players came out and handed it a cool bucket of water.

Delivered help

Spain, the host country, enjoyed the help of the referees to get through the first group stage. In the debut, on June 16 at the Luis Casanovas stadium in Valencia, the local squad fell behind to Honduras, thanks to a goal from Héctor Zelaya in the seventh minute. At 67 minutes, the Argentine referee Arturo Ithurralde called a foul on Enrique Saura, an offense the invisible man must have committed, and Roberto López Ufarte capitalized with a goal. After the shameful draw, Spain faced an old acquaintance: Yugoslavia. The Balkan squad opened the score thanks to a header from Ivan Gudelj. Four minutes later, the Danish referee Henning Lund-Sorensen (assisted, what a coincidence, by the Argentine Ithurralde as linesman) whistled another unusual penalty after Miguel Ángel *Periko* Alonso was knocked down by Velimir Zajec . . . out of the penalty area! "On TV it was very clear that it was outside," Alonso himself acknowledged years later. López Ufarte settled, kicked . . . and sent the ball wide. Lund-Sorensen ordered the penalty kick repeated, supposedly because the Balkan goalkeeper Dragan Pantelic had come off the goal line by stepping forward. The farce did not end there: López Ufarte took the ball and gave it to Juanito, the same player who had received a bottle in Belgrade five years before against the same rival. "You take it now," he ordered. Juanito scored and, in the second half, Saura got Spain's only triumph in his World Cup. With no more gifts forthcoming, however, the Iberian squad lost to Northern Ireland 1-0, Germany 2-1 and drew with England 0-0 in the farewell to their own party.

Champion of the pasta

Italy almost had to go without pasta, its traditional food, to invigorate its players. It happened that the Barcelona customs did not allow the entry of the large number of packages of noodles that they'd brought with them from Naples. When the delegation arrived in the Galician province of Pontevedra, its chef had to go to a supermarket to stock up. Fortunately, the hams, cheeses and olive oils imported by the delegation did not suffer the same restriction as the pasta.

Sheik

There were only ten minutes to go in the match that saw France comfortably defeat Kuwait, 3 to 1, when the French midfielder Alain Giresse received a delicious pass from the great Michel Platini, cut through the defense like a blast and, with a fine touch, placed the ball in one of the corners of the goal defended by Ahmad Al-Tarabolsi. While the French celebrated, the eleven players from the Persian Gulf pounced on the Ukrainian Miroslav Stupar, the match referee, claim their defenders had stopped out of confusion after hearing a whistle from the stands that sounded like the ref's. In the midst of the struggles, the head of the Kuwaiti delegation, Sheik Fahad Al-Ahmed Al-Jaber Al-Sabah (president of the country's soccer federation and Olympic Committee, as well as the brother of the head of state) entered the field of play, accompanied by his burly body-guards. He mingled among the enraged footballers and threatened Stupar with his dagger. Result? The judge annulled the goal and signaled a restart to the match, which ended 4-1 in any case.

And the French? They were furious despite the huge victory: coach Michel Hidalgo angrily retired to the changing rooms after the canceled goal, did not appear at the press conference and threatened to withdraw his team from the competition. The referee? After being shaken like a tow doll by the entire Kuwaiti squad, he only admonished the Arab midfielder Fathi Marzouq. His weak response was noticed by the organizers of the tournament and he was not called up to work another match. The sheik? He demanded entry to the French dressing room to talk, but FIFA delegates forbade him. "The mafia is small next to FIFA. I do not care about the sanctions. I will go and someone else will cover my position. I did not force the referee to annul the goal, he did it because he was convinced," were his parting words. Fahad Al-Ahmed Al-Jaber Al-Sabah died eight years later during the first Gulf War: defending the Dasman Palace, he was hit by shrapnel from the Iraqi troops.

Scandal

On June 25, Germany and Austria starred in one of the most disgusting matches in World Cup history. It came about because of Algeria's surprise 2-1 victory over Germany on June 16 in Gijón in the opening round of Group 2. By the end of the round, given the say the scores had gone, Germany would need a 1-0 victory over Austria to go through. With that result, the Austrians would also make it through to the next round, and Algeria would be out. What happened on the field of play that afternoon was an insult to the fans, the Algerians, FIFA and the world of soccer. The Austrians—perhaps as an "apology" for having eliminated the Germans in

Argentina '78—allowed German Horst Hrubesch to score the only goal of the match in the 10th minute. From there, the two teams co-starred in a charade to which goals were not invited. After letting the clock run, the two European teams achieved their mission and the poor Africans had to go home.

The arrangement was so rude that a Gijón newspaper published its sports pages in the crime section. The German daily *Bild* headlined "We passed, but what a shame". For *Der Spiegel*, "Germany and Austria made fun of the public." The international press posted photos of Algerian fans in the stands showing Spanish banknotes to signal that the match had been fixed. The German coach, Jupp Derwall, denied that there had been an agreement and assured that his players went eighty minutes in defensive mode simply "to avoid a draw that would have been fatal." More embarrassing was the Austrian coach Georg Schmidt's explanation: "At halftime we decided to keep one to zero because it was enough for us to qualify."

Down two

The delegation from El Salvador arrived in Spain on June 9 with only twenty players, despite the fact that the competition regulations allowed for twenty-two. In his first press conference, coach Mauricio Rodríguez Lindo was very sincere: "We came with only twenty players simply due to financial difficulties, there is no other reason." El Salvador not only lost their three Group 3 matches, but was the loser in the biggest win in World Cup history, 10-1, against Hungary.

Boozer judge

On June 18, in the middle of the clash between Italy and Peru at the Balaidos stadium in Vigo, the burly Andean defender José Velásquez accidentally hit German referee Walter Eschweiler. The blow was so hard that the judge could not get up, while Velásquez looked at him without extending his hand to help him. At the end of the match, which finished 1-1, the Peruvian defender was asked by the press about his attitude: "He had whistled a lot against Peru. As I had no obligation to lift him, I did not do it," was his reply. Acid, but honest.

But the "Eschweiler case" did not end there: When a group of journalists returned to the Mexico team's hotel in Vigo, an employee asked them how the referee, who was also staying there, had acted in the game. "Wrong," the reporters said. The woman was not surprised: "Men, how could he have acted well? Four hours before the game, during lunch, he drank no less than three liters of wine . . . alone!"

The fan

A week after Argentina's defeat in the opening match against Belgium, the Belgian goalkeeper, Jean-Marie Pfaff, appeared at the Montiboli hotel in Villajoyosa, Alicante, where the South American delegation was staying. Pfaff had surprisingly arrived by private car from Elche—the city where the Belgian national team was staying, about 80 kilometers away—and when he appeared before one of the Argentine managers, he explained he wanted to "fulfill one of the dreams of my life: to photograph myself with Diego Maradona. He is an extraordinary player, the best in the world. At least, I would like to shake his hand." After waiting for a half an hour at the reception, Pfaff was allowed to go into one of the rooms. Fifteen minutes later, the goalkeeper came out exultant, the more so for having received as well, as a souvenir, a shirt signed by Argentina's number 10. Four years later, he would exchange his jacket with Maradona at the end of the semi-final that Argentina won 2-0 over Belgium at the Azteca stadium in Mexico.

Bump

The duel between Germany and France for the semi-finals, on July 8 in Seville, was probably the best match of the Cup, along with the one between Brazil and Italy in the quarter-finals. The meeting was dramatic, exciting, with goals for all tastes. The Germans opened the scoring in the 17th minute via Pierre Littbarski, but at 26 minutes the French star Michel Platini equaled with a penalty. The ninety minutes ended with no change to the score, so extra time had to be played. In the first half, France went up 3-1 but once again the German miracle arrived: first Karl-Heinz Rummenigge scored 102 minutes and then Klaus Fischer's spectacular scissor kick tied it up. It would be the first World Cup match decided by penalty shots. In the frantic series, goalkeeper Harald Schumacher saved two penalties and became a hero.

But in France he was public enemy number one, and not exactly because of his efficiency in the goal. At 60 minutes, when the game was still 1-1, France's Patrick Battiston, in a quick counterattack, was one on one with the rival goalkeeper. Battitson advanced the ball but he did not elude the goalkeeper: Schumacher knocked him down with a violent kick. It was so brutal that Battiston was knocked unconscious and rushed to a nearby hospital. It was Schumacher's penalty and a red card, at the very least. For the Dutch referee Charles Corver, however, it was only a goal kick. "Everyone saw it: the players, the spectators . . . except the referee," Giresse complained to the press after the match. The goalkeeper never came to see what happened to his opponent—who had also lost several teeth in the crash—and even dared to make fun of the French fans who, behind his goal, expressed their annoyance. At the end of the match, when the journalists informed him of the serious situation suffered by the French defender, Schumacher, undeterred, fired back: "If that's all that's wrong with him, I'll pay him the dentures."

Champion, scorer and top star

Italian striker Paolo Rossi was not going to play in the 1982 World Cup. The forward, a Perugia celebrity in "Serie A", had been found guilty in 1980 of having "arranged" some matches at the request of the *mafia* that controlled the illegal sports betting business. Rossi was suspended for two years, and his sanction expired just two months before the World Cup. Although the striker had lost his competitive rhythm, coach Enzo Bearzot decided to bet on "Pablito" to set up his attack. In the first round, Rossi played poorly, which provoked strong criticism for his performance and also for his "godfather," for having caused his long absence from high-level play.

Italy qualified for the second stage almost miraculously, without victories and with only one goal more than Cameroon. And Rossi seemed to wake up, playing well against Argentina and exploding for three goals against the powerful Brazil team. Rossi was unstoppable again in the semi-final in Barcelona, scoring two against Poland, and in the final, in Madrid, he opened the way to the consecration with a goal at 57 minutes. Rossi found the net in only three of the seven games his team played, but always at the moment when his

Paolo Rossi woke up when he was needed.

squad needed him the most. The gale of goals, essential for Italy to win the title, not only established Paolo as the top scorer of the tournament, but also as the winner of the Ballon d'Or for the best player. Tournament champion, top scorer and top player—three titles that had only ever been won by the same man at Kempes four years earlier—fell to Rossi. This triple honor was never repeated at the World Cup.

Bitter victory

After the lap of honor, the celebrations and the champagne, the Italian players had to endure the bad taste of a judicial investigation from by a Milanese prosecutor. The official, Alfonso Marra, prosecuted the 22 champions and ordered their passports to be withdrawn, after accusing them of having introduced foreign currency into Italy illegally. Marra initiated the case after questioning the former general secretary of the Italian Football Federation, Darío Borgogno, who admitted that the players had received an award in dollars from the French sportswear firm Le Coq Sportif, which dressed the squad. That reward had not been declared upon arrival in the country from Spain.

The footballers had traveled to Rome with the President of the Republic, Sandro Pertini, in his own official plane. Photos from the time showed the premier playing cards with midfielder Franco Causio, goalkeeper and captain Dino Zoff, and coach Enzo Bearzot, at a comfortable table on the aircraft. One of the Italian newspapers ran the headline "Under Pertini's nose" about the case, and specified that the champions carried in their suitcases about $350,000 in payment Le Coq Sportif. As the European Union did not yet function as a free transit area at that time, athletes had to declare the cash when passing through customs at Leonardo da Vinci airport in Fiumicino, outside Rome. The prosecution alarmed several of the players who, without passports, were prevented from participating in European tournaments.

But before Marra managed to get a judge to convict any of the accused, the Italian parliament modified the laws on importing foreign currency, and increased the allowed amount. As the prize money, per-player, was below the maximum limit, the cause was forgotten.

MEXICO 1986

No player had a greater performance in a World Cup than Diego Maradona in Mexico '86. In a sport characterized by collective play, the Argentine squad led by Carlos Bilardo went down in history as a team made up of "Maradona and ten others." Pelé had Garrincha, Vavá, Jairzinho or Tostao as musketeers. In fact, Brazil was champion in Chile '62 almost without the "King", who barely played the first two games in that tournament. Diego was not only the captain and driver of his team, but also its scorer: When the opposing goal seemed closed off, Maradona took the ball and, alone, eluded half of the rival team to score. He did it against England, repeated it with Belgium, and almost tripled the feat against Germany, if he had not been fouled after being surrounded by four rivals. Diego was the head, the heart, and even the hand of the Argentine squad. "La mano de Dios"—The hand of God—his famous play against the English gave Argentina a fraudulent first goal of the match. It's left for his detractors to insist that moment overshadows the wonderful dribble that, minutes later, left scattered more than the half of the English team.

The thirteenth edition of the Cup was not only the dribbling and the hand of Maradona. Many journalists agreed that Mexico was a World

Maradona did everything for Argentina.

Cup featuring many epic battles: Brazil 1-France 1 (the Europeans won on penalties), Belgium 4-Soviet Union 3, Spain 5-Denmark 1, Argentina 2-England 1, Belgium 1-Spain 1 (the Belgians won on penalties), and the final, Argentina 3-Germany 2, are just a handful. The funny thing was that all these good shows took place in the middle of the oppressive heat. As in 1970, most of the matches were scheduled for midday, in a very hot area, and more so in summer, to accommodate European television.

In this tournament, the format was changed for the eighth time: six zones of four teams were arranged. For the second round—a draw from the round of 16 with direct elimination—the first two teams of each group qualified, and the best four from the third position. Thanks to this, teams like Bulgaria or Uruguay went through without winning and with only two draws in their harvest.

The Cup had, as in each edition, many notable events: the Uruguayan José Batista went down in history for having seen the red card just 53 seconds into his game against Scotland. French referee Joel Quiniou possibly rushed to dispatch Batista, a defender with a reputation. Meanwhile, the Paraguayan Cayetano Ré became the first coach sent off in a World Cup. Ré walked to the dressing room early in the game against Belgium on June 11 after his complaints and insults broke the tolerance of Bulgarian referee Bogdan Dotchev.

Bye Colombia, hello Mexico

When the '82 World Cup ended, FIFA was sure that the next edition would take place in Colombia. But on October 26, 1982, the country's president, Belisario Betancur, announced that Colombia was not in any economic condition to organize the tournament. He stressed that his country had been designated as host eight years earlier, when 16 teams were involved, but with the increase to 24 participants, ten large stadiums were needed and Colombia simply did not have enough venues. The president of the North, Central American and Caribbean Football Confederation (CONCACAF), Joaquín Soria Terrazas, applied in December of that year for Mexico, which had hosted twelve years earlier, to fight alongside the United States and Canada for the honor. Perhaps due to the friendship of the president of FIFA, Joao Havelange, with the Mexican businessman Guillermo Cañedo—FIFA vice president and director of the giant Televisa Network—Mexico became the first organizing country with two World Cups on May 19, 1983.

Although in the political arena it seemed Mexico had easily won the tug of war, the result was strong criticism from five continents. There were complaints about the "repetition" of Mexico to the detriment of other countries that had never hosted, such as the United States and Canada. Even the players and coaches objected to the oppressive weather they were sure to face. But the heat was nature's only intrusion: in September 1985, less than a before kickoff, a violent earthquake shook the entire country, especially Mexico City.

It killed some 10,000 people—unofficial tallies in some media put the death toll at 40,000—and it destroyed thousands of homes and buildings in the center, south and west of the country. But, just as the heat did not overwhelm the protagonists, the earthquake could not stop the ball either. Miraculously, the twelve stadiums designated for the competition were intact.

Broken heart

Wales and Scotland squared off in Cardiff on September 10, 1985, for the right to play Australia, first in the Oceania zone, for a World Cukp berth. Trailing 1-0 Scottish coach Jock Stein bet on all or nothing with a last substitution: at 61 minutes he sent David "Davie" Cooper onto the pitch to replace Gordon Strachan. Nine minutes before the end, when everything seemed cooked, the referee whistled a penalty for Scotland. Cooper, who had not much intervened of the game, called for the ball, put it on the eleven meter mark and, after a short run, fired a soft shot that fooled Welsh goalkeeper Neville Southall, who dived to the other way. Scotland held the tie and won the right to take on Australia for a place in Mexico '86. It was a heart-stopping finale. Literally. When the referee whistled the end of the astonishing game, Stein, excited, grabbed his chest and fell next to the bench. The trainer was taken to a stretcher in the visiting locker room, on which he died minutes later. Stein had coined a famous phrase: "Every coach dies a little in every game." He died completely at that point.

To face Australia, the national federation decided to summon the young Aberdeen FC coach, Alex Ferguson, who had achieved the miracle of leading his team to the league title twice (1983/4 and 1984/5) under the nose of Rangers and Celtic, the two greatest clubs in the country. From the hand of Ferguson—who would later become multi-champion with Manchester United—Scotland qualified for Mexico after winning 2-0 on November 20, 1985 at the Hampden Park stadium in Glasgow, and equalizing at zero on December 4 in the Olympic stadium in Melbourne. Finding itself in the World Cup "group of death" Scotland could not accomplish much in Mexico. They came last behind Denmark, Germany and Uruguay. But the story did not end there: Davie Cooper, Cardiff's hero on the day of Stein's death, also died on a pitch. It was on March 23, 1995, when he suffered a stroke at Broadwood Stadium in the city of Cumbernauld, where he was watching a youth practice. He was 39 years old.

So much trouble for that?

At the 59th minute of the Ireland-Denmark qualifier on November 13,1985, in Dublin, visiting coach Sepp Piontek ordered a change: midfielder Soren Lerby was replaced by Jens Bertelsen. Lerby had not suffered any injury, nor was he playing badly: Piontek, happy with the 3-1 victory that ensured first place in Group 6 and a ticket to the Cup, something Denmark had never achieved, wanted to fulfill his pledge to Bayern München sports director Uli Hoeness. The Bavarian club had asked that Lerby be allowed to play, that same day, in a match for the German Cup in Bochum. Due to the wide time difference between the two games—the international started at 1 p.m., and Bayern's with Bochum, at 8 p.m.—Lerby was able to contribute to the victory in Dublin (in fact, the score ended wider, 4-1), take a quick shower and drive with Hoeness to airport escorted by an Irish police motorcycle. The player and the manager traveled on a private flight to Düsseldorf, and upon landing—an hour before the kickoff of the second match—they got into another car to quickly cover the nearly fifty kilometers that separated them from Bochum.

As fate would it, a traffic jam stopped them only two kilometers from the Ruhrstadion. With just minutes left, Lerby had no choice but to get out of the vehicle and run to the stadium, where he arrived with a margin of just seconds to put on the red shirt, while his team-mates waited for him at the tunnel to the pitch. However, so much effort was in vain for the poor Dane: coach Udo Latek informed him that he would seat him on the bench. Lerby played just a few minutes of the second half, which were not enough to break the tie game. Five days later, in the rematch in Munich, and with Lerby from the start, Bayern won 2-0. That triumph served as the founda-tion stone for the Munich club to win the German Cup that season.

Phone waiting

Canadian coach Tony Waiters had a lot of trouble assembling his team. First, because of the icy climatic conditions in his country, eleven-man soccer was hardly practiced, so there are not many footballers to select from. Eight of those summoned were actually soccer-5 players, a specialty that takes place indoors. Others came from foreign leagues: the United States, Switzerland and Belgium. Even so, Waiters did not get to collect the 22 that he could take to Mexico, but only 18. The list was completed, but with four boys who remained in their country, close to the phone so that, in case of an emergency, they could be requested urgently. It would not be necessary. The Canadian stay in Mexico was very short. The North American squad lost all three of their Group C games—to France, Hungary and the Soviet Union—and said goodbye without scoring a single goal.

A "collaboration" please

A few days before the start of the Cup, Bulgaria and Uruguay played a friendly match to finalize some last details for the competition. Leaders of both teams had agreed that the match would be held "behind closed doors" and the police were called to prevent the public from getting in. The request was unsuccessful, because people filled the stands anyway. Moreover, having summoned the police was counterproductive, because the agents themselves were the ones who let the people pass . . . after receiving a few pesos to thicken the pockets of their uniforms.

Reality is the only truth

Weeks before the start of the 1986 World Cup, the soft drink company Coca-Cola released a series of advertisements related to the championship in Mexico. In the different commercials, there were boys playing soccer, fans celebrating victories, and spectators performing the wave at the Azteca stadium. The star of Mexico's national team and of Real Madrid, forward Hugo Sánchez, participated in several of the shorts. In one of them, Sánchez executed a penalty against a team dressed in yellow socks and black shorts. The action ended in a goal celebrated by a boy who was washing his car, the employees of a restaurant and a dozen people stationed in front of televisions in the window of an appliance store. Very cute. But reality is not governed by scripts.

On June 7, Mexico and Paraguay were tied at one. Luis Flores had opened the scoring three minutes but Paraguay's Julio César Romero had equalized at 85. With two minutes left, Guarani defender Vladimiro Schettina and the local striker Hugo Sánchez collided at the edge of the visiting area and both ended up sprawled inside the rectangle. The English referee George Courtney sanctioned a highly debatable penalty kick: the charge by Schettina didn't seem illegal, and contact looked to have taken place outside the penalty area. Sánchez simply placed the ball and took a run. The situation replicated the scene of the emotional Coca-Cola ad, but the outcome was diametrically different: Sánchez kicked and goalkeeper Roberto Fernández cleared the ball with his right hand.

Wet reaction

Iraqi player Hanna Basil was severely sanctioned by FIFA for spitting at the referee in a match against Belgium. The incident occurred in the 52nd minute, with the Belgians leading 2-0, when Basil applied a strong kick to an opponent. Colombian referee Jesús Díaz Palacio showed the yellow card to the Middle Eastern midfielder who, in response, expectorated on the face of the man in black. He was suspended for one year.

Justified hammering

According to the Uruguayan coaching staff, the overwhelming 6-1 defeat against Denmark on June 8 in Neza had an explanation: Almost all the players had suffered an epidemic of enterocolitis a few days before caused by something they had eaten or drank. The squad doctors had to work hard to combat the disease, which did not leave the players in their best condition. One of those who suffered most was defender José Batista, whose participation was in doubt until a few hours before the game.

Nudist tour

Its draw against Uruguay and elimination from the Cup did not keep the Scottish players down for long. They left the stadium and went to a hotel in the city of Nezahualcóyotl to drown their sorrow in whisky and beer. Well loaded, the Scots decided that, despite the setback, they still deserved to take a victory lap. And so they did, completely stripped of clothing. The drunk boys spread their celebration" throughout the hotel facilities, showing their attributes to every woman who crossed their path.

Problems in Portuguese

The Brazilian and Portuguese squads were both embroiled in disputes with their respective associations. On the one hand, the South Americans were told not to make statements to the press, after Socrates, the Brazilian midfielder, accused FIFA in an interview of "organizing world championships in a corporate way," of "favoring the strongest teams, not only in the game but from the commercial point of view," and of wondering how such an event was organized in a country submerged in a deep economic crisis. The Brazilian federation initiated a process against Socrates Brasileiro Sampaio de Souza Vieira de Oliveira—it was easier to just say "Socrates"—and another against the right back Leandro, who resigned from the World Cup seconds before the delegation traveled to the town of Guadalajara. Leandro—who coach Telé Santana saw as a solid starter—said that he resigned in solidarity with the forward Renato, who had been pre-selected but was ultimately left off the list of twenty-two players. The defender's gesture sparked a series of articles in Brazilian newspapers, in which it was claimed that Leandro and Renato were more than just good friends.

Meanwhile, the Portugueses athletes announced that they would participate in the Cup "under protest," because the managers had not accepted their demands for a salary increase. The players, who refused to play preparation games before the championship, considered the $20 a day salary and the $666 dollars per game offered by the Lusitanian federation to be a mockery.

Doping without penalty

Spain's 2-1 victory over Northern Ireland, on June 7 in Jalisco, in Group D, was tainted a few hours later when news broke that Ramón María Calderé del Rey, known simply as "Calderé", had failed and anti-doping test. However, after FIFA studied the case, it decided to fine the Royal Spanish Football Federation (RFEF) and not the athlete. A letter sent by FIFA secretary, Joseph Blatter, to the RFEF, explained that the player was released from all blame for not knowing the medications the team doctor Jorge Guillén gave him to treat salmonellosis. The doctor had included the drugs on the completed C-1 form prior to the match. Guillén argued that the tablets Calderé consumed had been prescribed by a doctor at the Guadalajara headquarters, but the Spanish federation had to pay a fine of 25,000 Swiss francs for negligence since Guillén should have known that the drugs contained substances banned by FIFA. Calderé was not even suspended for the competition. After the clash against Ireland, the Barcelona striker scored two goals in the next match against Algeria.

Gave a hand

After Argentina's brilliant 2-1 quarter-final victory over England, several British gambling agencies decided to return the money to those who had bet on a tie between the two teams, judging that Diego Maradona's first goal, scored thanks to the "hand of God," had not been legal.

More than twenty years after that match, a resentful English gambler named Ian Wellworth tried to attack Maradona when he made his debut as a coach for the Argentine national team in Scotland on November 19, 2008. The man, out of his wits, was arrested by the police when he tried to enter to Hampden Park stadium armed with a machete to "cut off the thief's head." Wellworth, 43, told police that, in 1986, he had bet a lot of money on an English victory. After Diego's two goals, he'd gone into debt and his wife left him.

Every cloud has a silver lining

English officials had some reason for modest relief after the loss to Argentina: They saved the twenty thousand pounds that a charter flight costs to fly the wives and girlfriends of the players from London to Mexico. Footballers and managers had agreed that this trip would be a prize for reaching the semi-final.

Morocco's players also had reason not to feel too much pain for being eliminated. Although they fell to Germany due to a free kick goal by Lothar Matthäus—just three minutes before the end of the match—the North Africans did not lose their good humor. When they returned to the locker room, they crossed paths with the Germans to ask for autographs and take photos. The cordial Germans agreed to pose with the smiling Moroccans, albeit with a serious expression on their cold faces. For having qualified first in Group F over power teams such as England, Portugal or Poland— something that an African squad had never achieved before—the Moroccans had received numerous prizes and rewards. The strangest came from a tobacco company, which gave each player enough cigarettes to set up a well-stocked kiosk.

Who lives by the sword, dies by the sword

The night of June 18 was tough for Denmark's ailing squad. After losing to Spain 5-1 and being eliminated from the competition, they had to listen the Spanish victory party taking place . . . in their own hotel. It was very difficult for the Danish to fall asleep, since the Spanish chants, music, and shouts of joy continued until dawn. Two days later, Spain moved to Puebla, where they had to face Belgium in the quarter-finals. Upon arriving at the hotel that had been assigned to them, the delegation found a surprise. The Germans, who were supposed to play in Monterrey against the local team, had not left their rooms because they planned to return immediately after the match. With no place there, the Spanish were forced to move to the "Mansión de los Ángeles", where their rivals, the Belgians, were also staying. On the night of June 22, the Spanish received a good dose of their own medicine, having to go to bed with the anger of defeat in their souls and the revelry unleashed by the Belgians, who had eliminated them on penalty spot, in their ears.

Brazil served the cake

When Northern Ireland faced Brazil on June 12 in the first round, Irish goalkeeper Patrick Jennings was turning 41. The Verdeamarela squad did not let him celebrate his birthday: they scored three goals on him. Days later, on the 21st, in the quarter-finals, the Brazilians showed more love for the Frenchman Michel Platini, who blew out 31 candles that day, by wasting three penalties: one in the game, fired by Zico, and two in the shootout after 120 electrifying minutes of a game that finished 1-1. Brazilian bad aim allowed the Gauls to qualify for the semi-final. Another curious fact of that clash was provided by Platini himself: he scored the tying goal for France at 40 minutes, but he sent the ball into the clouds in the penalty shootout.

Don't say "oui", say "ja"

France looked like a runaway train to the title. In the round of 16, it had dispatched Italy, the defending champion. In the quarters, Brazil, one of the favorites and former champion on Mexican soil. At the semi-final, the French squad arrived hungry for revenge. Again, it would face Germany, its executioner in the same instance four years earlier. In addition, Patrick Battiston would once again be "face to face" with goalkeeper Harald Schumacher, with whom he had a pending account since the fierce blow in Spain that sent him to the hospital. The Germans did not arrive in the best way: They had eked out a meager victory against a weak Morocco, 1-0, and had eliminated the host squad on penalties after 120 minutes without goals or really much compelling soccer. The captain and star of France, Michel Platini, who two years before had led his team to victory in the final of the European Championship played in Paris, was convinced that all was in place for his country to lift the World Cup.

But that conviction evaporated before the ball began to roll. "I realized we were in trouble when, after the toss of a coin (with Italian referee Luigi Agnolin and his colleague Karl-Heinz Rummenigge), the linesmen (Serbian Zoran Petrovic and Hungarian Lajos Nemeth) wished me luck in German," Platini revealed later. With goals from Andreas Brehme and Rudolf Voeller, Germany beat France and reached the grand final for the second time in a row.

The sadness of the champion

The Argentine dressing room at Azteca stadium was an overflowing furnace of joy. All the members of the team celebrated the conquest of the highest title in world soccer. Well, not all: the coach, Carlos Bilardo, only distilled bitterness. Amid the laughter and shouts from the players, Bilardo was trying to find an explanation for the two German goals that almost appropriated Argentine glory. For the strict coach, the two German scores, both headers that got past goal-keeper Nery Pumpido, were two sharp knife-wounds that cut off the desire to celebrate the World Cup.

Rituals

Argentine coach Carlos Bilardo is considered one of soccer's personalities most obsessed with rituals meant to attract good luck.

Throughout the World Cup in Mexico, and by arrangement of the coach, the blue and white team incorporated an intense series of unusual customs, generally driven by coincidence, which had to be strictly respected until the end of the contest. Before the first match, against South Korea, the delegation visited the Perisur shopping center. In one of the bars, a group shared a coffee and the goalkeeper Nery Pumpido, one of the few who had brought Mexican money, paid for the drinks. Argentina won by three to one, so the ritual was repeated religiously before each game, always with the same participants, and in all cases Pumpido was in charge of paying the bill. Another superstition consisted of enjoying a barbecue prepared by Maradona's father and father-in-law, Don Diego and Coco Villafañe, at noon the day before each game. Likewise, after each match, the delegation dined at the Argentine restaurant Mi Viejo, owned by a former Estudiantes de la Plata player and Bilardo's teammate, Eduardo Cremasco.

One afternoon before the duel with the Koreans, a hairdresser named Javier Leiva, a friend of goalkeeper Héctor Zelada, appeared at the Club de Futbol América's training camp, where the South American squad had been installed. Leiva cut the hair of several players, and also of Bilardo. The day after the initial victory, the coach asked Zelada to call the stylist and order him to return to the premises to cut his hair before each game. "For the final with Germany, he had seen me six times in less than a month. I had no hair to cut, but he still managed to get some fluff out!" revealed the obsessive manager in his autobiography, Doctor and Champion. Another habit was born in the round-of-16 match against Uruguay. Upon returning victorious from the Cuauhtémoc stadium in Puebla—1-0 on a goal by Pedro Pasculli—one of the members of the squad noticed that no one had prepared their suitcases for the eventual return home, which would have been immediate in the event of a defeat. This incident, therefore, was repeated against England,

Belgium and before the final against Germany, even though the return was planned anyway a few hours after the end of the closing game.

But the most surprising ritual was related to trips by bus to the fields. In addition to everyone maintaining their places throughout the event, on the day of the first transfer to the Olympic Stadium in Mexico City, the Argentine bus was preceded by two motorcycle policemen named Tobías and Jesús, whose mission consisted of opening the way for the vehicle. After the three-to-one victory, Bilardo expressly asked the organizers of the tournament that these two officers perform the same service in each of the six remaining matches. In fact, for the final against Germany, the police sent twenty troops on motorcycles, so the coach ordered that only Jesús and Tobías ride in front, and that the rest circulate alongside and behind the bus.

The incredible bouquet of curious habits did not end there: during the ride to the stadium ride prior to the duel with Korea, one of the players gave the driver of the bus a cassette with music by Argentine interpreters to make the trip to the field more pleasant. The songs, all very emotional, were playing until the arrival at the coliseum. Bilardo noted that the last one, which had accompanied the final section of the route, the entrance to the parking lot and the stop of the vehicle, was one by singer-songwriter Sergio Denis—"Gigante, chiquito"—which ended just as the bus slowed down. In each successive trip, the coach asked the driver to regulate the speed of the bus so it would always pull in to the last chords of "Gigante, chiquito." The problem came when Argentina had to change venues for the quarter-final, semi and final matches, all at the Azteca stadium very close to the América Club's camp. As the song was longer than the normal route, barely a kilometer and a half, the driver had to drive very slowly so he entered the parking lot of the coliseum just as the moving song ended.

Champions without playing

At this World Cup, Argentine Héctor Zelada became the eighth and last world champion footballer who never played in a match for his national team, not even a friendly. The other seven are: Juan Carlos Calvo (Uruguay-1930), Giuseppe Cavanna (Italy-1934), Pietro Arcari (Italy-1934), Aldo Donati (Italy-1938), Bruno Chizzo (Italy-1938), Luis Alberto Rijo (Uruguay-1950) and Washington Ortuño (Uruguay-1950).

Some Maradona teammates shared in his glory without touching the pitch.

ITALY 1990

In a country famous for its artistic heritage, with such masterful works as the Colosseum, Leonardo da Vinci's "The Last Supper", or Michelangelo's "David," World Cup Italy 1990 lacked beautiful soccer completely. The quality of several fantastic players did not come through on the playing fields. Statistics testify to the poverty of the soccer: 115 goals in 52 games, the lowest average in history. Ultra-defensive strategies led many of the matches in the second round to end goalless, and be decided by penalty shots. The two semi-finals, for example, were decided by shootouts after finishing 1-1. The final between Germany and Argentina—for the first time the same teams faced each other in two consecutive finals—also had two negative firsts: One of the two teams, Argentina, did not score in the defining match—all previous losers had one goal—and a player was sent off for the very first time in a final (two, actually: Pedro Monzón and Gustavo Dezzotti, both from Argentina). For Germany, this triumph had a special flavor: it was the first time they had lifted the Cup undefeated, since they had lost a game in 1954 (8-3 to Hungary) and another in 1974 (1-0 to the East Germany), both in the first round.

The tournament had other notable firsts. For the first time, FIFA authorized a team to modify its official list: it allowed Argentina

Unheralded Cameroon becomes the first African squad in the quarter-finals.

to change goalkeeper Nery Pumpido, who had suffered a double tibia-fibula fracture in the second match, against the Soviet Union, for Ángel Comizzo, who joined the squad at the third game, against Romania. Cameroon became the only team to win a group from the opening round of a Cup with a negative goal differential: they defeated Argentina 1-0 (one of the most surprising results in World Cup history), Romania by 2-1 and fell in the third game 4-0 to the Soviet Union. Cameroon finished the first phase with three goals scored, five conceded and a -2 goal differential. On the plus side, Cameroon would become the first African squad to reach the quarter-finals: there they were eliminated by England 3-2 in the best match of the tournament. Another pearl: The goalscorer and great star of the team, Albert Roger Mook Miller (known by his nickname "Milla") had not been originally called by coach Valeri Nepomniachi, a Russian, but he was part of the delegation that traveled to Italy by a decree of the president. Milla scored both goals in the 2-1 victory against Romania and repeated the double success against Colombia in the round of 16. Those scores allowed him, at that time, to become the oldest scorer in the history of the Cup, at 38 years and 29 days. Meanwhile, the Italian goalkeeper, Walter Zenga, reached the record for a goalless streak —517 minutes. It ended off the foot of Argentine Claudio Caniggia in the 67th minute of the semi-final played at the San Paolo stadium in Naples.

With the German victory, Franz Beckenbauer equaled the Brazilian Mario Zagallo in having become world champion first as a player and then as a coach. After two falls in the finals of Spain 1982 and Mexico 1986, for Germany the third time was the charm.

Complicated qualification

Two American countries had to be severely sanctioned in the qualifying stage because of embarrassing irregularities. On September 3, 1989, the historic Maracanã stadium in Rio de Janeiro was the scene of scandal. Brazil and Chile were playing for the right to travel to Italy for the World Cup. In the 67th minute, with the match 1-0 in favor of the locals, the visiting goalkeeper, Roberto "Cóndor" Rojas, was struck down and next to him was a flare thrown by a fan, a 24-year-old "torcedora" named Rosamary Mello Nascimento. The Chilean doctors treated Rojas, who was removed on a stretcher with a bloody face and shirt, and then the entire visiting team left the field to protest the "attack." The match was suspended by the Argentine referee Juan Carlos Loustau, and the Chilean officials and players said they would claim, from FIFA, the points, a sanction for Brazil and a place in Italy.

But soon an investigation carried out by the international federation— which included a photograph that showed the flare had fallen within a meter of the goalkeeper, and not on his head—determined that the visitors engaged in deception to obtain a victory off the field that they couldn't achieve on it. Rojas's injuries were real, but they had been caused by the goalkeeper's own hand: he'd cut himself on one eyebrow with a small scalpel that he had hidden in his glove. "Cóndor" explained in an interview later that "the idea came two days before the game. I asked [team captain Fernando] Astengo if he dared to do something and he answered yes. When I saw the flare, I remembered the scalpel that was hidden in a glove and I cut myself. It was a single cut, but very deep, that's why so much blood came out. In the locker room I called Astengo to take out the scalpel. He took my gloves off, then the kit-man Nelson Maldonado took them, who had them at his house 15 days before giving them back."

Everything was overturned: the game was declared lost, Chile was out of the 1990 World Cup, it was fined 100,000 Swiss francs and it was disqualified from participating in the qualification for the next World Cup, United States 1994. In addition, Rojas—who at that time wore the Brazilian club Sao Paulo's shirt—was suspended "for life" from professional play, and coach Orlando Aravena and doctor Daniel Rodríguez were punished for five years. At the beginning of 2009, the British newspaper *The Times* published a list of the "greatest actors" in the history of soccer, and Roberto Rojas took first place. Twelve years later, FIFA lifted the sanction against Rojas, but it was too late: the "Cóndor" was 43 years old, too old to play again as a professional. What happened to the beautiful Rosemary? After spending a few hours in police custody, she agreed to pose nude for Playboy magazine.

A little further north, the Mexican team also lost its chance to participate because of its own reprehensible, though very different, behaviour. In the qualifying tournament for the U-20 World Cup in Saudi Arabia 1989, which was held in Guatemala in April 1988, Mexico had four boys over the maximum age of 19—one of 20, two 22 and another 24. The deception, known as "the case of the cachirules" (in Mexico an illegitimate son is called "cachirul"), was discovered by a journalist, and FIFA suspended Mexico for two years from all international competition. The sanction was lifted a few months before the start of the World Cup, but by then the Mexican squad had missed the qualification round.

Maradona, the diplomat

On June 8, 1990, a few hours before the Argentine team faced Cameroon at the opening of the World Cup, President Carlos Menem met with the squad at the Giuseppe Meazza stadium in Milan. There, Menem gave Diego Maradona an official passport and appointed him "ad honorem advisor" to the government "for sports matters and dissemination of the Argentine image abroad," as formalized by a presidential decree published on May 11, 1990. "This type of appointment should have imitators," declared the then head of state. Maradona thanked the delegation and expressed his joy "for my dad and my mom, who will surely be proud of me today." The footballer's "diplomatic" career ended several months later. On March 17, 1991, after the match in which Napoli defeated Bari 1-0, Maradona was chosen by lottery for the anti-doping control. Twelve days later, after carrying out two analyses, the Italian Federation reported that traces of cocaine had been found in his urine.

Maradona returned to Argentina almost immediately, while FIFA sentenced him to fifteen months of inactivity, until June 30, 1992. Maradona's addiction to drugs caused a true scandal worldwide. To "detach" from the disgraced idol, Menem signed a new decree, on April 25, 1991, which annulled the previous diplomatic designation. Exactly 24 hours after the signing of this second legal regulation, Maradona was arrested by members of the Superintendency of Dangerous Drugs of the Argentine Federal Police in the Buenos Aires neighborhood of Caballito. Two friends of the player, who shared the raided property with him, were also caught. After this incident, Maradona distanced himself from the government, which he denounced on more than one occasion for using his image for political purposes. He was right. But a short time later, the brilliant player agreed to approach Menem again. With Maradona's support, the president was reelected in 1995 for a second term. That same year, Maradona was summoned to be the central figure in the "Sol sin Droga" ("Sun without drugs") program carried out by the Secretariat of Programming for the Prevention of Drug Addiction and the Fight against Drug Trafficking.

Double Negative

As against Belgium in Spain '82, Argentina began the defense of the title with a defeat, but in this case the fall was much more surprising: In Milan, they lost 1-0 against Cameroon, supposed to be very inferior to the champions. The blue and white squad could not avoid the humiliating failure despite finishing the match with two more men than its rival: Africans Andre Kana and Benjamin Massing were sent off at 61 and 89 minutes, respectively. For the Argentine captain, Diego Maradona, the pain was twofold. In addition to repeating a bitter fate, this time with Cameroon—number 10 had been part of the team that fell to Belgium in the opening of Spain 1982—he lost a diamond earring on the pitch that his wife Claudia had given him on his last birthday, worth about $5,000.

Zoo

The exceptional performance of the Cameroon national team is said to have been directly linked to a zoo. The story began when the heads of its delegation chose a hotel in the southern city of Brindisi to house the squad during the Cup. Upon arriving, the players asked the managers to move to another accommodation, which was next to a zoo. It was safari style, with loose animals. The footballers justified their demand by pointing out that, near lions, giraffes and other denizens of the African savanna, they would feel a little closer to home and their families. The leaders agreed and the players, at every spare moment, would go around the park to lift their spirits. "The atmosphere is not African but it helps not to miss the family or our landscape," said defender Emmanuel Kunde. The remarkable performance of the Cameroonians fully justified the change, and showed that the soul feeds on more than exercise and videos.

Green toilet

Question: What could be more inconvenient than an intense intestinal colic while playing soccer? Anwer: An intense intestinal colic while playing soccer . . . at the World Cup, before the eyes of hundreds of cameras and millions of viewers. That extremely uncomfortable situation afflicted English striker Gary Lineker—World Cup top scorer in Mexico 1986—during his team's debut against the Republic of Ireland on June 11, 1990, at the Sant Elia stadium in Cagliari, on the island of Sardinia. Lineker, who had opened the scoring in the 9th minute, began to feel uncomfortable in the second half. "I already felt bad during halftime. There was an attack on the right wing, I tried to overtake an opponent, I stretched and, when I fell to the ground, I relaxed," the forward said during an interview several years after the tournament. Lineker took advantage of his stay on the grass to free himself from acute suffering without even touching his shorts. Before rejoining, the player tried to clean himself in a very original way: "I rubbed against the grass like a dog. It was the most horrible experience of my life. Luckily, I was fortunate that it had rained the night before, which allowed me to do something like that, but I was still very dirty," he acknowledged. The misery of the "smelly" Lineker did not end there: Ireland managed to equalize a little while after the unusual evacuation. Ten minutes later, the English striker was replaced and went straight to the showers.

Canteen and wedding

One incident took on great significance during the 1990 Italian Cup was the complaint by Brazilian left-back Cláudio Ibraim Vaz Leal, known as Branco. According to the defender, the Argentine "water man" Miguel di Lorenzo, nicknamed Galíndez, gave him a canteen with a "vomiting" liquid, which caused him nausea and drowsiness in the middle of the South American classic of the round of 16. The incident was never officially explained, however a camera recorded the instant in which Galíndez, during a game interruption, handed Branco a plastic bottle similar to the one used by members of the Argentine team to drink, but with a white adhesive tape that clearly differentiated it from the others.

Several Argentine players, including Diego Maradona, claimed to have been aware of this maneuver and even celebrated it. "All the good ones came to drink. I said 'come on, drink, drink'. And Vasco Olarticoechea took it . . . 'Vasco, don't!'," Maradona said his companions yelled to him. "Careca and Valdo were saved," he lamented, and finished: "Someone grinded a Rohypnol." The version was always denied by coach Carlos Bilardo. According to the Argentine magazine *El Gráfico*, Bilardo, days before the duel, told a journalist: "I'm going to invent something, I don't know what, but there will be something. We have to win this match with the Brazilians." Maradona's comment was also rejected by the former Argentine Football Association president, Julio. Asked during a radio interview about Maradona's revelations, the past leader replied: "Maradona was not in his right mind." "He wanted to make a joke . . . and sometimes the joke backfires." "Which canteen?" Grondona wondered, and added humorously: "We are going to have to go get the canteen to see what it says about all this. You have to make an inspection of the canteen, to see if it was altered." He continued: "They are classic situations that occur in Argentine soccer, which are commented on as a joke and then everything comes out seriously. It's like when one jokes with another and does not take the joke as such, but in the wrong sense." Argentina prevailed in that difficult duel by a score of 1-0, with a great goal from Claudio Caniggia after a tremendous pass from Maradona.

In his autobiography, Bilardo makes no mention of that incident, but he does attribute part of the victory to an outside event: a wedding. "I did not tolerate the idea that Brazil was the team that would kick us out of the World Cup. I wanted to banish forever that complex that had arisen through a chain of bad results: we had faced Brazil in Germany 1974, Argentina 1978 and Spain 1982 with a goalless draw at home and two defeats in the European cups". "When we left Trigoria [a location next to Rome, where the Argentine squad had its camp] to travel to Turin, we did not pack our luggage, as we had used to do in Mexico. When we arrived in Turin, the day before the game against Brazil, the city looked like São Paulo or Rio de Janeiro. In the streets, everything was samba and carnival, yellow and green. In hotels, in squares, everywhere you could see Brazilian fans singing, dancing and celebrating a victory in advance. They had enormous faith!

"When we arrived at the Turin hotel, we discovered that, the night before to the South American classic, a wedding party was being held in one of the halls. In Italy there is a saying that my grandparents had always mentioned to me: 'Fidanzata porta fortuna,' the bride brings luck. We had to touch the girl to bathe us with her good fortune! After dinner, I sent the players to the hall to take pictures with the bride. The brand new consorts were happy for the surprise. Me too, and I even asked the bride for a bouquet of flowers, who graciously handed it to me. Nothing could go wrong the next day. "

Bad habits

Players smoke too, it's nothing new. But what did attract attention was that one of the footballers was caught smoking . . . on the substitute bench. It was the Italian Andrea Carnevale, exposed by a "paparazzo" as he smoked out of anger for not being a starter against Czechoslovakia, after having started in the team against Austria and the United States.

Asian method

European journalists who had access to the Korean camp in Udine were surprised by the extravagant training systems of coach Hoe Taik Lee. The manager made his players get up at five in the morning and only allowed them to have breakfast at four in the afternoon. After intense sessions that included martial exercises, the footballers were massaged with strange creams made from onions. Those who suffered from the high humidity of the Friuli region were provided with a huge glass containing olive oil mixed with brandy. These original recipes did not prove to be very useful in practice: Korea lost all their three matches of the Group E against Belgium (2-0), Spain (3-1) and Uruguay (1-0).

The bet

On October 27, 1989, SSC Napoli and Sporting Clube de Lisboa decided a UEFA Cup match with a shootout. The Italian team was up 3-2 and it was the turn of its captain, Diego Maradona. If the shot of 10 ended in the net, Napoli triumphed. When the Argentine took the ball to place it on the mark, the Yugoslav goalkeeper of the Portuguese team, Tomislav Ivković, approached him and proposed to bet one hundred dollars, convinced that he would make the save. Diego accepted, but had to pay at the end of the match, because Ivković guessed the direction of his shot, on his left post.

On June 30, 1990, for the quarter-finals of Italy '90, Ivković and Maradona returned to face each other, again in penalties, after the Argentina-Yugoslavia match ended 0-0 after 120. This time there was no bet, but the keeper again beat the South American 10: he contained the shot Maradona fired. As at the San Paolo Stadium, Ivković's feat could not be complete, as the Argentine team finally prevailed three to two.

Public bathroom

Nerves and that long game against Yugoslavia complicated matters for goalkeeper Sergio Goycochea: when the goalless match finished, Goyco was dying to go to the bathroom, but did not have enough

Goalkeeper Goycochea had personal business to take care of.

210

time before the shootout. Desperate, he asked two companions to cover him, knelt down and, moving one of the sleeves of his shorts, urinated on one side of the playing field. Unloaded, the goalkeeper saved two of the rival shots and Argentina went on to the semi-final.

In that instance, the duel against Italy—the fifth World Cup in a row they'd faced each other, a record—was again tied, in this case 1-1. Argentina had to shoot one more time from the eleven-meter spot. This time, Goycochea did not feel the same pressure, he repeated the "piss-on-the-grass" ritual on the orders of his obsessive coach, Carlos Bilardo. Believe it or not, after the strange procedure, the goalkeeper saved Roberto Donadoni and Aldo Serena's shots that allowed the Argentina to defeat the host team and reach its second consecutive World Cup final.

Years later, on June 27, 1993, Goyco faced a new series of penalty kicks in the Copa América in Ecuador, against Brazil for the quarter-finals. The South American duel ended 1-1 after two hours of play in the Monumental stadium of Guayaquil. While the two teams were preparing for the shoot-out, the Argentine coach Alfio Basile approached his goalkeeper and asked: "Did you piss or not?". Goycochea realized that he had not copied the Italian ceremony. Encouraged by Basile, he did it again under the protection of some of his teammates. Emboldened, Goyco contained Marco Antônio Boiadeiro's shot, which gave the victory to Argentina by six to five.

Four days later, in the same tournament, Argentina and Colombia did not score goals after 120 minutes of semi-final action. Uruguayan referee Jorge Nieves called for a new shootout and the goalkeeper, obedient to Basile's insistent claim, once again performed his duties. Surprisingly, Goycochea saved Victor Aristizábal's shot that allowed Argentina to win six to five. Three days later, the National Team defeated Mexico by two to one, without the need for penalties or magic discharges, and won the last of their titles at the "major" level.

Dry

England coach Bobby Robson ordered his men not to engage in exaggerated displays of jubilation after each goal. "Those provocative scenes are detrimental to the sport, the fans, and are also dangerous. We don't want to curb the natural enthusiasm, but a pat on the shoulder and a 'well done' would be enough. After all, the players are only fulfilling their obligation and are paid for it," said the sober coach. The "energy savings" in the celebrations paid off: England came out first in the tough Group F, beat Belgium in the round of 16, Cameroon in the quarter-finals and fell in the semi-finals to Germany, the champion, on penalties.

The oversight

The first 90 minutes of the semi-final between Italy and Argentina, played at the San Paolo stadium in Naples on July 3, ended level in one goal. So, French referee Michel Vautrot ordered the extra time consisting of two halves of 15 minutes each. However, the first of those segments was extended more than necessary: it reached 23 minutes. At the end of the duel—which remained tied after 120, or 128 minutes, and Argentina won in the shoot-out—Vautrot acknowledged the extra extra time was due to his absurd clumsiness: "I just forgot to look at my watch."

The shoes

The Italy 1990 final between Argentina and Germany offered a varied menu of curiosities. The first, that it featured the same two teams in consecutive World Cup finals. The second had to do with the appointment of the referee for the game. FIFA's initial choice was the Brazilian José Roberto Wright, considered the best qualified, but the German delegates demanded that another ref be chosen. Why? Because the German team had lost the two previous finals with a Brazilian ref on the pitch: with Arnaldo Coelho in Spain 1982, they lost 3-1 against Italy, and with Romualdo Arpi in Mexico 1986, 3-2 against Argentina. FIFA accepted the claim and, then, it appointed the Uruguayan nationalized Mexico native Edgardo Codesal, son of José María Codesal who had refereed in the 1958 World Cup in Sweden.

An unusual moment came when there were six minutes to go in the final at the Olympic Stadium in Rome. Argentine Néstor Sensini crossed German Rudolf Voeller inside the box. For Codesal, there were no doubts: penalty. For some, it was not even close; for others, at least confusing, but the punishment had already been decided by the referee. Until that moment, the person in charge of executing the penalty in the German squad was Lothar Matthäus, who the only goal that say the quarter-final against Czechoslovakia, and had also scored in the penalty shoot-out against England, in the semi-final. But to the amazement of the entire stadium and the millions of TV viewers, Matthäus took the ball, passed it to his teammate Andreas Brehme and ordered: "You take it."

Many wondered if the German captain feared coming face to face with Sergio Goycochea, a specialist in stopping shots from eleven meters. The reason was quite different: Matthäus had come out onto the pitch with a pair of boots that he had used for some years and had perfectly adapted to his feet. But during the game, one of the studs on his right foot broke. At halftime, the German midfielder put on a new pair, but he wasn't feeling comfortable, certainly not enough to take a shot as momentous a this—with four minutes to go in a tied World Cup final.

The damaged shoe had an additional story. It had been used two years before by . . . Diego Maradona, Matthäus's rival that day, although in a benefit match in which both had taken part. The

Argentine had forgotten the boots and the German lent him that pair, new and worn by Maradona for the first time. When Diego returned the shoes, Matthäus found that his colleague had passed the laces in a different way. By putting them on, he noticed that he felt more comfortable and decided to incorporate that technique until the end of his career.

The rest of the story is known: Brehme, a defender with a great shot who'd scored in the shootout against England, accepted the responsibility and with a precise shot put the ball out of reach of the goalkeeper, who had not had time to repeat his urinary ritual. This single goal gave the German team the title.

Sixteen years later, Brehme himself assured that Sensini "did not commit a penalty. Before that play, they had committed one to Klaus Augenthaler, but the one I scored on goal was not a foul. It was a correct tackle, although dangerous at the time for having made it inside the area." In case Codesal had any doubts.

Postman

Due to Sergio Goycochea's popularity in the Cup, thanks to his skill in stopping penalties, Correo Argentino ran into a problem managing the tens of thousands of fan letters sent to the goalkeeper. To expedite the large quantity of envelopes, the company decided to assign the Goycochea family's house a unique zip code: 0004 Lima, Buenos Aires. The selection of the number was not accidental: Goyco had saved four shots in the shootouts against Yugoslavia and Italy.

UNITED STATES 1994

The choice of the United States as the venue for the World Cup drew numerous criticisms. It was the first time that a World Cup had been played in a country where soccer was not—and never had been—the most popular sport. In fact, it is also not the second,

Americans surprised the world by coming out in droves to watch soccer.

nor the third, nor perhaps even the fourth in public preference, despite the fact that the U.S. had received an enormous number of Latin American and Asian immigrants who do love soccer. The supposed general ignorance of the discipline led the local organizers to publish a "guide for the uninitiated," with some basic notions of the game and its history.

This apparent disinterest disappeared with the first kick of the ball. United States 1994 recorded the highest attendance at stadiums in World Cup history. The 52 matches drew almost 3.6 million spectators, an average of almost 69,000 per match. The total number is close to that registered in Brazil 2014±with a total of 3,386,810 attendees, but in 64 games, twelve more than in the United States.

The fifteenth edition of the World Cup—the first to award three points to a game winner, and the first to feature player names on the jerseys—had three outstanding events, two of which were not necessarily sporting. First, Brazil's triumph after 24 years, in the first goalless final in history, after 120 minutes. Never before had a World Cup been decided by shots from the penalty spot. Roberto Baggio, Italy's top player, and author of penalty shot over the crossbar that gave Brazil the Cup, confessed years after that final: "I think it was Ayrton Senna who took the ball high." Senna was the legendary Brazilian Formula 1 driver who had died in an accident two months before the soccer championship.

The second notable incident was the positive doping test of Diego Maradona, revealed after Argentina's 2-1 victory over Nigeria. The sight of Maradona going from the field at Boston's Foxboro Stadium to doping control—led by the hand by Sue Carpenter, a nurse employed by the tournament organizers—was one of the emblematic images in the history of the contest. Five prohibited substances derived from ephedrine appeared in his urine. FIFA immediately expelled the Argentine Captain and handed him with a fifteen-month suspension.

The last of the resonant events was the murder of Colombian defender Andrés Escobar, one of the most horrific cases of violence in soccer. The defender had scored an own goal in a loss to the United States, and was blamed for the country's elimination from the tournament. After returning home, he was shot twelve times after an argument with a man outside a restaurant, where a group of fans reproached him for the unfortunate move. The murderer, Humberto Muñoz Castro, was sentenced to 43 years in prison, although he was released on October 6, 2005 after having spent just eleven years in a penitentiary.

Even before Escobar's crime, the spectre of violence had plagued the Colombian camp. Hours before the fateful game with the United States, player Gabriel Jaime Barrabás Gómez received death threats against himself and his family. A mafia group, allegedly involved in unofficial sports betting, blamed Gómez for Colombia's loss to Romania in their World Cup debut, and said a bomb would be planted in his house if he stepped on the field during the Cup again. After this incident, coach Francisco Maturana resigned, but changed his mind thanks to the support of the officials and the players. The one who did not appear at the Rose Bowl stadium in Los Angeles was Gomez. He told his coach he was willing to play despite the threats, but Maturana decided that the midfielder, whom he considered one of the keys to his team, should prioritize his safety, and that of his family. Before the match, the midfielder held a press conference to announce that he was abandoning not only the national team, but also soccer as a player. "I am very sad. I am leaving soccer after seventeen years of career. I can not take it anymore. I am afraid for my family, not for me. I am not afraid of death," he said.

Singular situation

On September 8, 1993, shortly before stepping onto the pitch to face Denmark in a qualifying match, Albanian coach Bejkush Birce gathered his men and urged them not to exchange their jerseys with the Danish players after the game: "We have only one set left and we don't have the money to buy another for the game against Spain." At the end of the match, which the visitors won by a meager 1-0, poor Birce collected the jerseys to wash them and found that three of his players had disobeyed him. Desperate, the coach took an extreme step to prepare his team for the last game of the series, against Spain: he picked up the phone and called his Spanish colleague, Javier Clemente, to ask him to bring an extra set of shirts to Tirana. Clemente did, and contributed fifty meals for his impoverished rivals as well. His gesture was well rewarded: on September 22, 1993, with the two teams on the pitch with their bellies full and their hearts happy, Spain won 5-0.

That was not the only precaution the Spanish took in their Albanian journey. Apart from deciding to make a round-trip on the same day, so as not to spend the night in one of Tirana's extremely poor hotels, the delegation's cook carried his own food and mineral water and hired two guards to prevent his supplies from being stolen. Chef Xabier Albizu said he did not want a repeat of "what happened in Latvia, where part of my food was stolen." The Spaniards, moreover, had learned that the Danish squad had come out to play against Albania having only eaten an apple because their provisions had been pillaged.

English spectacle

The qualifying series was horrific for England. The English squad not only was out of the Cup, beaten by the Netherlands and Norway, but it took a slap from San Marino, one of the worst national teams in the world. On November 17, 1993, England traveled to the Renato Dall'Ara stadium in Bologna, Italy—San Marino did not have a suitable coliseum for international matches—and after eight seconds they were already losing: defender Stuart Pearce played a ball towards his goalkeeper, David Seaman, but it fell short and San Marino striker Davide Gualtieri easily sent the ball to the back of the net. England recovered and finally won 7-1, but had suffered the fastest goal in its history and in the World Cup, including the qualifiers.

French spectacle

After failing to qualify for Italy 1990, France put together a great team so as not to miss the United States cup. Led by the notable Eric Cantoná and many of the stars who would be champions in 1998, the French squad started the qualification round successfully, and with only two games left—both at the Parc des Princes in Paris—a simple draw would be enough to make it. But two fatal seconds crossed the path of "Les Bleus," two tiny moments that forged a nightmare that would last for four years.

The catastrophe began to develop on October 13, 1993, with a match that seemed won before it started. France had already beaten Israel easily 4-0 in Tel Aviv, and Israel was already eliminated with two draws and five defeats. But a biblical flood prevented a normal game, and under a curtain of water the visitors took an advantage thanks to a goal from Ronen Harazi. The French, embarrassed, soon put things in their place: still in the first half, Franck Sauzée and David Ginola made it 2-1 and seemed to consolidate the classification. But Eyal Berkovic drew the Israelis even at 83 minutes. When three minutes of added time were played, Reuven Atar hit the final slap: surrounded by three defenders, the Israeli took a left-footed shot that beat goalkeeper Bernard Lama. The locals barely had time to get out of the way: Northern Irish referee Alan Snoddy whistled the end a second later as a thunderous whistle of disapproval enveloped the stadium.

But France had one more chance. On November 17 they hosted Bulgaria, who in the first leg had won by 2 to 0. Once again a draw would give the Gauls a happy ending. Cantoná, at 32 minutes in the first half, opened the account that calmed the spirits. But the Bulgarians, led by the great Hristo Stoichkov, immediately tied it up on a shot by Emil Kostadinov. The locals held the draw until the 90th minute, but when referee Leslie Mottram raised the whistle to his mouth to lower the curtain, another missile from Kostadinov, from about 35 meters, hit the left post and finished in the net. With no time for more, the visiting players erupted in a crazy celebration while insults and violent threats rained down upon the French. "We are donkeys", acknowledged Didier Deschamps, on one of the blackest nights in French sporting history. It is said that soccer always gives revenge, and Deschamps and most of the "donkeys" would have it, although they would have to wait until July 12, 1998 to lift the World Cup in Paris.

Autograph

Shortly before the start of the World Cup, Argentine captain Diego Maradona took advantage of a free morning to distract himself from the pressure with a visit, along with his wife, daughters and a friend, the journalist Adrián Paenza, to the Faneuil Hall Marketplace in Boston. In the food court, the group had pizza for lunch with a former student of Paenza's, Gerry Garbulsky. At the end of the meal, Diego asked Gerry to accompany him to a Foot Locker close by, since he needed to buy shoes. Already in the store—decorated for the World Cup with posters of different soccer players, none of them the Argentine number 10—Maradona was amazed by the great variety of brands and assortment of models, so he began to try on different shoes helped by Gerry and a young salesman. After choosing eight pairs, Maradona went to the cashier to pay for his purchase. The employee, happy with the volume of the sale, gave the Argentine a World Cup key ring. "I don't know if you know," the boy confided in English, "but the soccer World Cup is about to begin here in the United States. This keychain has the tournament logo on it." Gerry translated the comment, Maradona thanked him for the gift, and the two Argentines left the store.

Seconds later, Paenza entered the same shop with Claudia Maradona, who had forgotten to ask her husband to buy sneakers for their daughters. The journalist noticed the soccer decoration of the place, very appropriate for the proximity of the championship, and asked the happy salesman: "Do you have any idea who just was here?" He didn't. Paenza continued: "The best soccer player in all of history." The young man was embarrassed, but quickly recovered, grabbed a paper and pen and hurried out of the place, shouting after his recent clients. There was no way he could miss getting the autograph of such a glittering sports star. When the salesman reached them, he extended the paper and pen and excitedly asked for the signature of Gerry Garbulsky!

FIFA vs. UN

Not for nothing does FIFA boast of having more members than the United Nations, and that the power of soccer is often greater than that of politics. Just ask United Nations Security Council. The session of Tuesday, June 21 had to be delayed because almost all the representatives of the countries stayed in their offices watching the clash between Germany and Spain. The day before, Brazilian ambassador Ronaldo Mota Sardenberg got his colleagues to approve, by a large majority, that the UN Peacekeeping Mission's treatment of the war between the African nations of Uganda and Rwanda be advanced several hours "so that it does not overlap with the Brazil-Russia match."

TV overdose

The first weekend of the Cup proved fatal for a Chinese citizen living in the then Portuguese colony of Macau. Because of the time difference, Law Chon-Yin, 37, spent two nights without sleep so as not to miss any of the tournament. So much soccer passion was not good for his health, and he passed out, and then died, on Monday while he was serving in his restaurant, which at that time was full of diners.

Meanwhile, according to the book "Soccer's most wanted", by John Snyder, a Swedish woman killed her boyfriend by sticking scissors in his neck after he woke her up at dawn on June 20 to watch Sweden-Cameroon match that was about to start in Los Angeles . . . on June 19, due to the great time difference. The young woman murdered her partner and went back to sleep. When the police arrived, alerted by a neighbor who'd overheard them arguing, they found her still sleeping next to her boyfriend's corpse, in a sea of blood. The two were resting in peace.

Benches in the stand

The clash between the U.S. and the Swiss teams on June 18 at the opening of Group A had a very particular scenario: for the first time in a World Cup, a match was played in a fully covered stadium. The battle was fought at the Pontiac Silverdome in Detroit, where the Lions play American football, which was specially adapted for soccer. Artificial turf was replaced with natural grass, but the dimensions caused an even bigger change: because an American football playing field is fifty meters wide, and the soccer grounds for international matches must be between 64 and 75, the side lines were practically glued to the stands. For this reason, the architects in charge had no choice but to place the substitute benches in one of the stands, as is the case in most English stadiums.

A most unusual bet

According to the Spanish newspaper *El Mundo*, it seems that an Albanian man, a lover of soccer but much more of gambling, did not have enough money to calm his itch. Convinced that Argentina, with Diego Maradona and Claudio Caniggia, would easily surpass Bulgaria in the third game of Group D, he decided to bet it all and risk . . . his own wife. Unfortunately, without Maradona or Caniggia, the South American team was easy prey for the inspired Hristo Stoichkov and his teammates. And so his wife disappeared arm in arm with the happy winner. Evicted from his house, the defeated man appeared at a police station to demand the return of his spouse, but it was not a police matter. The woman had already announced "no more bets."

Records and more records

When they met on June 28, Russia and Cameroon were already eliminated, making the match unimportant for Group B at the World Cup. But that day, at Stanford Stadium in San Francisco, two World Cup records were reached: with his goal scored in the 46th minute, Cameroon's Roger Milla broke his own 1990 mark by becoming the oldest player (42 years and 39 days) to score in a Cup. On the other team, forward Oleg Salenko scored five goals, a mark never reached by another player in a single World Cup match. Salenko—who shared the Golden Boot with Bulgarian Hristo Stoichkov, who had six goals—also established himself as the only World Cup top scorer to play fewer than three games in the tournament.

Red records: Italian Gianluca Pagliuca was the first goalkeeper to be sent off in a World Cup. It happened at 21 minutes in the June 23 clash between Italy and Norway in Group E in New Jersey. Despite playing with one less player after that, Italy won 1-0. Meanwhile, in the opening match on June 17, Bolivian Marco Etcheverry became the substitute to see the red card quickest. The Diablo was ejected three minutes after having replaced Luis Ramallo, eight minutes from the end and with his team losing 1-0 to Germany. Etcheverry did not play in the Cup again. A week later, Cameroonian Rigobert Song became the youngest player to be sent off during a World Cup game. That June 24, Song was 17 years and 358 days old. Brazil beat Cameroon 3-0 in Group B at Stanford Stadium. Also against the Verdeamarela team, again at Stanford but on July 4, the American Fernando Clavijo, 37, became the oldest player to be sent off in a World Cup. It wasn't red, but it was a record: On June 24, at the Pontiac Silverdome in Detroit, Russia's Sergei Gorlukovich was booked in the first minute of the game against Sweden.

Black mark: Frenchman Joel Quiniou was the referee with the most games worked in World Cups. Quiniou led a total of eight matches over three Cups: one in 1986, three in 1990 and four in 1994. His farewell came on July 13, 1994, in the Italy 2-Bulgaria 1 semi-final played at the Giants Stadium in New Jersey. His mark was surpassed in 2014 by Uzbek judge Ravshan Irmatov, who worked 9.

Perfect penalty kicks: Throughout the World Cup, fifteen penalties were sanctioned and *all* were scored. Some shots were missed from the eleven-meter mark, but only those shootouts that ended tie games after extra time.

Finally, Bulgaria finally broke a streak of futility: on June 26 they won their first World Cup match against Greece, 4-0. Until then, they had suffered eleven defeats and six draws. In Mexico 1986 they got through the first round, although with two draws, against Italy and South Korea, and one defeat, against Argentina.

Diana missed

In the previous section, it was said that, without counting the shootouts from 11 meters, throughout the American Cup 15 penalties had been fired and all had been scored. There was, however, one well-noted miss. During the official opening ceremony of the championship, on June 17 at Soldier Field in Chicago, everything was set for one of the artists invited to the party, Diana Ross, to kick a ball into a goal while she sang. The show was planned so that the plastic goal, when the ball hit, broke in two and allowed Ross to continue running up into the grandstands. The distance between the ball and the goal was just three meters. But, unbelievably, Ross missed the shot and the goal collapsed anyway! Ross continued her song and her choreography like nothing was wrong, but her blooper was recorded for eternity as the funniest in the history of World Cup opening shows. It could also be said that "officially" it was the only failed penalty of the contest.

French arrest

Bad temper caused a very bad moment for France's Eric Cantona. The forward, who at that time was playing for Manchester United, went to the Rose Bowl in Los Angeles to serve as a commentator on English television for the semi-final between Brazil and Sweden. Arriving at the coliseum well in advance of the start, Cantona mistakenly took a seat in the wrong sector of the grandstand. When a police officer approached him to point out the mistake, Cantona, a man with a healthy ego and propensity for running over people, insulted the guard. Within seconds, several officers appeared to assist and immediately beat and handcuffed Cantona. The forward was taken to a Pasadena detachment and missed the game.

Gay team

On June 26, after his team was beaten 4-0 by Nigeria in their second Group D appearance—an identical score to their first match loss against Argentina—Greek coach Alkis Panagoulias stormed out of the locker room. "I have a team of homosexuals," he complained loudly, not caring that the anteroom was packed with journalists and television cameras from around the world. "We are a not very serious people," he continued barking, calling his players "innocent little girls" for the mistakes made in the two games.

Reward

Saudi Arabian players were well rewarded for qualifying for the round of 16 at a World Cup. A Saudi businessman, Wafaa Zawawi, acquired 22 of the latest models from Volvo to give one to each player. Zawawi was convinced the $700,000 expense was not frivolous, but a fair reward for such success. The inspired Arabs had already each earned $25,000 dollars and a Mercedes Benz car for qualifying for the World Cup.

Saudi players were well-compensated for their 1994 World Cup performance.

Misbehavior

Two players at the World Cup were expelled from their national teams by their own coaches. The first was Romanian midfielder Ion Vladoiu, who was sent home after getting a red card for a violent kick to Switzerland's Stephane Chapuisat, three minutes after replacing Ilie Dumitrescu. "The Federation fired Vladoiu from the team considering, first, the harsh foul committed against a rival player, and also the bad behavior he had with one of the team's coaching staff," explained coach Anghel Iordanescu. For the serious offense, the FIFA Disciplinary Committee sanctioned Vladoiu with a three-game suspension and the Romanian federation with a $5,500 fine.

The second was the German Stefan Effenberg. On June 27, after being replaced by Thomas Helmer in the game against South Korea, Effenberg made rude gestures to his country's fans who were jeering him from the Cotton Bowl stands in Dallas. "Effe" left the pitch with the middle finger of his right hand extended towards the stunned German supporters. The midfielder was tossed from his team by order of coach Berti Vogts, who justified the measure by saying that "an international player cannot perform that gesture."

Chain alarm

The half-times of the World Cup matches caused a particular headache across the Atlantic in Berlin. According to the city's sanitation corporation, every time a referee marked the end of the first half, the massive use of the city toilets caused sewage pipes to overflow.

Maradonian claim

Diego Maradona's expulsion from the World Cup for a positive doping test caused strange demonstrations around the world. In Israel, an eleven-year-old boy from the city of Haifa went on a hunger strike and had to be hospitalized after spending three days without food or drink. In Bangladesh, people took the streets to demand FIFA revoke the sentence, and burned an image of the organization's president, Joao Havelange. A lawyer there, Mohammed Anwarul, also filed a lawsuit against Havelange, demanding payment of 1,000 taka (about $25) as compensation for the "mental disorders" caused by the expulsion of the Argentine captain. In India, workers from a food company boycotted a wedding in protest.

Diego's power could also be measured in tickets sold: in Dallas the Cotton Bowl's 64,000 tickets for the game between Argentina and Bulgaria were sold out well before game day, before the drug test and the ban that prevented him playing on June 30. The two previous games in Dallas didn't come close. Spain and South Korea on June 17 drew 56,000 fans, while Nigeria vs. Bulgaria on June 21 attracted barely 44,000.

Reward and punishment

The 90 minutes had passed, and the extra time nearly finished at Foxboro Stadium in Boston, on July 9, where Italy was beating Spain 2-1. In the last Iberian attempt, the Basque Jon Goikoetxea launched a cross towards the front of net but it found the end line. Meanwhile, the Spanish striker Luis Enrique was stretched out on the pitch, his face bathed in blood from a treacherous elbow from defender Mauro Tassotti. Everything suggested that the Hungarian referee Sandor Puhl would whistle a penalty and would send off Tassotti. But neither Puhl nor his assistants saw what they had to see, and the match finished despite angry Spanish protests and the obvious infraction painted on Luis Enrique's face.

Two days later, the FIFA Disciplinary Committee analyzed a video of the match to review the incident, which did not appear in the referee's report, and made a historic decision. Never before had the entity used a tape to study an incident that occurred on the field of play during the World Cup: Tassotti was punished with an eight-game suspension—a penalty that, unbelievably, Luis Enrique himself found "excessive"— and a fine of 20,000 Swiss francs. But for the Spanish, justice was late, since they had already returned home eliminated. It was unclear why no punishment was applied to the oblivious Puhl, much less why he was designated for the grand final between Italy and Brazil.

Kilometric support

Bolivia's participation in the Cup was not very happy. The squad was quickly eliminated after losses to Germany and Spain, and a goalless draw with South Korea. But for their goalkeeper—the naturalized Argentine Carlos Trucco—there was at least one beautiful consolation: a letter of support seven kilometers long. The delightful and original initiative came from thousands of fans, who expressed warm messages on several reels of paper. The huge letter was delivered to Trucco by the Bolivian National Post Office, with its corresponding stamps and security seals.

Wig by final

Bulgarian goalkeeper Boris Mihailov was as effective as he was flirtatious. A great star of his team in the round of 16—he saved two penalty kicks against Mexico—and in the quarter-finals, in the historic 2-1 victory against Germany—Mihailov also stood out for his vanity. In addition to his gloves, the gatekeeper wore a neat toupée. He admitted the use of the hairpiece, which remained attached to the head despite all the tumbling. But perhaps to downplay his vanity, he promised that if his team beat Italy in the semi-final, "I will throw it to the stands. Without a doubt, I change my toupee for a chance at the final game." But fate would have Bulgaria lose to Italy, and then again to Sweden in the match for third place, so Mihailov kept his shiny bald head safe.

France 1998

Twenty years after Argentina 1978, a host country raised the Cup again. France, with a solid team defense and a lethal attack, was probably the best of the host-winning countries since 1930. It was the World Cup champion with the with the greatest goal difference in history, thirteen, and with the fewest goals allowed—only two. Nor can anyone credit politics or help from the referees for the French win: France suffered three red cards, the most for a Cup winner until Russia 2018. The men who had to leave early for the showers were Marcel Desailly (double yellow in the final), Zinedine Zidane (direct red for stepping on a rival from Saudi Arabia, which resulted in a two-match suspension) and Laurent Blanc (also direct red, in the semi-final). The tri-color success was so laudable that, the day after the victory over Brazil in the final, the sports newspaper *L'Equipe* sold 1,600,000 copies!

This tournament was full of records. First of all, the number of teams. For this edition, FIFA determined an increase from 24 to 32, in eight groups of four each, and that the first two of each quartet go to the second round. Meanwhile, the 37-year-old German veteran Lothar Matthäus reached the mark for the most games played, with twenty-five in five World Cups—another record, although shared with Mexican goalkeeper Antonio Carbajal. Cesar Sampaio scored the fastest goal in a Cup opener game, in the fourth minute in Brazil's 2-1 win over Scotland. Denmark's Ebbe Sand scored the fastest goal in World Cup history by a substitute. Sand sent the ball into the net just 16 seconds after stepping on the grass at the 59th minute against Nigeria, in the round of 16. Denmark won 4-1. In addition, the replacement of Alessandro Nesta by Giuseppe Bergomi four minutes into the match against Austria—on June 23, for Group B— was the fastest in the history of the World Cup. Nesta had to leave the field at the Saint-Denis stadium in Paris on a stretcher due to a torn cruciate ligament in his right knee, which left him out of the competition.

Argentine striker Gabriel Batistuta achieved an interesting mark: he was the first to get a "hat trick" in two World Cup tournaments. Bati scored three goals against Greece in United States 1994 and three against Jamaica at the Parisian Parc de Princes. For this edition, the controversial "golden goal" was established, which determined that, if a match ended even after 90 minutes, the team that scored first in extra-time would win the match. The only game decided in this way was the clash between France and Paraguay in the round of 16. French defender Laurent Blanc gave the bleu squad the golden victory in the 113th minute.

The final between France and Brazil was the first time the organizing nation and the defending champion met in the ultimate game. It was also the first World Cup final to be umpired by an African referee: Moroccan Said Belqola. Another African, the Cameroonian Rigobert Song, became the first to be sent off in two consecutive World Cups: Against Brazil in USA '94, and in the meeting with Chile in Nantes on June 23. Four countries debuted at the World Cup in 1998: Japan, Croatia, Jamaica and South Africa. The draw determined that the first three were in the same initial group, Group H, with Argentina. A final interesting tidbit: To mark the World

Cup, the French Post launched a series of round stamps, the first issued in that format by any European country.

A sound thrashing

In the qualifying phase, on June 2, 1997, Iran recorded the most lop-sided win that had ever been registered between two national teams in a preliminary round match: It crushed the Maldives Islands by 17 to 0. Iran scored six times in the first half and eleven in the second, and striker Karim Bagheri was the top artilleryman with seven goals. Maldives Islands, which shared Group 2 with Iran, Syria and Kyrgyzstan, finished the series with a very poor record: six games, six defeats, zero goals scored and 59 against.

Forced labor

When the regime of Iraqi dictator Saddam Hussein ended—overthrown in 2003 after the invasion of allied forces from the United States, the United Kingdom, Australia, Spain and Poland—a terrible story emerged: the players who had participated in the qualifiers for France 1998 and Korea-Japan 2002 had been punished severely for failing to qualify for both competitions. Several players reported that Uday Hussein, one of Saddam's sons and self-appointed president of the local soccer federation, resorted to torture, jail time

Uday Hussein with his father, the dictator Saddam Hussein.

and forced labor sentences to punish his athletes. According to the complaints, Uday personally whipped soccer players and witnessed cruel abuses such as plucking nails, or plunging boys headfirst into barrels with rotten water or excrement. Prolonged lockdowns without food, or forcing players to kick cement balls were other methods. A few months before the fall of the Hussein regime, when the European press collected testimonies from some athletes who had fled their country, FIFA launched an investigation to try to determine what was happening and asked the Iraqi federation for an explanation for the accusations. In response, Uday replied that his players were only "invited" to a retreat to participate in "spiritual exercises."

Pardon

Some months before the World Cup in France, the great Saudi star Sayeed Al-Owairán was caught drinking from a glass full of liquor with several women on his arm, in Ramadan, the Muslim holy. Al-Owairán went to jail, but was later pardoned so he could train and arrive in perfect condition to wear the 10 jersey in the important competition. The midfielder had been the star of his team in the United States and had scored a "Maradonian" goal against Belgium that qualified Saudi Arabia for the round of 16.

Gourmet complaint

A French chefs association complained about the designation of McDonald's as the "official restaurant" of the championship. The U.S. corporation had signed a massive sponsorship contract with FIFA to win the designation, and the ire of the best chefs in the world. "This alliance between soccer and fast-food is not a gastronomic issue, in which a lot of money is at stake," said the chefs.

"French gastronomy is world renowned. We cannot let a hamburger replace us." On the other hand, precisely because France is the world capital of gourmet food and wine, it was astonishing that most of the participating teams carried in their suitcases native food and drink that the athletes consumed during the competition. The Italians, for example, arrived at their neighbors with a truck packed with 1,300 kilos of pasta, 300 kilos of Parmesan cheese, 500 kilos of packaged peeled tomatoes—to prepare about 7,500 sides of spaghetti with sauce—80 legs of Parma ham, 120 liters of olive oil, 5,000 liters of mineral water, 400 of Italian wine (wasn't French wine the best in the world?), several boxes of soda and beer, 400 kilos of sponge cakes, 100 kilos of sugar and 120 kilos of flour. All these products were treated by the prodigious hands of chefs Franco Soncini and Gino Delle Donne, in charge of preparing the daily menu.

Hot TV

Most coaches prefer that their men abstain from sex, at least the night before their matches. When Brazil arrived in France, they were undefeated for almost a year, a series that had started after a defeat in Oslo against the Norwegian team. Coach Mario Zagallo had blamed the fatigue produced by seventeen hours on the plane and "excess sex on television" for that 4-2 defeat. Zagallo, a forward on the Cup winning teams of Sweden '58 and Chile '62 and coach of the glorious team that prevailed in Mexico in 1970, confessed that before the match against Norway his boys spent the night "with their eyes open, watching explicit sex films on the TVs in the hotel rooms." This caused "the physical disposition of the players to be less than the expected," he explained. So that this situation would not be repeated during the World Cup, the coach ordered the management of their hotel to provide a package of "innocent" movies, such as "Lion King", "Maximum speed" or "Terminator I and II."

But Zagallo had to review his strict measures on the advice of the head of the Brazil's medical department, Lidio Toledo. The doctor authorized players to have sex and drink beer, but in moderation. The specialist remarked that "in the 1974 World Cup, the technical staffs of Germany and the Netherlands gave these freedoms to their players. We maintained a rigid scheme and did not achieve anything. Making love is scientifically recommended for athletes." He remarked that the consumption of two cans of beer maximum per day "serves to alleviate the anxiety" produced by 40 days of pre-tournament training.

The doll

Minutes before the Belgian delegation left for France, right-back Eric Deflandre told a journalist that in his suitcase he carried his cleats and "an inflatable doll because a month without a woman will be difficult." This quickly found its way into the Belgian newspapers, forcing Club Brugge's defender to clarify that he was, in fact, just joking. The "red devils" were eliminated in the first round and Deflandre returned home much earlier than planned. It is not known what explanations he gave to his girlfriend, who waited for him "inflated" with anger over the scandal his confessions produced.

Heartbreaker

Scotland's starting goalkeeper Andy Goram did not have an immaculate résumé in matters of the heart when, a month before the start of the Cup, a sex scandal broke out, knocking him out of the competition. While his team was preparing in the United States, newspapers in the United Kingdom filled pages and pages with the tears of the good Goram's girlfriend, disconsolate because her lover had impregnated another girl. At the same time, a prostitute came out to shout from the rooftops that she had provided her services to the goalkeeper, but in exchange she had not received the 200 pounds previously agreed upon. Burdened by the exposure of his private life, Goram decided to return home to Glasgow. The Scottish coach, Craig Brown, had to call up Jonathan Gould urgently, and promote Jim Leighton as the new starter.

Clean Fans

It came as a surprise to the Cup organizers that the stadiums where Japan and South Korea played each match ended cleaner than before their doors were opened. The Asian fans—possibly to burnish their image prior to the World Cup four years hence in those two nations—brought blue plastic bags for the papers, food scraps and other detritus generated during the games. On the field of play, the two teams weren't as sharp as their fans. Both finished last in their zones. Japan lost its three games (against Argentina, Croatia and Jamaica), and Korea only rescued a draw with Belgium, after being defeated by Mexico and the Netherlands.

Mexican tortilla

The Mexican team led by Manuel Lapuente had a curious performance: In the first round, for Group E, they defeated South Korea 3-1 after being down, and tied with Belgium and the Netherlands at two after being down 2-0. In the quarter-finals, when they were finally able to open the scoring against Germany, they could not maintain the advantage and fell 2-1, a result that meant their elimination.

Guarani

The Guarani language was an important tool for the Paraguayans who faced Spain in Group D. They played to a goalless draw that allowed them through to the second round and sent the Spanish home. They credited much of their success to their players using Guarani, the native dialect of their land, and not the Spanish brought by the Iberian conquerors, to direct the actions on the field. The Spanish noticed the successful tactic and tried to make it their own, since almost all spoke a second Iberian language. Of course, the trick did not work, because the use of Catalan, Basque or Galician led to confusion more than a solution.

Seasoning

During this World Cup, the Thai embassy in Paris offered a consignment of its best curry to spice up the spirits of the Nigerian team. Thailand did not qualify for the final series played in France, but both its government and its people followed the performance of the Africans with great passion. They felt united by the stomach: Nigeria was the main buyer of Thai rice.

Marriage

When the draw determined that Brazil and Norway were to meet on June 23 for Group A, a couple decided to set a date and begin the process to make their dream come true on the green grass of the Velodrome in Marseille. The Norwegian Oivind Ekeland and the Brazilian Rosangela de Souza contacted FIFA officials and requested permission to marry that day, in the center circle of the pitch, minutes before the kick-off of the game. FIFA analyzed the strange request and, perhaps inspired, allowed the ceremony to take place.

Spokesperson Keith Cooper stressed that "we have always said that soccer should bring people together in a spirit of love, friendship and brotherhood, so we accept. We only asked (to the bride and the groom) not to notify to the press because we did not want a flood of similar requests, of Moroccans marrying Paraguayans or God knows what." An hour before the start of the match, Oivind, in a sober black tuxedo, and Rosangela, in a long white dress, were declared "husband and wife" by a Catholic priest and blessed by the applause of the crowd that filled the coliseum. The joy was double for Oivind: Norway beat Brazil 2-1 and advanced to the round of 16.

One scorer and two homelands

By sending the ball into the net at 53 minutes into the match against Jamaica in Lens, Croatian Robert Prosinecki became the first player to score goals in the World Cup tournament for two different countries. The midfielder had worn the Yugoslav jersey in Italy 1990, in which he scored against the United Arab Emirates. For a few decades, FIFA had prohibited a player from wearing the national shirt of more than one country, but it had to relax this rule in the face of the political changes in Europe after the fall of the iron curtain. Prosinecki was born in Germany, but at age 14 he moved with his family to Croatia, which at the time was part of Yugoslavia. In 1991, Croatia declared its independence and Prosinecki switched to wearing the red and white checkered shirt. In France 1998, the Croatian squad had Davor Šuker and Robert Jarni, two others who'd played in Italy 1990, but the first did not play in a game and the second saw only a few minutes action against Colombia.

Until that moment, only five footballers had competed in a World Cup with two different teams, playing at least one game with each squad: the Argentines Luis Monti—he scored two goals for the 1930 runner-up, but not with the Italian shirt in 1934—and Atilio

Demaría, who failed to score with Argentina in 1930 and Italy in 1934. Ferenc Puskás scored four times for runner-up Hungary in Switzerland 1954, but not for Spain in Chile 1962. José Emilio Santamaría went goalless with Uruguay in 1954 and Spain in 1962, and Juan José Altafini had two with Brazil in Sweden 1958, none for Italy in 1962.

Testing one, two, three . . .

After the match that South Africa and Saudi Arabia played on June 24 at the Parc Lescure de Bordeaux, a controversy arose: Several newspapers claimed that the defender and captain of the African team, Pierre Issa, was in radio contact with his coach, the Frenchman Philippe Troussier, using a headset in his right ear. FIFA reacted with great surprise when it discovered in various journals a photo of the player in action with something in his ear. FIFA began an investigation by asking the South African Federation for explanations and summoning the Chilean referee, Mario Sánchez Yanten. "I didn't notice it," the umpire excused himself. Although an incident of this nature was not foreseen in the regulations, FIFA considered it unsportsmanlike to transmit radio instructions from the substitute bench. Finally, after all the commotion, it was determined that the issue had been generated by a simple optical illusion. FIFA Press chief Keith Cooper said that, after an exhaustive inquiry, it was found that the photograph had taken the exact moment when Issa's necklace had lifted and covered his ear, giving the appearance that the defender wore a headset.

Better later than never? Not always . . .

The Austrian team scored three goals in the Cup, one per game and all in overtime in the second half. Anton "Tony" Polster tied the match with Cameroon and Ivica Vastic with Chile. Meanwhile, Andreas Herzog scored a penalty against Italy, although the goal was not enough to prevent a 2-1 defeat, which meant their elimination.

Coach changes

When he came to the locker room after the 4-0 loss to France, Brazilian Carlos Alberto Parreira, the Saudi Arabian coach, suffered another headache. Prince Faisal, son of King Fahd of the wealthy Persian Gulf nation and president of the Soccer Federation, had made him the first coach to lose his job during a World Cup. Parreira, who had been champion four years earlier with Brazil, was replaced by Mohammed Al Kharashy after two defeats, to Denmark (1-0) and France (4-0). Two days later, this situation was repeated with the Korean Bum Kun Cha: the leaders of the Korean Soccer Association dismissed him after the losses to Mexico (3-1) and the Netherlands (5-0). "For Cha, this ended now, right here," said Chun Hanjin, deputy director of the South Korea's technical committee for national teams. It wasn't just the losses. Cha's statements prior to the Dutch game fell very badly: "I am satisfied with a draw," he had said. Cha was replaced by his assistant, Pyung Seok Kim. Another who had to pack his bags before the end of the first round was the Henryk Kasperczak, relieved by Ali Selmi after Tunisia's two defeats against England (2-0) and Colombia (1-0). The unusual thing is that all three brand new coaches got draws in their tournament farewell: Korea with Belgium, 1-1; Tunisia with Romania by the same score; and Saudi Arabia with South Africa, 2-2.

Brave heart

At the age of twenty, Nwankwo Kanu was enjoying success. From his impoverished native Owerri in Nigeria, he had reached the pinnacle of soccer thanks to his surprising moves. He was a three-time champion with the Dutch club Ajax; he won the Champions League, the Intercontinental Cup, and the European Super Cup. He was also essential to the Nigerian national squad that conquered the 1993 U-17 World Cup and the gold medal at the 1996 Atlanta Olympics. So many titles and a stellar reputation made caused Italy's Inter Milan club to spend a fortune for him to wear the blue and black.

But when Kanu, days after the Olympic final, arrived in Milan and underwent a thorough medical examination, the flame went out. A cardiologist discovered that the African star had a serious heart valve failure in the aorta, which not only would prevent him from playing professional sports, but also put his life at risk. The diagnosis was confirmed by other doctors consulted by Inter, so the midfielder traveled to a medical center in Cleveland to have an artificial valve placed to supplant the damaged natural one. After more than a year of study and recovery, Kanu was able to travel with the Nigerian "green eagles" to France. On June 19 at the Parc des Princes, against Bulgaria, when Serbian coach Velibor "Bora" Milutinovic called him to replace Daniel Amokachi, at 67 minutes, the talented midfielder was welcomed back on a pitch by a standing ovation from more than 45,000 people. Although he did not play a great World Cup—he started only on the day Nigeria was knocked out in the round of 16, against Denmark—he showed that he had a heart with more courage than muscle.

Alcohol control

During the preparation stage for the Cup in Spain, England's Edward "Teddy" Sheringham decided to take full advantage of a rest day and took a plane to visit the beautiful Portuguese city of Algarves for the night. The next day, several London newspapers published a photo of the striker with a beautiful woman, a glass of whisky in one hand

and a cigarette in the other. *The Sun* criticized the then Manchester United forward: "It is 6.45 in the morning and Sheringham leans his elbow and smokes, before sleeping with a blonde. Teddy, you are an idiot." The scandal angered coach Glenn Hoddle, who nevertheless forgave the player: "I am disappointed in what he did, but Teddy understood that he made a mistake, he apologized and that is why he will continue with the team."

Hoddle had not reacted in the same way to a similar event starring Paul Gascoigne. A month earlier, while the England team was participating in the Hassan II tournament in Morocco, Gascoigne, then a Glasgow Rangers FC player, returned one night completely drunk to the camp. Hoddle, enraged, fired Gascoigne from the team and removed him from the list for the World Cup in France. "I need players who can run the 90 minutes and, today, Paul is not in a position to do it," the coach said. Several members of the national team met with Hoddle, pointed out that everyone had consumed more beers that day and demanded a pardon for Gazza. "Paul wasn't the only one who was drunk. There were quite a few. Actually, we were all drinking," goalkeeper David Seaman said. Despite the intervention, Hoddle was adamant.

Fed up with the alcohol scandals, the coach swore that, upon arriving in France, such incidents would not happen and established a harsh prohibition at the Hotel du Golf Saint-Denac in the town of La Baule, where the English team stayed. Hoddle ordered the removal of beer cans and whisky bottles and other spirits from the rooms' fridges and from the bars throughout the complex, including the one on the golf course. And even more: he demanded that his cooks not use any alcoholic beverage as an ingredient for their sauces or meats. Hoddle did not want to suffer the saying that claims "never twice without a third." For all that, his team barely reached the round of 16, where it was defeated by Argentina in a shoot-out.

Saved by the draw

The Polish prosecutor Skarzysko Kamienna, who carried out numerous cases against the mafia in his country, decided on June 30 to stay a while longer in his office so as not to miss the exciting clash between Argentina and England. Kamienna had to go to court in his official car, but he resolved that that afternoon a good World Cup soccer match was a priority, and postponed his departure until the game was over. The prosecutor enjoyed the ninety minutes with relish, which ended 2-2, and loosened his tie to watch the extra time between the two teams, favorites to reach the Cup final, more comfortably. When the second half of the extra time was playing, Kamienna was shaken by an explosion that came from the parking lot of the courthouse: his car had been detonated by a bomb. The prosecutor's life thanks to his passion for soccer, but especially because Argentina and England had not ended the match in 90 minutes.

Defeated pub

The owner of a pub in the city of Brighton, on the south coast of England, claimed compensation from the talented midfielder David Beckham. He held him responsible for the economic losses suffered by his business after the English were eliminated in the round of 16, against Argentina and on penalties. Beckham was punished with a red card after kicking the South American captain Diego Simeone. Paul Murray, a 45-year-old bartender, told the British newspaper *The Sun* that Beckham's send off not only cost England its participation in the tournament, it cost his establishment customers and money because there were no more games to watch at the bar. "England could have advanced to play another three games, including the final", said Murray, who filed documents in a Brighton court for Beckham to pay him a token compensation of . . . 100 pounds.

A very interesting detail of the penalty shootout that left England out was that midfielder David Batty, who missed the last shot, later admitted that he had never taken a kick from eleven meters as a professional. "I had never kicked a penalty before, but I really wanted to and I asked the coach to do it. I don't regret it and I would do it again," said the courageous midfielder who was playing in Newcastle at that time.

Stay home, Chancellor!

When the German players saw Chancellor Helmut Kohl appear at their squad's camp in Nice, they immediately recalled that four years earlier, in the United States, the head of state supposedly brought bad luck to the team. They were eliminated by Bulgaria in the quarter-finals, the worst Die Mannschaft performance since the World Cups had started again after World War II. Unfortunately, the German players could neither avoid Kohl's visit, nor twist their destiny: They were defeated again in the quarter-finals, this time by Croatia.

God's anger

Shortly before the start of the Cup, all the members of the Romanian team made a curious promise: if the team qualified for the second round after the first two games, against Colombia and England, the players would bleach their hair and the coach, Anghel Iordănescu, would shave his off. As it happened, Romania beat Colombia 1-0 in Lyon and England 2-1 in Toulouse. Iordănescu, a very superstitious and religious man, begged his boys to dispense with the crazy pact, fearful that the new look of the squad would affect their performance on the pitch. But promises, as we know, must be kept.

Adrian Ilie, author of the winning goal against Colombia, related that "some players refused, but then it was decided that we would all do it, since we were all part of the national team, so we asked the hotel employees to find us two local hairdressers to bleach our hair the night before the match against Tunisia . . . We did it after the last training session and no one saw us. In fact, when we returned, the hotel people thought we were part of another team. Our relatives could not believe it." Gheorghe Craioveanu recalled in an interview that the chemical product used by the stylists burned their scalps. "They really wrecked us. It hurt so much that I could only sleep on one side of my body for three days," he revealed. When the team took to the field to face Tunisia in the last match of the first phase, they surprised the fans with all their silver-plated players, except the bald goalkeeper Bogdan Stelea. Iordănescu, meanwhile, covered his bald head with a cap. The unusual bet also affected the press: "It was impossible to differentiate the players on the field", said Emil Grădinescu, the commentator on Romania's national television.

The colorful story had a dark ending. The Romanians did not win again: they drew with Tunisia and then were eliminated in the next round after losing to Croatia in Bordeaux, 1-0. Iordănescu, disappointed, regretted not having acted more firmly in trying to convince his players. "We have angered God," he protested.

Convulsion

When the final was already a memory and the French popped the champagne corks on the Champs Elysées, the Brazilian press reported that striker Ronaldo had been seriously ill hours before the game and that he'd been included in the line-up due to pressure from the sponsoring companies of the South American team. According to the official version of events, Ronaldo suffered convulsions the night before the culminating match and, after numerous medical tests carried out in a Parisian clinic, coach Mario Zagallo, backed by doctor Lidio Toledo, decided to put him in as a starter. It

Ronaldo's illness was one of the great mysteries of the 1998 World Cup.

was a last minute decision, to the point that in the first list of players designated for the match that afternoon, Edmundo appeared as a forward. Zagallo asserted that it was Ronaldo himself who asked to be a starter.

Much of the Brazilian media, however, believed the coach had been forced by the president of the Brazilian soccer confederation, Ricardo Teixeira. It was even confirmed that Zagallo and Texeira argued loudly in the Saint-Denis stadium dressing room moments before the final game. These versions were denied by all involved, and by Nike, official clothing sponsor of the squad. The company told the author of this book that "Nike never has an opinion or influence on which players should make up a team, since this decision is the responsibility of the technical staff. In the previous moments to the France 98 World Cup final, Nike was unaware of Ronaldo's physical condition and his inclusion in the team, until that was publicly announced." For his part, Ronaldo, who had a very poor performance in the 3-0 loss to France, explained that "when I got to the stadium I was fine and I wanted to play. I don't know what happened to me. Roberto Carlos spoke of a lot of pressure. It can be, as it can be anything else. Some journalists wrote that I was afraid. But it is one of the many lies that are written about me. [Because of the convulsion] I felt terrible fear. I lost the World Cup, but I won the Life Cup. I'm sad about the end, but life counts for so much more."

Bouquet of sevens

French midfielder Emanuel Petit enjoyed a blast of glory related to the number 7. At the age of 27, and a week after lifting the World Cup in Paris, where he scored his team's third goal against Brazil in the final, Petit traveled on vacation with his girlfriend to Monaco, in the Mediterranean Riviera. There, he visited the famous Monte Carlo Casino, and with just a ten-francs piece (around two dollars at that time) he won a bounty of 170,000 francs. British newspapers noted that that same season Petit won the English league and the F.A. Cup with Arsenal and the World Cup, all with the number 17 on the back of his jersey. The 170,000 francs fell after the magic combination 777 appeared on the slot machine Petit was playing.

KOREA AND JAPAN 2002

Seventy-two years had to pass for the World Cup to cease to be exclusive to Europe and America. And, at the same time, to a single host nation. The combination of South Korea and Japan made possible a technologically brilliant World Cup, with twenty stadiums, the most in history. Despite the supposed friendly relationship between the two organizing nations, some political clouds appeared, the product of old animosity between Japan and South Korea. (Japan had annexed and occupied Korea in the first half of the 20th century, and for many Koreans that dispute was still fresh.)

The Japanese emperor, Akihito, snubbed his associates by not attending the Seoul stadium box to witness the opening ceremony. "The opening ceremony is like a marriage bond," said the president of the Korean soccer federation, Chung Mong Joon, who said Akihito's absence was "as if the bride or groom does not show up to a wedding. It is not a matter of taste but of obligation." Still, the tournament moved past this rudeness and proceeded smoothly.

FIFA made some changes for this championship, like increasing the number of players per team to 23, and determining that the champion would no longer qualify directly for the next World Cup. As the ball rolled along, new curiosities and records emerged. The

Seoul Plaza during the 2002 FIFA World Cup.

final between Brazil and Germany, won by the South Americans with two goals from Ronaldo—who had his revenge from the previous edition—marked the first World Cup clash between these two nations. It was remarkable, really, because they were the two national teams with the largest number of World Cukp matches played—86 and 84, respectively, before crossing into the final—and the most appearances: Brazil played all the World Cups, and Germany only missed Uruguay 1930, when they refused to travel, and Brazil 1950, when they'd been excluded for their crimes against humanity committed during World War II. Brazil won all its games on the way to the ultimate victory, something that had only occurred before in 1930, when Uruguay ran the table, 1938 (Italy) and 1970 (also Brazil).

France, defending the title, was eliminated in the first round something that had not happened since England 1966, with Brazil.

The French experience was much more humiliating: they scored no goals, barely tied a match with Uruguay, and finished last in Group A. In England, Brazil had at least beaten Bulgaria. Argentina's quick departure, in what was called "the group of death," was also surprising: they beat Nigeria, fell to England and drew with Sweden—not much for a team that had swept the qualifying stage.

Among the records, the Turkish captain, Hakan Sukur, did something that will be very difficult to beat: he scored the fastest goal in the history of the World Cup, just 10.8 seconds into the third-place match against South Korea on June 29, in Daegu. On June 4, the Korean Doo-Ri Cha also broke a mark, although without much applause: he was cautioned only twenty seconds after entering the field. Cha replaced Ki Hyeon Seol 89 minutes into the match with Poland, with the score 2-0 for the host squad and twenty seconds later he performed a kick that, in the eyes of Colombian referee Oscar Ruiz, deserved the card. A black . . . or yellow record: On June 11, during the match between Germany and Cameroon in Shizuoca, Japan, Spanish referee Antonio López Nieto showed his caution card to 14 players. As the German Carsten Ramelow and the Cameroonian Patrick Suffo were reprimanded twice, the yellows were 16 and the reds, two. On June 16 in Suwon, Korea, American Jeff Agoos and Portuguese Jorge Costa joined forces to score two own goals in the same game. The Americans triumphed 3-2, a victory that allowed them to go through the second round and, at the same time, send the Portuguese home.

Game of fear

Austria and Israel had to close out Group 7 of the European qualification round in Tel Aviv. Spain had already won the group, but the meeting was not unimportant: it decided the second-place finisher in the zone, who would then go to the European playoffs with

Turkey for a place in the World Cup. It was a tricky thing, because the Austrians had a three point advantage but the Israelis had a better goal differential; with a victory they would go through. On October 2, 2001, five days before the scheduled date for the important duel, nine Austrian players informed their coach, the Croatian Otto Baric that they would not travel to Tel Aviv for fear of being attacked. They abandoned the training camp in Vienna. "In the current political situation, we cannot think of traveling to Israel to play a soccer game. It's too dangerous," Walter Kogler told the reporters. The players highlighted the fact that, three weeks earlier, UEFA had authorized two clubs, Anzhi Makhachkala of Russia and he Rangers of Scotland, to change the venue for a match to avoid possible violence: Makhachkala, capital of Dagestan, was very close to Chechnya, a state that at that time was starring in a separatist war with the Moscow government.

Despite the Austrians' arguments, FIFA confirmed the date and place of the meeting. Then, on October 4, three days before the game, a Russian commercial airliner which had left Tel Aviv for Novrosovick fell into the Black Sea with 78 passengers, after being hit by a missile. The incident led to the immediate suspension of the game. Two weeks later, when it was determined that the aircraft had been hit by mistake by a Ukrainian rocket and not by a terrorist missile, FIFA rescheduled the match for October 27 at the Ramat Gan stadium in Tel Aviv. Austria traveled without its nine defectors and achieved a miraculous 1-1 draw on Andreas Herzog's goal in the second minute of extra time in the second half. For the play-off with Turkey, Baric only called up one of the nine who had refused to go to Israel. With their team diminished, the Alpine squad fell 1-0 at home, on November 10, and 5-0, four days later, in Istanbul.

53 goals in two games

The Oceania qualification zone was a very simple matter for Australia, to the point of scoring 53 goals in just two games. On April 11, 2001, they recorded the biggest win of all time in an international match by beating American Samoa 31-0. That afternoon, Archie Thompson scored thirteen goals, while David Zdrilic scored another eight. Australia thus shattered the previous record, which also belonged to them. Two days before overwhelming Samoa, they had beaten Tonga 22-0. On that occasion, Thompson scored a single goal, and Zdrilic "just" two. Of course, these numbers have an explanation: Coach Frank Farina had to organize two mostly different teams for the two games so close together, and had only repeated the four defenders. Against Tonga, Thompson and Zdrilic had played as substitutes, going in with only a few minutes remaining. Australia qualified for the inter-confederation playoffs with South America after playing six games, all victories, with 72 goals scored and just one surrendered. Against American Samoa, Thompson achieved another record: he scored two "hat tricks" (three goals in a row by the same player, none of them from a penalty and no other goal between them). The first took five minutes, and the other eight, all in the first half, in which he scored another two goals for a total of eight. In the second half, he "just" scored five more times.

Cook

"I fear that our team will be intoxicated. Food could be poisoned, as happened to the New Zealand rugby delegation in South Africa in 1995." This is how the president of the Australian Soccer Federation, Ian Knop, justified the appointment of the most important member of his team for the second leg match of the inter-confederation playoffs with Uruguay, on November 25, 2001: the chef. Knop's statements went over very badly in the South American nation, as did the visit of the Australian ambassador in Buenos Aires, Sharyn Minahan, who demanded greater security around the hotel where the Oceanic delegation would be staying. Australia had beaten Uruguay 1-0 in the first leg at the Melbourne Cricket Ground. Australia had one foot in a World Cup after 28 years. But all the precautions were useless: Uruguay was vastly superior, won by 3-0 thanks to two goals from Richard Morales and one from Darío Silva, and qualified for Korea-Japan.

Attack

At the beginning of May, before leaving for Asia, coach Luiz Felipe Scolari must have had a bad drink. While walking from the head-quarters of the Brazilian Confederation, in Rio de Janeiro, towards his car, which was in a nearby parking lot, the coach was surrounded by a hundred fans who began to demand the inclusion of the attacker Romario on the national team. Scolari did not react and quickly got into his vehicle, which was surrounded by the "torcedores." The enraged boys quickly went from insulting to kicking and punching against the windows and body of the car. The coach was rescued seconds later by a group of policemen. Scolari remained firm, however, and did not call Romario, a 1994 hero and a star at that time of the Rio de Janeiro club Vasco da Gama. With Ronaldo and Ronaldinho, Brazil to become five-time champions.

Alcoholics non Anonymous

The English players' reputation for enjoying a drink was proven in the days leading up to the World Cup. In May 2002, the English team did a three-day preseason session in Dubai, ahead of the tournament. In those three days, the bar tab alone amounted to about

$55,000. According to the *Sunday Mirror*, each of the 120 members of the delegation, including the players, consumed $135 of beer a day. Each pint cost $6.40, so each manager, coach, kit-man or player drank twenty pints, equivalent to ten liters of beer, every day.

Defeated before play

The Chinese team started the tournament very badly: they considered themselves defeated before the ball started to roll. In an unusual move, on May 24, 2002, ten days before their debut against Costa Rica, the spokesman for the Chinese delegation publicly released an "open letter" to anticipate what was believed to be a certain bad performance in the Cup. "We are afraid we will not obtain, due to lack of experience and skill, the results that could satisfy the public," the absurd note said. The defeatist spirit transferred to the field: China fell 2-0 to Costa Rica, 4-0 to Brazil and 3-0 to Turkey. With no points or goals scored, the Chinese squad was one of the worst in the tournament, along with Saudi Arabia.

Beware of supplication to God

The Chinese appearance produced more curiosities than good soccer. Their Serbian coach, Bora Milutinovic, confessed during an interview with the German newspaper *Süeddeutsche Zeitung* that before traveling with his team to the World Cup, he had a very particular experience. "I went into a church to talk to God. He asked me 'What do you want, Bora?', and I said: 'Achieve the same as France'. And God kept his word. France and China were both in that World Cup the only countries that did not score goals. Of course, I was referring to achieving what France had done in 1998." A small oversight, with a lesson: you have to be very precise when you ask God for something . . .

Aromatic injury

Santiago Cañizares was having a fantastic season. A brand new club champion with Valencia, he had been confirmed as Spain's starting goalkeeper for Korea-Japan by coach José Antonio Camacho. Finally, after two World Cups sitting on the bench, with the 13 jersey, he had the opportunity to play with the number 1. But everything fell apart when an unusual incident combined vanity with clumsiness: on May 17, 2002, while training with the national team, and staying in their hotel in Jerez de la Frontera, Cañizares tried to apply a little Acqua di Gio cologne, by Armani, but the bottle slipped from his hands (this just happens to a goalkeeper . . .), fell to the ground and exploded into pieces. One of the fragments of glass dug into a toe and cut a deep tendon. The player was immediately taken to a nearby hospital, where he underwent surgery. The severity of the injury forced Camacho to remove Cañizares from the team and appoint the young Real Madrid goalkeeper, Iker Casillas, as the starter. "Santi," again, watched the World Cup sitting on a chair.

More clumsiness

There was probably no more stupid reason in the history of the World Cup for being left out of the tournament than what befell Brazilian midfielder Emerson, an undisputed starter and a fundamental piece in coach Luiz Felipe Scolari's game plan. On June 2, the day before their debut against Turkey, the South American team visited the Munsu Stadium in Korea to examine the playing field. Joking around, Emerson put on gloves and tried to imitate Marcos, the starting goalkeeper, before Rivaldo's powerful shots. But when he flew to the right post to make a save on one of the balls, he landed awkwardly and dislocated his shoulder. "He fell bad because he is not a goalkeeper," Rivaldo tried to justify. As his type of dislocation requires a four-week recovery, Emerson—who coincidentally had played the World Cup in France due to Romario's injury—was sent back home, his place taken by Ricardinho, Corinthians midfielder. Emerson paid dearly for his clumsiness: he missed the World Cup and being part of Brazil's "five-time championship."

Missing

The Irish national team had to face the Cup with one less player: team captain Roy Keane was sent off by coach Mick McCarthy. McCarthy took that hard measure after the player criticized the team's training conditions in the press. Although the midfielder regretted and apologized, the coach did not back down: "As long as I continue to be the national team coach, he will not come back. If he arrives, several players would leave with me," he said. The Irish Association tried to replace Keane with Colin Healy on the World Cup list, but FIFA rejected the request because the deadline for submitting the rosters had expired. According to the rules, a player can only be changed in the event of injury or an exceptional circumstance, such as the death of a close relative.

Unsuccessful order

Jeong Man-Yong, a Protestant pastor of a Seoul church, went to court to request that the use of the term "red devils" for Korean fans be banned from soccer stadiums. The religious man justified his claim by saying that this name "represents evil" and is "a religious affront." Man-Yong asked fans to call themselves "the red tigers" or "the white angels." But, despite the effort, the thousands of fans who packed the stadiums before each home team game proudly sang their status as "red devils." Even more so with each triumph of the Korean squad as it reached the semi-finals, something no team from Asia had ever accomplished.

Flirtatious

To try to win the Cup, Swede Sven Goran Eriksson carefully selected 23 players, physical trainers, doctors, kinesiologists, a cook, and a hairdresser. The coach brought Scott Warren, a famous coiffeur from the London borough of Mayfair, to Japan. The barber did not travel alone: as he had to serve the entire delegation, he flew accompanied by three of his colleagues from the Daniel Hersheson salon. Eriksson was a regular Warren customer, although he never visited his premises because the stylist cut his hair in his own home.

The only head that Warren could not touch was that of David Beckham, who had brought his own stylist, Aidan Phelan, who designed a kind of cockscomb that quickly gained popularity among the Japanese public. The hairdressers of the Far East could not cope with the demands of thousands of young people who wanted to reproduce the original "pompadour" on their heads.

Crime without punishment

On May 27, four days before the opening match between France and Senegal, the famous Bobby Moore case in Colombia in 1970 had its remake when a Daegu jeweler reported that an African player, Khalilou Fadiga, had stolen a gold necklace valued at about $250. The Senegalese footballers had passed through the store the previous Friday, during a walk through the center of the Korean city, and on Monday, when he noticed the necklace missing, the owner of reviewed the tapes of his security camera. Fadiga was arrested by the local police, and released shortly after having acknowledged the theft: "I did it just out of curiosity," was all the midfielder told the press. Meanwhile, the president of the Senegal Soccer Federation, El Hadj Malick Sy, tried to minimize the incident by claiming that "it was a bet between the players."

Fadiga was kept on the team, which was making its debut in a World Cup. On May 31 they beat France, the previous champion, 1-0 in Seoul. Shortly thereafter, on June 4, the Daegu prosecution dropped the charges against the Senegalese number 10, saying the decision was meant to let the player and his teammates focus exclusively on the tournament. Interestingly, the merchant sent Fadiga a small gold-plated pig, used as a good luck charm by Koreans, along with a letter wishing him success in the World Cup. It inspired the African team: Senegal qualified second and undefeated in Group A, behind Denmark (Fadiga scored a penalty goal in a tie with Uruguay), defeated Sweden in the round of 16 and finally fell to Turkey 1-0 in the quarter-final. Not bad for their first time at a World Cup.

Dangerous fashion

The English boys found the shirts with Japanese symbols very amusing and bought several, all the same, one for each. The shopkeeper told them the writing expressed praise to the gallant subjects of the British Crown. Proud and arrogant, that night the group went out wearing their new shirts to walk the streets of the city of Sapporo, where two days later they'd face Argentina in Group F of the first World Cup round. What they didn't know, due to their ignorance of Japanese writing, was that across their chests, their T-shirts said: "Passive English gay looking for an ardent muscular Japanese lover."

More fashion crimes

An executive with Nike complained to Korean authorities about fake Brazilian national team jerseys being sold in the city of Ulsan. The jerseys were offered at about $33 each, almost half the price of the licenced originals, and according to the indictment they featured "false logos of the Brazilian Soccer Confederation and the sports company." What most outraged the Nike representative was that the fake shirts were exhibited in a shop inside of the Hyundai hotel, where the Brazilian delegation had been staying.

My left foot

The first blow, literally, was suffered by David Beckham. The English midfielder, playing for Manchester United, was violently fouled by Argentine Aldo Duscher, a defender with Deportivo La Coruña of Spain, in a match for the European Champions League played on

David Beckham on the turf with a foot injury.

April 10, 2002. Beckham suffered a fractured metatarsal bone on the left foot, which put his World Cup participation at risk. Two weeks later, a teammate of Beckham's in Manchester and on the national team, Gary Neville, suffered the same injury in the same place, but in the semi-final of the European League, against Bayer Leverkusen of Germany. But the metatarsal curse didn't end there. Ten days before the opening of the 2002 Korea-Japan Cup, during a friendly between England and South Korea, Liverpool midfielder Danny Murphy also fractured a metatarsal bone in his left foot. England's Swedish coach, Sven Goran Eriksson, couldn't believe his misfortune: three starters with the same injury. Fortunately for him, one of them, Beckham, recovered in time thanks to a bone reconstruction therapy which was usually applied to racehorses. What's more, he scored the winning goal against Argentina in the initial phase, with a penalty kick.

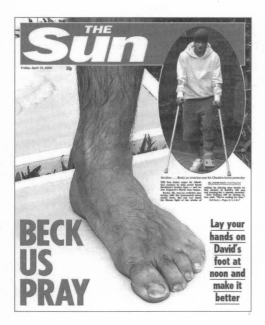

News of Beckham's foot
filled five pages in the Sun.

A little bit of luck

When the first half of Uruguay's match against Senegal ended, on June 11 in the Korean city of Suwon, everyone considered the Uruguay team eliminated from Group 1. They were down 3-0, having had a goalless draw with France and another defeat, 2-1 against Denmark. With all but lost, the South American squad went onto the field for the second half just looking top play good soccer. With contributions from two forwards who until then had been warming the bench, Richard "Chengue" Morales and Diego Forlán, the Uruguayans combined touch and heart to narrow the gap. Morales and Forlán quickly scored a goal each and, with just two minutes remaining, Alvaro Recoba equalized with a penalty kick. When the last minute of additional time was played, a last Uruguayan pass fell into the Senegal box. Goalkeeper Tony Silva muffed the play, and the ball came free for a header by Chengue with the goal empty and a spot in the next round served on a silver tray . . . but Morales missed the target and the ball went by the post and off the pitch. This time, the renowned "Charrúa courage" just lacked a bit of luck.

Red from the bench

To the Argentine humiliation of being eliminated in the first round of a World Cup, which hadn't happened since the 1962 edition in Chile forty years earlier, was added the unusual expulsion of forward Claudio Caniggia. El Pájaro (The Bird) saw the red card in the 47th minute for having insulted Emirati Arab referee Ali Bujsaim from the substitute bench. "I think I said 'the fucking mother', I don't know," Caniggia said in an attempt to explain the referee's decision. Bujsaim didn't hear the insult—in fact, he did not understand the language—but it was reported to the ref by the fourth official, the Jamaican Peter Prendergast, who did speak some Spanish and was a few meters from the chair on which Caniggia was waiting to play in his third World Cup.

The punch

Argentine referee Ángel Sánchez may have expected a quiet game between South Korea and Portugal on June 14 at the Incheon stadium. A draw qualified the two teams for the round of 16. But with the running of the ball, the Portuguese started an incomprehensible rough game. At 26 minutes, midfielder Joao Pinto made a violent tackle from behind on Ji Sun Park. Sánchez, as the regulation indicates, sent him off directly. Pinto, enraged, approached the referee and punched him in the abdomen. "Joao Pinto hit me so hard that the FIFA doctor took a photograph of me to record the blow from the bruise that he had left me," Sanchez said after the match. Joao Pinto was suspended for six months and fined 50,000 Swiss francs, plus another 15,000 "for costs and expenses." He got off cheap, since he was given the lighter penalty stipulated in the regulations, which provide for a maximum punishment of a one-year suspension.

Demolishing changing rooms

The French players found no better way to vent their anger over the scoreless draw with Uruguay than by destroying all the furniture in the dressing room at the Asiad Main stadium in Busan, Korea. The violent reaction of the Gauls forced their coach, Roger Lemerre, to apologize to the local authorities and FIFA.

Extra hours

On June 21, American forward Landon Donovan quickly left the stadium in Ulsan after his team's loss to Germany in the quarter-finals. The abrupt departure of the American star was not due to problems with the squad or the coaching staff, led by Bruce Arena, but because he had to take a plane to California to join the San José Earthquakes team, which the next day had to face the Colorado Rapids in the Major League Soccer (MLS) tournament. After having played the ninety minutes against the Germans and slept uncomfortably on the plane, Donovan joined the bench of substitutes for San José. He cameod in the second half to help in the 4-0 win over Colorado.

Confused bald

For the semi-final against Turkey, Brazilian striker Ronaldo had a very particular haircut: The top and back of his skull were shaved, and a kind of diamond about four inches wide was left on his forehead. "I did not do it for any special reason. I grabbed the machine and cut myself to change a bit. I hope it gives me luck to reach the final," the forward told to the press. Shortly after, the real reason for the change emerged. The player learned that, during the quarter-final game with England on June 21, his little son Ronald approached the television and, while babbling "papa, papa", gave a kiss to the image . . . of defender Roberto Carlos. Until then, both Ronaldo and his partner had completely shaved heads. Distraught by the confusion of his first-born son, Ronaldo decided to get a distinct new hairstyle so his boy would not give his love to any stranger.

Undiplomatics

Before returning home after being eliminated by Turkey on June 22, the Senegalese players agreed to travel to Taiwan to participate in a diplomatic act in support of the island nation's independence. Senegal was one of 28 countries that recognized Taiwan as an autonomous nation. The attitude of the players, however, was not the most courteous. They appeared at the government palace in shorts and sandals, refused to play a friendly match with the local team, and during the two days the visit lasted they rarely left their hotel, where, according to the Taiwanese press, they were visited by 37 beautiful women.

Men in black

As in Italy '34, England '66 or Argentina '78, the performance of the referees was strongly questioned, especially in games featuring the two host teams. The European media were especially critical of Ecuadorian Byron Moreno and Egyptian Gamal Ghandour, who were accused of favouring Korea in their matches against Italy, in the round of 16, and Spain, in the quarter-finals, respectively. Moreno was questioned about having annulled a legitimate goal scored by

Christian Vieri during extra time and having sent off Francesco Totti for no apparent reason. Taking advantage of the extra man, Korea won 2-1 with a goal in the 119th minute. Several Italian newspapers accused the Ecuadorian referee of having markedly increased his personal assets, without apparent justification, after the World Cup.

Ghandour, meanwhile, did not concede two legitimate goals scored by the Spaniards and whistled unusual off-sides of the European attackers, who were eliminated in the quarter-final by penalties after 120 minutes of a 0-0 tie. In their defense, the Koreans assured that the secret of their good performance was in a preparation called "stamina food," which included extracts of fish, medicinal herbs and ginseng, which the players ingested in the form of pills three times a day.

Brazil was also put under the magnifying. In its first round match against Turkey, on June 3 in Ulsan, Korean referee Young-Joo Kim did not send Rivaldo off even though he'd simulated a blow to the face from to a ball that actually hit him in the knee. FIFA analyzed the video of the match and ordered the Brazilian number 10 to be sanctioned ex officio for his deception, but only imposed a financial fine of 11,500 Swiss francs. In the round of 16, on June 17, the future champion was favored again, when Belgium had a legitimate goal disallowed while the score was blank. Brazil ended up winning 2-0. So many scandalous arbitrations annoyed even former world chess champion Garry Kasparov, who, embarrassed, said that he had "never seen a sports scam like that."

Computer boycott

The scandalous elimination of Spain at the hands of Korea, in a match plagued the favoritism of the Egyptian referee Gamal Ghandur, provoked different manifestations of repudiation in the Iberian Peninsula. The most curious came from the computer retailer PCBox, which suspended the sale of all items made in Korea for two days. On July 1 and 2, the 70 PCBox stores did not sell computers, monitors or other IT supplies manufactured or assembled in the host country of the World Cup.

Ghandur's controversial performance also had repercussions in England, where a gambler sought the return of the 40,000 pounds sterling he'd put down on Spain. Adrian Fitzpatrick, from Birmingham, would have won £945,000 if José Antonio Camacho's team were champion. "I am not a bad loser, but everyone agrees that Spain was robbed by incorrect decisions, and there have been many in favor of South Korea," Fitzpatrick argued. He was right about that, but the bookmaker did not refund a single penny.

Dangerous advertising

In almost every major city in the world, complaints are heard about the visual pollution generated by graphic advertisements on buildings, streets and avenues. But in Tokyo, the Japanese capital, the ads were much more damaging during the Cup. A giant ball, which accompanied a poster mounted on a skyscraper, fell off and landed on a pickup truck. By a miracle, the gigantic ball did not hurt anyone, although the streets of Tokyo are not characterized, exactly, by having clear sidewalks.

Escape to freedom

The interesting clash between Brazil and Belgium in Kobe, on June 17, was made good use of by 48 inmates in a prison in Sumatra, Indonesia. The detainees took advantage of the twelve prison guards watching the match to attack them by surprise. After handcuffing the jailers and seizing their weapons, the inmates escaped, but not before thanking the Verdeamarela scorers Rivaldo and Ronaldo for their return to freedom.

Unusual Awards

Korea's arrival at the semi-finals was as surprising as it was well rewarded. The sporting achievement allowed the Korean players to be excluded from compulsory military service. Dutch coach Guus Hiddink, meanwhile, was awarded free beer for life by a Seoul hotel, the Westin Chosun.

Germany 2006

If you are looking for a tango title at the 2006 World Cup in Germany, none would be better than "Por una cabeza" (By a head). The French captain Zinedine Zidane, who seconds before the final had been awarded the "Ballon d'Or" as the best player in the Cup, did not tolerate the insults of Italian Marco Materazzi and applied a vehement header to his chest that left only one injured: the sport of soccer.

Zidane and Materazzi had scored the two goals of the culminating match. From there, the match would stay tied until it was decided in a shootout, for the second time in history. Except for the Italians, who won their fourth World Cup, and the French, who were embittered by the defeat, there was little talk of the game but much about the head of the angry Frenchman.

Zidane's great career, which included the 1998 World Cup, the 1996 Eurocup, and two Intercontinental club Cups, among other achievements, was overshadowed for days by that backlash inside Berlin Olympic stadium. The Gallic number 10 had opened the scoring from the penalty spot with an exquisite touch, Panenka-style, to deceive goalkeeper Gianluigi Buffon. But his magic could not prevent honor from being caught in a spider web. After the game, Zidane said he did not regret his reaction: "They were very harsh, very serious words that touched me to the core. I'd rather be punched in the face than hearing that. My gesture is unforgivable, but if I was punished, the real culprit, the one who caused it, should also be punished. It was a reaction to a provocation. Do you think that ten minutes before my retirement, I was going to do something like that for the mere pleasure of doing it?" he asked. One report had it that the Italian had told the French that his mother was a "terrorist whore" (Zidane was of Algerian descent), but Materazzi denied it. "I lost my mother when I was 15 years old and today I still get emotional just talking about her. I insulted him, it is true, but with an insult of the kind that is used regularly and that I hear at least ten times per game. I didn't call him a son of a terrorist bitch." What a good boy.

In a European World Cup, with two finalists from the home continent, there were, however, two South American joys. The Brazilian Ronaldo scored three goals—two against Japan on June 22, for Group F, and one against Ghana, five days later, in the round of 16— to surpass German Gerd Müller as the top scorer in World Cup history. Ronaldo had already achieved four goals in France 1998 and eight in Korea-Japan 2002. Some say that Ronaldo should be denied a 2002 score, against Costa Rica, which occurred on June 13 in Suwon, Korea. In his report, the Egyptian referee Gamal Ghandour assigned that goal to the "Tico" defender Luis Marín, as an own goal, but then, at the request of the Brazilian confederation, FIFA awarded it to the striker. Meanwhile, the Argentine referee Horacio Elizondo had the honor of being the first to umpire the opening match and the final of the same Cup. Along with the Mexican Benito Archundia, Elizondo also achieved the mark for the most matches refereed in the same World Cup: five.

Negative records: Germany 2006 was the most violent tournament in history, with 28 red cards and 307 yellow cards. The match between Portugal and the Netherlands for the round of 16 in this edition—won by Portugal 1-0 on June 25—saw the highest number of players sent off in a single World Cup match: four. In addition to the red cards, Russian referee Valentín Ivanov showed another 16 yellows, which equaled the Germany-Cameroon mark in 2002.

Other details: The opening match was not played by the previous champion, but by the home team, as had been established four years earlier. Paraguayan defender Carlos Gamarra scored the fastest own-goal in World Cup history, inside three minutes of the first half of the match that Paraguay lost to England 1-0 on June 10. In its game against England, Sweden's Markus Allback scored the 2,000th goal in World Cup history. A previous chapter noted that Switzerland, in 2006, joined the list of those who were eliminated from a Cup without losing, after drawing against Ukraine in the round of 16 and falling in the penalty shootout. For the Swiss team there were two extra sore points: the squad returned home without having given up a single goal (in the first round it had drawn 0-0 with France and defeated Togo and Korea 2-0, and with Ukraine it reached penalties with the score 0-0), and it became the first in Cup history to not score once in the shootout. Meanwhile, Portuguese goalkeeper Ricardo became first to stop three shots in a World Cup penalty shootout, when the Portuguese squad eliminated England in the quarter-finals.

Why did you protest?

On September 3, 2005, Uzbekistan defeated Bahrain 1-0 in an irregular "first leg" match for the final spot in the Asian qualification round. The winner would face Trinidad and Tobago, fourth in CONCACAF, in the inter-confederation playoffs for the Germany World Cup. Why was this match irregular? Because the Japanese referee Toshimitsu Yoshida annulled a penalty goal for Uzbekistan for encroachment and, instead of repeating the shot, he whistled an indirect free kick for its rival. The Uzbek federation protested Yoshida's ruling and FIFA, after studying the case, agreed and ordered the match to be repeated.

The game was held again in Tashkent, the capital of the Central Asian nation, but this time the score was a 1-1 draw. In the return match, at the National Stadium in Manama, in Bahrain, the duel also ended level, albeit with a blank scoreboard. By having scored more goals as a visitor, the Arab team went to the next stage. If the Uzbeks had not protested, they would have won the key with a victory and a draw. It was perhaps some consolation that Bahrain was later eliminated by the Trinidadian team, which thus qualified, for the first time in its history, for a World Cup.

Bomb

A week before the start of the tournament, the Berlin press center had to be evacuated due to the discovery of a World War II bomb on the grounds of the Olympic stadium. The artifact had been found by a gardener working at the site. The scribes were ordered out as a precautionary measure, until it was determined that the bomb had no explosive charge. FIFA assured that the journalists who worked there were not in danger at any time. Spokesman Keith Cooper said that "it is something normal in Germany, because it suffered many bombings by the allies" during the war.

Thank you for not smoking

Shortly before the start of the 1998 World Cup in France, FIFA argued it had no power to prevent members of a team's coaching staff from smoking during the course of a match. "You cannot violate the freedom of the individual," said the spokesman Keith

Cooper when an advocacy group asked for a ban. "The only thing that we can do, and that we have already done, is to beg them not to do it, or at least to hide the cigarette when they notice the presence of a television camera. But a soccer stadium is not a non-smoking area and each person has the right to do what they consider appropriate with their habits," Cooper argued, adding, "it is difficult for a smoker to quit a habit, but it is even more so for a coach at a time of such stress as is a soccer game."

Eight years later, this position changed radically for the 2006 German Cup: FIFA ruled that smoking on the perimeter of the playing field, "in the technical area and substitute bench," was prohibited, and warned that "the technical director who commits a fault, the first time he will be cautioned and the second time, sanctioned." The first coach to be warned was Argentine Ricardo La Volpe, Mexico's manager, after he was seen smoking during the game against Iran. FIFA communication director Markus Siegler reported that La Volpe received a warning "in writing" which said that "the coaches and players have to be an example."

FIFA also advised fans not to smoke during the World Cup. "Nicht Rauchen, bitte (please do not smoke)" was the slogan of a campaign that was broadcast over the loudspeakers at the venues, where brochures were also distributed to explain the damage caused by cigarette smoking. The proposal had the support of the German government and, although the entry of tobacco to the stands was not banned, FIFA stressed that it hoped "to keep nicotine consumption away from the world soccer festival in Germany."

Privileged

Japan's Hidetoshi Nakata had a curious privilege during the Cup. The forward did not stay with his teammates at the Japanese camp, but rather rented, at his own expense, a suite on the top floor of a luxurious hotel in Bonn. The Bolton FC player only met the rest of the squad for practice and games. Nakata was a starter in the three matches that his national team played, but had a weak performance and did not score. The Japanese team was eliminated in the first round after falling 3-1 to Australia, drawing goalless with Croatia and losing 4-1 to Brazil.

I don't want to go with my dad

Serbia and Montenegro defender Dusan Petkovic resigned from the Cup because, he admitted, "it was too much pressure" for his father. Of course, Dusan's father was not just a spectator, but Ilija Petkovic, coach of the Serbian national team. The player refused to join the team after media criticized his inclusion as nepotism by the coach. "It's too much pressure for me, for my father and for my teammates," Petkovic junior said. Serbia finally arrived in Germany a man short: the spot could not be filled by another player because, according to FIFA, it was not a case of "force majeure", such as illness or injury.

In the name of the Father

Mexico's Pavel Pardo found it strange that the display on his mobile phone announced a call from Esperanza del Toro, the wife of his friend and roommate Oswaldo Sánchez. "I don't know what to do, help me," the woman said from Guadalajara, desperate to find a way to announce the worst news: Felipe Sánchez Carmona, father of the starting goalkeeper, had just died of a heart attack. "I want to tell him, but please don't leave him alone, don't be separated from Oswaldo for a second," Esperanza begged. Pavel, distressed by the situation, brought the cell phone to his compadre, who did not understand why his wife had not called him directly. As he listened, he understood what had happened. The news was devastating.

Especially because the goalkeeper had spoken with his father a few hours earlier, that same June 6, five days before the debut against Iran. "He told me: 'Son, I want to tell you that I am very proud of you. See you there in three or four days.' I wanted to answer 'I love you very much,' but it did not come out," recalled the goalkeeper.

The message spread to the rest of the squad and the entire team of coaches, officials and players appeared in Sánchez's room to console him and give him a warm hug. Immediately, the coach Ricardo La Volpe and the captain Rafael Márquez decided with Oswaldo that he should returnn to Guadalajara for the funeral. "If you arrive [back] an hour before the game, you play," La Volpe told him.

After the cremation at the Recinto de la Paz cemetery in Guadalajara, Sánchez returned to Germany with his mother, his wife, his brothers . . . and the ashes of his father. The goalkeeper returned to the camp set up in Göttingen the day before the clash with Iran. La Volpe included him in the team that came out onto the pitch at the Franken-Stadion in Nuremberg and won 3-1, with two goals from Omar Bravo and one from Antônio Naelson Matias Sinha. Sánchez, who gave a stupendous performance, broke down at the final whistle. He knelt down, kissed his palms, and spread his arms skyward, as if to envelop the spirit of his father. In the stands, the goalkeeper's mother, Alma Rosa, followed the game hugging the vessel that held the ashes of the undoubtedly proud Felipe.

·

The mask

The 90 minutes were up and Ecuador, beating Costa Rica 2-0 in Hamburg, would qualify for the round of 16. On the last attack, Edison Méndez sent a cross to Costa Rican territory and Iván Kaviedes sent it to the back of the net. As he ran to the corner flag to celebrate, the striker pulled out of his shorts a mask similar to the one used by Spiderman in comics and movies, and put it on. When

FIFA Communications Director Markus Siegler was asked whether the Ecuadorian forward could be sanctioned for his unusual celebration, he replied: "It is expressly forbidden to remove the shirt, but no mention is made of the masks. Therefore it's not forbidden . . . It was an isolated event, and it was fun, an expression of joy. Besides we must not be mean: the player explained why he did it."

Kaviedes said he was paying tribute to striker Otilino Tenorio, a former teammate on the national squad and the Emelec club, who had died a few months before in a traffic accident. Tenorio, who was 25 and had participated in several qualifying matches, was known as "el mascarado" (the masked man) for celebrating his goals by putting on a traditional red Spiderman mask. "The spirit of Otilino is with us, he gives us energy," added Kaviedes, who was responsible for the last Ecuadorian goal in the Cup. The South American team then fell to Germany 3-0 in the last game of Group A, and to England 1-0 in the round of 16.

One player, four cards

Murphy's Law holds that if something can go wrong, it will. During the clash between Croatia and Australia, on June 22 in Stuttgart, English referee Graham Poll showed three yellow cards to the same player. How could it be possible? Croatian defender Josip Simunic saw the first warning in the 61st minute, and the second in the 90th minute, but he continued on the field without the referee, his linesmen, or the fourth official noticing. Two yellows, of course, are equivalent to one red, and all officials are to register each card in their notebooks. In the 93rd minute, the "good" Simunic misbehaved again: he rudely protested a ruling from the referee and was cautioned again. The third time was the charm, and the yellow one was followed by a red one.

How to get caught for stealing

At noon on June 18, 42-year-old Eva Standmann called desperately to her husband: a thief had just stolen her wallet that, among other belongings, contained her ticket for Brazil-Australia game that afternoon at the Allianz Arena stadium in Munich. The victim had planned to meet her husband, Berndt, inside the arena, because he was going straight from work. Eva told her husband she was fine and convinced him that, despite her unpleasant experience, he should go and enjoy the game. When Berndt reached the stadium, he noticed that a young man was sitting in the seat that would have been his wife's. He discretely approached two policemen and told them what had happened. The uniformed officers detained the man, who was still carrying the stolen valuables, including the ticket, from Eva's bag. A Munich police spokesman told reporters that "the thief found the ticket in his wallet and decided to watch the game. He did not expect to sit next to the husband of his victim." Housed in his cell, the foolish rascal cursed his soccer passion and reproached himself for not having resold the ticket.

Forgiveness

Seconds after Brazil's 2-0 victory over Australia on June 18, Aussie striker Harry Kewell approached German referee Markus Merk to complain about his performance, which he thought was biased. Perhaps because he was unable to communicate verbally, due to the language barrier, Kewell decided to end the "discussion" with a rude gesture that involved an extended finger. Merk did not show any card to the Australian at that moment, but when he returned to his dressing room, he reported the incident on the official form, explaining how the forward, then a player on the English club Liverpool, had insulted him. Despite the referee's complaint, the

FIFA Disciplinary Committee did not sanction Kewell because of inconsistencies in Merk's report. The "forgiven" Kewell was thus able to play against Croatia, a situation which was not funny for the Europeans. On June 22, in Stuttgart, Kewell scored the final goal in what would end a 2-2 tie, which qualified Australia for the round of 16 and sent Croatia home.

International conflict

Nobody imagined that celebrating a win against the Czech Republic would cause so many headaches for the government of Ghana. At the end of that match, one of Ghana's players, John Pantsil, celebrated by displaying an Israeli flag. The gesture caused considerable discomfort to part of the Ghanaian population, 16 percent of which is Islamic, and became a minor international incident. Ambassadors from several Muslim countries—including Egypt, Libya, Morocco, Saudi Arabia and Syria—complained to Foreign Minister Nana Akufo-Addo. In addition, several Ghanaian embassies in Arab countries, like Libya, received bomb threats. Akufo-Addo apologized for "a regrettable isolated act by an individual who was completely ignorant of the political and democratic implications of his act." Pantsil, who played for Hapoel Tel Aviv, clarified that his gesture was only meant to dedicate the win to some Israeli friends who had traveled to Cologne and were in the stands.

Captains

The captain's armband gave fans a lot to talk about during this Cup. The case of Angola was the most curious. Against Portugal on June 11, Fabrice Maieco Akwa started as captain, but when he was replaced in the 60th minute by Pedro Torres Mantorras, the armband passed to Paulo Lopes Figueiredo. But he was replaced as well, in the 80th minute, by Marcos Joaquim Miloy, so the band went to André Makanga, where it stayed. Ten days later, history was repeated in almost the same way: Akwa left at 51 for Flávio Amado, Figueiredo at 73 for Rui Marques but this time João Pereira Jamba took over the armband until the end.

On June 14, the day in which Tunisia and Saudi Arabia tied at two, the Saudi captain Hussein Sulimani decided to pay tribute to his teammate Sami Al Jaber, a famous striker who played 163 international matches and participated consecutive World Cups, in the U.S., France, Korea-Japan and Germany. In the 82nd minute, when Al Jaber replaced Yasser Al Kahtani, Sulimani passed the armband to the veteran attacker, without leaving the pitch. Al Jaber had retired from the national team in 2002, but returned in 2005 encouraged by the new coach, Argentine Gabriel Calderón. This recognition was repeated on June 19 against Ukraine (Al Jaber entered in the 82nd for Mohammed Noor). In the game against Spain, four days later, it was not necessary: Al Jaber started and played all 90 minutes.

The Tunisian Riadh Bouazizi, meanwhile, was the only captain who came out in all the games: against Saudi Arabia he was replaced by Mehdi Nafti; against Spain, by Alaeddine Yahia; with Ukraine, by Chaouki Ben Saada. Coincidentally, in this last match, the Ukrainian captain, Andriy Shevchenko, also left his place, at 88 minutes, to Artem Milevskiy.

No national anthem

Togo's players, coaches and official were furious at the 2-1 loss to South Korea on June 13 in Frankfurt. All the more because, in their World Cup debut, the players could not sing their national anthem. The sound man at the FIFA World Cup Stadium made a mistake and played the Korean anthem twice. The blunder generated a formal protest from Togolese officials. Another who could not sing the anthem was the Italian Mauro Camoranesi, but for a different reason. When journalists asked him why his lips didn't move while it played, Camoranesi, who was born in Argentina, said simply: "I don't sing the anthem because I don't know it".

German miracle

The three young Argentine men were desperate to get their tickets for the first round clash between their team and the Netherlands, on June 21 in Frankfurt. Resale was tight and the few tickets available cost a fortune. It was a difficult challenge for young men who had traveled to Germany with meager capital. Then the light bulb went on: they rented three wheelchairs for a handful of euros and showed up at the stadium pretending to be disabled. In this way, the scoundrels acquired tickets for disabled patron, which were still available and inexpensive. The shameless young men were led to the disable section of the stands and everything was fine until, early in the match, the Argentine fans intoned their now traditional chant: "Who does not jump, is an Englishman!" One of the three "disabled" fans, named Ernesto, was carried away by the atmosphere and began to jump uncontrollably, while his desperate accomplices tried to contain him from their special seats without abandoning their ruse. The patron most moved by the display, however, was a disabled German gentleman located a few inches from the mischievous South American fanatics. He returned to his house convinced that he had witnessed a miracle.

Coherent

Trailing 2-0 at the end the first half in their round-of-16 match against Brazil, Ghana's coach, the Serbian Ratomir Dujkovic, approached the Slovakian referee Lubos Michel and asked him if, in the second half, he planned to continue helping the Brazilians, perhaps wearing a yellow jersey instead of a black one. Michel, implacable, immediately sent off the coach. At the end of the match, which finished 3-0, Dujkovic told the press that the referee had asked Ronaldo if he could have his shirt. The coach based his accusation on the words of one of his men: he had told him that, offering Ronaldo to exchange the jerseys after the game, the Brazilian refused because he had already promised his to the referee. Why did the Serb complain? Hadn't Dujkovic asked Michel to wear yellow?

The shorts of defeat

There are imponderables that outperform the most obsessive coach. For its game against Portugal on June 25, Dutch manager Marco Van Basten instructed midfielder Mark Van Bommel that, in every rival free-kick close to the orange penalty area, he should mark the Portuguese Maniche. He did so from the start, but at 23 minutes, Destiny—or the gods, or who knows what strange forces of fate— acted, and in the intense heat of the game, Van Bommel's shorts ripped and were rendered unusable. The midfielder had to leave the field momentarily to change. At that moment, a Portuguese pass fell into the Dutch area, the defense made a poor clearance and the ball went to the feet of Maniche, who without opposition scored the only goal of the match. The Netherlands returned home chewing the anger of the elusive destiny, and Portugal continued on its good path that later crowned with fourth place.

German invention?

FIFA officially reported that the settling of matches by shootouts from the penalty spot was devised by a German referee named Karl Wald. At the end of the 1960s, outraged by the flipping of a coin to decide the winner—a method that was used in the Olympic Games and was planned for World Cups, such as the England 1966 tournament—the referee began proposing in friendly matches that each team shoot five penalties when a game ended with a tie. Soon after, in 1970, Wald presented his idea to the Bavarian Soccer Federation. Little by little it gained ground: first it was adopted by the German Federation, then by UEFA and finally by FIFA. The first major international competition in which this system was used was the final of the 1976 Eurocup, in Belgrade. Ironically, Czechoslovakia defeated Germany with its own invention. But every time Germany participated in a shootout in the World Cup, it won. The first time (also the World Cup debut of the method) was on July 8, 1982, against France. In that round, Uli Stielike's shot, saved by the French goalkeeper Jean Ettori, was the only one that the Germans ever missed. Four years later, Germany beat Mexico in the quarter-finals, and then in 1990, England in the semi-final, and Argentina, on June 30, 2006, all on penalties.

Spain, for its part, held that this procedure was born a few years before Wald came up with it. Several sources maintain that the shootout was proposed by the journalist Rafael Ballester in 1958, so that the even night matches of the Ramón de Carranza's Trophy, a friendly quadrangular tournament played every summer, would not be prolonged too long. On the other hand, the Rec.Sport.Soccer Statistics Foundation, an entity founded by sports journalists from northern European countries, determined the method is even older, adopted for the Yugoslavia Cup in the 1952/53 season.

A work of art

Many fans consider two saves by Germany's Jens Lehmann on Argentina in their quarter-final shootout a "work of art." But the local squad's advance was not an exclusive achievement of the

Lehmann of Germany did his homework on Argentina.

goalkeeper: before the series of shots began, Lehmann carefully studied a paper that was given to him by one of the assistants to coach Jürgen Klinsmann, on which were written the names of the designated Argentine players and the characteristics of their shots in other similar situations. The goalkeeper hid the list—on a very elegant paper from the luxurious Schlosshotel im Grunewald—between his sock and his shin guard, to keep it handy and review it before each shot. After the match, Lehmann donated the piece of paper to the Museum of Contemporary History in the city of Bonn, where it has found a home in the institution's permanent exhibition.

Evasion

Once again, the passion the World Cup arouses allowed a jailbreak. In this case it was an Italian prisoner identified as Roberto Loi, who took advantage of the fact that the guards were absorbed in the final with France to escape from the Alghero prison on the island of Sardinia. The 38-year-old convict used the distraction to escape ten years before his sentence for numerous crimes was set to end in 2016.

Television suffering

Before the start of the Cup, the appliance company Media World launched a promotion throughout Italy: anyone who bought a plasma TV in installments before the beginning of the World Cup could stop paying if Italy became champion. Fabio Grosso's shot that beat French goalkeeper Fabien Barthez not only gave Italy the fourth title, it caused a loss of ten million euros to Media World, which had sold ten thousand devices, each with a value between 900 and 5,000 euros.

SOUTH AFRICA 2010

South Africa 2010 made history. It was the first African World Cup. It was the first time Spain won the title. And it will be remembered for some extra soccer seasonings, such as the deafening vuvuzela, and a strange octopus that, from an aquarium in Germany, got all the results right with his predictions. The contest looked like a win for South America because, five teams went through the round: four as first in their group (Argentina, Brazil, Uruguay and Paraguay) and one, Chile, as second. In addition, the first four qualified for the quarter-finals, along with three European teams (Germany, Spain and the Netherlands) and one from the host continent, Ghana. Only from then on did the South American dream begin to crumble.

Spain, which won all four matches of the second round 1-0—including the final against the Netherlands, in extra time, with a goal from Andrés Iniesta—became the first European team to raise the World Cup outside its own continent (Germany would equal this mark in Brazil 2014). The red squad was also the winner with the fewest goals scored, eight, and the first to win a World Cup after starting with a defeat: a 1-0 loss to Switzerland on June 16 in Durban, in the opening match of Group H. In the quarter-finals, on July 3 in Johannesburg, the Iberian team could have been eliminated by Paraguay, when its goalkeeper, Iker Casillas, stopped a penalty shot by Oscar Cardozo while the game was even at zero. In that same match, Spain's Xabi Alonso wasted another 11-meter shot—turned away by Paraguay's Justo Villar—four minutes later. An accurate shot by David Villa ended the tie, which seemed eternal, at the edge of 90 minutes.

The defining match, very hard fought, registered the most cards for a World Cup final: 14 yellow and one red. However, South Africa was notably different in this respect from Germany 2006, with about half of the cautions and sent-offs.

For the first time, the choice of the "Ballon d'Or" for the best player in the championship fell on a footballer whose team did not arrive to the podium: Diego Forlán. The Uruguayan striker was the driver and top scorer (with five goals) of a courageous team that finished fourth, although it had needed a playoff win against Costa Rica just to get to South Africa.

South Africa, surprisingly, became the first organizing country eliminated in the first round. It tied Mexico 1-1 in its opener, fell 3-0 to Uruguay and beat France 2-1, but that was not enough to overcome the Mexican squad, which went to the round of 16 with better goal difference. It was surprising because the host team reached the World Cup undefeated in eleven games. To this negative mark, the South African coach, the Brazilian Carlos Alberto Parreira, added a positive one: he equaled the Serbian Velibor "Bora" Milutinovic in the number of different teams coached, with five: Kuwait in 1982, United Arab Emirates in 1990, Brazil in 1994 and 2006, Saudi Arabia in 1998 and South Africa in 2010. As he led Brazil twice, Parreira became the coach with the most World Cup appearances.

Another novelty was that some World Cup matches were played on artificial grass. The stadiums Mbombela (in Nelspruit) and Peter Mokaba (in Polokwane) presented a hybrid carpet that combined natural and synthetic turf.

Never before had a tournament had so many high scorers: German Thomas Müller, Spaniard David Villa, Dutchman Wesley Sneijder and Uruguayan Diego Forlan matched for first place, with five goals each.

Germany's team, which finished third, surpassed Brazil's—eliminated in the quarter-finals—in number of games played in World Cups: 99 to 97. This distinction is significant because the South American squad participated in all World Cups, while the German team did not attend Uruguay 1930 and was barred from Brazil 1950.

Italy and France, meanwhile, starred as the first "double" of defending champion and runner-up to be out of the Cup in the first round. In Group A, France tied Uruguay 0-0, lost 2-0 to Mexico and 2-1 to South Africa; Italy, in Group F, drew 1-1 with Paraguay and New Zealand, and finally fell 3-2 to Slovakia, who was making their World Cup debut.

Switzerland broke the record for minutes without conceding a goal in the World Cup, reaching 559. The run began on July 2, 1994, in the round of 16 of the World Cup in the United States, when the Swiss squad was eliminated by Spain. They made it all the way from there to their second game in South Africa, which they lost 1-0 to Chile on a goal scored in the 75th minute by Mark González which ended the streak. Serbian Dejan Stankovic achieved a different unusual mark: wearing the shirts of three different countries in three World Cups. Stankovic played for Yugoslavia in France 1998, for Serbia and Montenegro in Germany 2006 and for Serbia in South Africa 2010. This particularity was due to the constant political change that took place in the Balkans after the disintegration of the former Yugoslavia in 1991.

For his part, Ghanaian Asamoah Gyan was the first player to miss two penalties in two World Cups during regular time: one took place on June 17, 2006 in Cologne, against the Czech Republic. That day Ghana won 2-0. The second, on July 2 in Johannesburg, in the quarter-finals, against Uruguay. That shot, which he bounced off the crossbar, would have qualified Ghana for the semi-finals, as it came in the last second of the match. Gyan received death threats over the miss, although he was a top scorer and the great star of his national team. Argentina also set a record: by scoring against Greece on June 22, forward Martín Palermo became the oldest World Cup debutant to score a goal, at 36 years, seven months and 15 days.

Stingers

On October 10, 2009, upon arriving in Mexico for the Confederation of Football Association of North, Central America and the Caribbean (CONCACAF) qualifier for South Africa, the Salvadoran goalkeeper Miguel Ángel Montes knew he would come face-to-face with a tough opponent. What Montes never imagined was that the attack would come not from the front, but from behind. Seconds after the match against Mexico began at Azteca stadium, the goalkeeper ran alarmed to the center of the field to warn the referee that a swarm of bees had taken over his goal. The ref ordered the game interrupted so that a group of assistants armed with fire extinguishers could show the "red card" to the dangerous torrent of insects, which in addition to the net, had taken over a microphone and television camera pod behind the goal. Nine minutes later, with the swarm expelled, the game resumed. Montes's problems did not disappear, however, but moved from his back to his defense: the Salvadoran players could not contain the sharp Mexican forwards, who that afternoon scored four goals. Actually, there were three: the first was an own goal by the fullback Marvin González. Thus, the El Salvador team was eliminated from the Cup, unable to savor the sweet honey of success.

What a nuisance!

Defender Kakha Kaladze was stunned. He heard his rivals speak in Italian, saw his Milan club mates Andrea Pirlo and Gianluca Zambrotta on the same pitch, and felt like he was in his second home, the Giuseppe Meazza stadium. But that night of September 5, 2009 the fierce defender was not in Italy, but in the Boris Paichadze Coliseum in Tbilisi, and the two goals he scored were not for the red-black team but against his own national squad, Georgia, that was facing Italy for the World Cup qualification. The first goal, in the 57th minute, Kaladze deflected a free kick taken by Angelo Palombo from 35 meters with his head. In the second, ten minutes later, he changed the trajectory to a cross from Domenico Criscito. In both cases, the ball ended up in the bottom of the goal of the stunned goalkeeper, Giorgi Lomaia. The 2006 champions took a crucial victory to qualify for South Africa and Kaladze entered the record books as the only player to ever score two own goals in a single World Cup match, either in the tournament or the qualifiers. The only positive thing for poor Kakha was that the fans took his double mistake with good humor. That night, Georgia no longer had a chance of qualifying for the World Cup, having collected just three draws, all at home, in seven matches.

Home goals rule

For many years, in the majority of soccer tournaments in which two teams play each other twice, once at each side's home ground, the squad that scores more times as a visitor wins in the event of equal points and goals. This rule is also applied in knockout World Cup qualification games in which two countries face each other to resolve which one passes to the next round. In March 2008, this system had a curious outcome because it favored the local team. How could it happen? The Caribbean tie between the Bahamas and the British Virgin Islands was resolved with two matches played in Nassau, the Bahamian capital, due to a lack of appropriate venues in the Virgin Islands. On March 26, with the Bahamas performing at home, the match ended 1-1. Four days later, in this case with the Virgin Islands as host in their opponent's stadium, the clash was again tied, but 2-2. In this way, the Bahamas went through having scored more goals as a visitor, although they did them on their own court.

What Whisky will not cure . . . there is no cure for!

This old Irish proverb proved its worth during the European qualification round. In August 2009, a month before Russia traveled to Cardiff to face Wales in Group 4, the Russian Fan Association advised supporters traveling to the game the team "to drink a lot of whisky as a precaution to avoid the spread of the H1N1 flu," also known as swine flu. "That should cure all the symptoms of the disease," said Alexander Shprygin, president of the association. Shprygin said that "the health authorities say that the virus is very dangerous, but, as a fan that I am, I say that for any true fan there is nothing more important than the team. The Russians fear nothing or anyone, so the virus will not stand in our way to support the national team." Russia prevailed 3-1 and its happy fans "disinfected" themselves until dawn with excellent 40-percent-alcohol medicine.

Raiders of the lost striker

When traveling, one can lose a passport, cell phone, or handbag. It's natural, in all the comings and goings through hotels, airports, the nerves about the flight, the incessant flow of passengers—anyone can get distracted. But if the lost item is a player, the case is complicated, and may require professional help.

Such an episode began to unfold on Wednesday, June 10, 2009 in Medellín, Colombia, shortly after the local team defeated Peru 1-0 in the South American qualification group. After leaving the Anastasio Girardot stadium, the Andean team—which was already eliminated and finished last in the local tournament—returned to their hotel where they planned to spend the night. But upon arrival at the hotel, the head of the delegation was informed that the national team's charter flight, initially scheduled to depart on Thursday morning, had been advanced: it was an Air Force plane that was to return early to Lima, Peru's capital, at the request of the President of the Republic, Alan García. The players, the coaching staff and various officials quickly departed for the airport, got on the aircraft and started home. Shortly after landing, one of the footballers noticed that forward Hernán Rengifo, who played against Colombia as a substitute for the last three minutes, was not in the group. Rengifo, who at that time also wore the Lech Poznan Poland club's jersey, had not heard anything and had gone to sleep in his room. In the morning, he noted with dread that he had been left alone in the hotel. The directors gave him a ticket and the abandoned boy was finally able to return to Lima. To his consolation, he was called up for the remaining four games, and scored two goals, against Uruguay and Argentina.

Blatter, clueless

FIFA President Joseph Blatter made an astonishing mistake on December 4, during the lavish gala party at the Cape Town International Convention Center: during a live worldwide broadcast, Blatter was supposed to mention which city would host the opening game of the 2010 Cup but, perhaps nervous from the pressure and the cameras, he suffered a memory lapse and was struck speechless. He looked around desperately for someone to help him. After a few seconds that seemed like forever, South African actress Charlize Theron, host of the event, came to his rescue by telling everyone the championship would kick off at the Soccer City stadium in Johannesburg. Arguably, she also announced it to Blatter himself.

Oceania x 2

For the first time, Oceania had two representatives in a World Cup: Australia and New Zealand. It was made possible by the fact that Australia was accepted as a member of the Asian Soccer Confederation on March 23, 2005, a move FIFA endorsed. The international federation had already taken a similar measure, albeit for political reasons: since 1994, Israel has competed in the European group to avoid crossing with its Muslim neighbors—in previous editions it had also faced teams from Oceania and the Far East. The Australian officials decided to take this step because they thought they'd have a better chance of reaching the World Cup. Australia had only won entry into two before, coincidentally both played in Germany (1974 and 2006). FIFA historically awarded "half a place" to Oceania—its winner had to play a tough playoff to make it through, sometimes against a South American team, sometimes an Asian one. On its "new continent", Australia comfortably qualified in Group 1, eight points clear of second-place Japan.

And that was good for New Zealand, who had only played in one World Cup, Spain 1982. This time, the second best team from Oceania made it easily through the local stage and in the playoffs, against Bahrain, earned its ticket to South Africa thanks to a goalless draw and a 1-0 win.

Ecological T-shirts

At this Cup, Nike was dressing nine national teams, including Brazil, The Netherlands, Serbia and the U.S. And it was making its shirts with plastic bottles recycled as polyester—it took eight recovered bottles to make each of the official jerseys worn by the players. The total production, including those that were put on sale around the world especially for this tournament, required 13 million containers, enough to fill 29 soccer fields. According to Nike, if all these bottles had not been recycled, they could have stretched a distance of three thousand kilometers, greater than the length of the South African coast.

Family is the most important thing in the world . . . cup!

Rarely did a single World Cup have so many "familial" oddities. Perhaps the most dramatic involved half-brothers Kevin-Prince and Jerome Boateng. The two boys were born in Berlin, Germany, children of the same father—a man of Ghanaian nationality—but different mothers. The Boatengs became professional players and, when choosing a national team, Kevin, who had already performed for the German youth squad, decided on Ghana while Jerome preferred to wear the Teutonic jersey. By chance, Ghana and Germany shared the same World Cup group (D), which meant that the Boateng brothers went head-to-head on June 23 at the Soccer City stadium in Johannesburg, something that had never happened before in a World Cup. The duel had an extra spice: Kevin, who played for the English club Portsmouth, had doubly earned the hatred of the German fans—first, by defending the colors of Ghana and second, for injuring German star, and Chelsea striker, Michael Ballack, in the English Cup final. Ballack would be unable top play in the World Cup. "All I can do is apologize," said Boateng. "I was just too late and I hit him straight on. It looked stupid. I apologised to him twice on the field and now for a third time. I am sorry. It was not intentional." His stepbrother, speaking to a Berlin newspaper, tried to ease the tensión: "Kevin is a man who makes mistakes, but he had no intention of injuring Ballack."

Before the clash started, the brothers, who had a cold and distant relationship off the pitch, barely shook hands. Germany won that afternoon 1-0 and both teams qualified for the following round after eliminating the other two teams in the group: Serbia and Australia. The Boatengs, then, ended in peace.

More fraternal harmony could be found on the Honduras team, where Wilson, Jhony and Jerry Palacios, became the first trio of brothers to join a World Cup team. Several pairs of brothers had done the trick before, such as Germans Fritz and Ottmar Walter, the English Robert and Jack Charlton or the Dutch René and Willy Van der Kerkhof, among others, but this was something unique. Jerry Palacios, a 28-year-old midfielder who played on the Chinese club Hangzhou Greentown, was called up urgently by coach Reinaldo Rueda to replace the injured Julio César de León. In fact, the record could have been broken by a greater margin, since the Palacios were actually five footballers: Milton, at that time 29 years old, had played the qualifiers for Germany 2006 but was not chosen by Rueda; Edwin, who would have been 18 years old, had been murdered in November 2007 by a group of criminals who had kidnapped him from the family home. The criminals had asked for a ransom of $200,000 to free Edwin, at that time 15-years-old and and young star in the youth divisions of the Las Mercedes club. Friends and supportive fans gathered the money, and the criminals collected the ranson, but they shot the teenager anyway.

Another sad family episode involved the former South African president Nelson Mandela, who could not attend the opening ceremony of the Cup because, the day before, an allegedly intoxicated driver had run over and killed one of his great-granddaughters. The girl, 13-year-old Zenani Mandela, was returning from the opening concert of the World Cup, held on June 10 at the Orlando stadium in Soweto.

The World Cup in South Africa led to another strange situation: Argentine coach Diego Maradona's handling of Sergio Kun Agüero, the talented forward who at that time played for Atlético de Madrid and was the boyfriend of Giannina, Maradona's youngest daughter. "Kun is going to play when I think he has to play. If I think not, I wouldn't put him on the team even if Benja (for Benjamin, his grandson and the couple's baby) asked me to," Maradona said at a press conference. But Benjamin "does not speak yet, so he is not going to ask me," he joked. Agüero played in three of Argentina's five games: he replaced Carlos Tevez against South Korea, started against Greece, and replaced Ángel di María in the 4-0 loss to Germany that eliminated Argentina in the quarter-finals.

The Slovak national team presented a list with a curious repetition: Vladimir Weiss. One, as a midfielder (who played as well for England's Manchester City); the other, a former defender for Czechoslovakia (which split into the Czech Republic and Slovakia in 1992) in the World Cup in Italy 1990, who was now the coach. But, before the two of them, there was another Vladimir Weiss who, as a Slovak, wore the colors of Czechoslovakia's squad. The father of the coach and grandfather of the Manchester City player, the first Vladimir Weiss, was a defender who won the Silver Medal at the 1964 Tokyo Olympics, and participated in the qualifying rounds for the 1966 World Cup in England, although it did not qualify.

Speaking of grandparents, Javier Chicharito Hernández, who scored Mexico's first goal in their 2-0 victory over France on June 17 at Polokwane, was repeating the feat of his maternal grandfather, Tomás Balcázar. Balcázar had also scored a goal against France on June 19, 1954, in Geneva, for the World Cup in Switzerland, but that day history did not end happily for Mexico, as it fell 3-2.

Family didn't come first for New Zealander Chris Killen. The number 10 of the "All whites," a player for England's Middlesbrough, got married on Saturday 29 May in Loch Lomond, Scotland, but preferred not to go on his honeymoon but rather return to Austria, where New Zealand was training. "My wife (Hannah) would have been happier if they didn't call me, but she knows what playing this World Cup represents for me and that's why she accepted the sacrifice," said the forward. Against all odds, the New Zealand squad finished undefeated in zone F, with three draws against Italy, Paraguay and Slovakia. Although they were eliminated, they celebrated having finished third in the group, above defending champions, Italy. Killen returned to England and finally traveled to a warm beach with his new (and patient) wife.

Liver menú

As it's become clear throughout this book, the feeding of the players during the World Cup is no minor detail for the coaches. As soon as the group and venue draw was over, Japanese coach Takeshi Okada paid special attention to the fact that his team would have to face Cameroon in Bloemfontein and Denmark in Rustenburg, two cities located, respectively, at 1,400 and 1,500 meters above sea level. To adapt his men to a very different altitude than they were used to, Okada took his players to the small Swiss town of Saas-Fee, at 1,800 meters above sea level, in the canton of Valais. There, to the work carried out in the Alps for two weeks, the manager added an essential component to his boys' diet: cow liver. Throughout their stay, noon and night, the Japanese ate fried, boiled or roasted that organ rich in iron, an essential element for the body to produce hemoglobin, a heteroprotein that transports oxygen in the blood and helps to improve endurance. The liver-based regimen gave Japan excellent results: they defeated Cameroon 1-0 and Denmark 3-1. They reached the quarter-finals for the first time away from home (they had done it in 2002) and although they were eliminated by Paraguay, they fell honorably in a series of penalties after a very tough 0-0 tie after 120 minutes at 1,200 meters in Pretoria. The only game they lost, against the Netherlands by a narrow 1-0, was in Durban. In a city on the shores of the Indian Ocean, the liver didn't do much good.

Vuvuzelas

Along with the players, coaches and referees, the World Cup had a sonorous protagonist that stood out, a lot: the vuvuzela. Loved and hated, this unusual musical instrument, traditional on South African fields, took up far more column inches of newspaper space than most players. On the radio and television, on the other hand, it was the most listened-to sound. The trumpet—a long conical tube made of plastic—is said to have been created in the early twentieth century by a follower of a South African evangelical church, to replace antelope horns. Many players and coaches complained that the very loud sound of the vuvuzelas being blown by the fans, like a powerful swarm of millions of bees, prevented them from maintaining good communication on the field. For visitors, following the matches from the stands was devastating for the eardrums.

The sounds of the 2010 World Cup in South Africa.

Throughout the Cup, the sale of earplugs soared: a Cape Town merchant claimed that in two days he depleted his stock, although they barely reduced the sound from 120 to 90 decibels.

Curiously, despite the criticism, the vuvuzela went around the world and found its way into cell phones. A group of Dutch designers developed a ring tone with their sound for the iPhone, which became all the rage. Just hours after being uploaded to Apple's web page, the South African din was downloaded by 750,000 consumers.

In this game, the big winner was China, the country that produces 90 percent of these plastic instruments. Manufacturers doubled their orders across the globe. Four months before the start of the Cup, one million vuvuzelas arrived in South Africa.

The television networks, for their part, had to balance the amount of ambient noise from the stands with the voices of their commentators, without removing it completely so as not to give a feeling of an empty stadium. Some channels eliminated them completely. In Peru, the Professional Soccer Sports Association (ADFP) announced a ban on bringing loud vuvuzelas to all stadiums in the country, because "their thunderous sound prevents the normal performance of the referee, as well as that of the fans." A similar measure was taken by UEFA, which vetoed them on all pitches in Europe.

In Uruguay, on the contrary, the cornet captivated a couple, who requested authorization to register their daughter with the name of "María Vuvuzela." Have they thought carefully about the poor baby's future?

Not only the eardrums were affected by these bizarre rigs. From blowing so much, a South African woman broke her throat! Yvonne Mayer, a Cape Town resident, had to be hospitalized for three days without eating or speaking after injuring herself while she participated in a contest to see who could blow the hellish instrument the longest. Those three days, Yvonne's neighbors celebrated with champagne.

Excess and deficit

The Chilean team arrived in South Africa with excess baggage. In its luggage were a thousand official shirts. The care of coach Marcelo Bielsa and the team officials can well be considered exaggerated, since, if the red squad reached the final, those thousand jerseys meant an average of six per game for each of the 23 players. By contrast, footballers from Honduras were unable to swap shirts with their opponents from Belarus after their pre-championship friendly on May 26 because of the team's short supply. "We are ashamed because we could not exchange the shirts with them because we do not have enough sports equipment," admitted the manager of the Honduran National Team, Osman Madrid. He could have asked Bielsa for some.

God's buttocks

Diego Maradona's appointment as coach of the Argentina generated many curious situations. The first, and perhaps the one that caused the most noise, was an insolent press conference held in Montevideo the day Argentina defeated Uruguay and qualified for the 2010 World Cup in South Africa. "Keep on sucking" was one of the of the insults hurled by the former player, who in eight games had achieved four wins and four losses, including the historic and humiliating 6-1 defeat of Bolivia in the qualifying rounds. For his bad taste, Maradona was punished by FIFA with a two-month ban on any soccer-related activity and a fine of 25,000 Swiss francs. The sanctions, which included a ban on attending the tournament draw, held on December 4 in Cape Town, was questioned by the European media, which considered the penalties very light and denounced that the former player had received "idol treatment" from the FIFA's Discipline Committee.

During the World Cup, Argentina started with four wins in a row but in the quarter-finals they were a poorly prepared team, thrashed 4-0 by Germany. The poor play of Lionel Messi, who did not score goals, was especially surprising because, weeks before the start of the tournament, he had won the FIFA's award for the best player in the world.

Perhaps the most curious situation related to Maradona was due to the fact that, like a King Midas who turns everything he touches into gold (or almost everything, since he didn't achieve the success he longed for with his team), he turned a toilet into a bestseller in South Africa. It happened that, when the Argentine coach visited the facilities of the High Performance Center of the University of Pretoria, where the Argentine "bunker" was installed, he noticed that the toilets did not meet sufficient standards for comfort and health. He requested they be changed for a more modern model. The new toilet, called Bathroom Bizarre and made in South Africa, offered three drain speeds and a bidet with built-in hot water. As Maradona's strict requirement was published in the local newspapers, sales of this product multiplied ten times. In the sanitary wares businesses, the Bathroom Bizarre took over the shop windows along with Argentine flags. Almost everything Maradona touches turns to gold, and even a toilet can enjoy huge commercial success when favored by the "hand" . . . or, rather, "the buttocks of God."

Big Brother

England coach Fabio Capello had an idea on how to prevent his players from having sex during their stay at the luxurious "Vineyard Hotel and Spa" in Cape Town: install cameras in all hotel rooms. Well, not in all of them. There was none in his room, so that he could "privately" receive his wife, Laura Ghisi. The measure—diametrically opposed to that taken by other coaches, who did allow "intimate" visits for their men—was harshly questioned by the players' wives. The British press went further, highlighting that one of the "most watched" would be John Terry, who had sparked a media scandal a few months earlier when his affair with the wife of a Chelsea FC teammate Wayne Bridge emerged.

But it was not just the players' intimate lives that aroused media interest. Every four years, different polls analyze the relation between soccer and sex among the fans. Before the start of the South African championship, an investigation in Germany found that only five percent of men would exchange watching the World Cup final live for a night of pleasure with their partner. Fifty-two percent admitted that they would stop watching the final in case of an emergency, while 20 percent said that nothing would separate them from their televisions if the German squad reached the last game.

However, victory can add some spice to a fan's love life: the German birth rate increased nine months after the team defeated Portugal for third place in the Cup played at home in 2006. In Korea, the "red devils" qualification for the round of 16 in South Africa triggered the sale of condoms. The *JoongAng Daily* newspaper said that thanks to the festive atmosphere, the demand for condoms increased fivefold compared to the 2006 World Cup, in which the red team had been eliminated in the first round.

Electrifying matches

Zimbabwe did not qualify for the World Cup, but it had its "send off" nonetheless: the energy minister. Elias Mudzuri was expelled from the government due to the successive power outages during television broadcasts of the games. In Harare, the capital, it was almost a miracle to see 90 minutes in a row without interruptions in the power supply. Mudzuri had promised there would be no blackouts during the Cup, but the national electricity company Zesa could barely produce half the megawatts needed to meet the demand. Because he failed to fulfill his commitment, the minister was forced to resign ten days after competition began. The only winners were Harare bars, which had the foresight to buy generators to protect their customers and bring in new ones from the ranks of desperate home viewers.

Electrical problems also plagued Bangladesh, where hundreds of enraged soccer fans in Dhaka, the capital, took to the streets to destroy vehicles and smash windows because a failure in the energy flow had interrupted transmission of the Argentina-Nigeria clash on June 12.

Another inadvisable cut, also on June 12, made English fans choke on their beer as they watched their team's match against the United States on television. In the middle of the first half, with the game tied at zero, the broadcast by ITV suddenly cut to an advertisement for Hyundai cars. When the ad ended, viewers were amazed to discover that their team was winning 1-0, and that they had missed Steven Gerrard's goal. The owner of a Stockport pub said his customers began calling family and friends watching the match on other channels to tell them what had happened. The ITV network apologized, but it was not enough to calm the angry viewers. And they were angrier still after the stupid goal allowed by English goalkeeper Robert Green, which sealed the tie against the Americans.

You've Got (hate) Mail

Nigeria was comfortably leading Greece on June 17 in Bloemfontein, with a goal from Kalu Uche in the 16th minute, a nice recovery from their loss to Argentina in the opening match of Group B. At 33, minutes, midfielder Sani Kaita, inexplicably, kicked Vasilios Torosidis when both were off the court and without the ball in play. Colombian referee Óscar Ruiz did not hesitate and showed the

African a completely fair red card. Thinking quickly, Greek coach Otto Rehhagel took advantage of Kaita's outburst and immediately swapped defender Sokratis Papastathopoulos for striker Georgios Samaras. With numerical superiority, Greece equalized in the 44th minute and sealed the victory in the 71st with a goal from Torosidis, the same player who'd received the blow from the send off. The defeat brought Nigeria to the brink of elimination, which would come five days later with a 2-2 draw with Korea. A wave of fury the length and breadth of the African nation broke on the impulsive Kaita. The player received more than a thousand death threats in his email inbox. The 24-year-old's teammates came out to demand compassion from the fans: "He is a person who serves his team and his country in the best possible way," they said. Kaita, who had won the silver medal for his nation at the 2008 Beijing Olympics, apologized to the fans and all members of the Nigerian delegation for hurting the team, although he downplayed the intimidation. "I'm not scared. Only Allah decides who lives or dies. Everyone has their own destiny on earth," he declared. As if the situation did not have enough surreal touches already, the spokesman for the Nigerian team, Peterside Idah, called an international press conference to "clarify" that the spirits were very good at home. "In our language, 'I'm going to kill you' means 'I'm not happy with you.'"

Cheap . . . but expensive!

The fast (and surprising) elimination of Italy and France, winner and runner-up of the previous World Cup, generated a lot of fallout in both countries. Coaches Marcello Lippi and Raymond Domenech were quickly fired, and both teams returned to their homeland amid rejection and insults from fans. The French situation put the Gallic president himself, Nicolas Sarkozy, on edge. During halftime of the second game—against Mexico on June 17—Domenech argued loudly, inside the dressing room and in front of the rest of the team, with forward Nicolas Anelka. "Fuck you, you dirty son of a bitch," Anelka shouted to his coach, according to the sports newspaper *L'Equipe*. "Very well, you are coming out", answered Domenech, and ordered André-Pierre Gignac to replace him. France fell 2-0 (the two Mexican goals came in the second half) and was on the brink of elimination. Anelka was expelled from the squad that same day, and his teammates, in solidarity with the attacker, went on strike on Sunday, June 20, and refused to train for the third game, with South Africa on June 22. At a press conference Domenech revealed that he told his players "that what they were doing was an aberration, an imbecility, a nameless stupidity." Sarkozy, worried by the news coming out of South Africa, asked his Sports Minister, Roselyne Bachelot, to take action and meet with the team to "call them to order." "What is happening is a moral disaster" that "has tarnished the image of France," lamented the president. "The face shown by the French national team in South Africa was disastrous," he acknowledged. Dispirited, the "bleu" team also fell to South Africa, 2-1, and said goodbye to the Cup. At least the French players managed a gesture of decency: their captain, Patrice Evra, announced after the elimination that they were renouncing all bonuses. "It is difficult to forgive a team that fails to qualify in the first round. I don't forgive myself. We will not accept a single penny," Evra declared after the loss to South Africa. The slip came cheap to the blue federation.

The usual suspects

Every four years, criminals around the world take advantage of World Cup fever to get their cut. South Africa 2010 was no exception. A clever thief took advantage of the fact that all of Argentina was frozen in front of the television watching the debut match against Nigeria and seized two valuable paintings from the Argentine

Theater in the city of La Plata. The bandit's work was recorded by the security cameras, but the images were little help: the skilled intruder wore a huge coat with the collar turned up and dark glasses.

More forward-looking, the Brazilian Federation of Banks decided to change their opening hours in all locations to avoid surprises. In some cases, banks closed their doors before normal hours; in others, they shut down during the matches played by the Verdeamarela team.

In Mexico, six inmates from the Atlacholoaya prison, in the state of Morelos, escaped while the guards watched replays of their team's match against Uruguay. The prisoners took advantage of the guards' distraction to file the bars of their cell and leave the prison through one of its gates.

In South Africa, meanwhile, security measures were widely questioned. The local newspaper *The Star* denounced that the government had hidden from the press that, five days before the World Cup kicked off, a group of robbers had stolen more than a million dollars from Nedbank, one of the largest banks of the country. Despite an official campaign increase security, dozens of fans and even some participating delegations suffered theft of money and valuables from their hotels. Many foreigners were also assaulted on the streets. The thieves did not spare the stadiums either: a group stole seven replicas of the FIFA trophies that were in the offices of Soccer City in Johannesburg, scene of the final.

Goalkeeper with skirts

Spain's debut, on June 16 in Durban, was a real surprise: hardly anyone imagined that the defending European champion would be defeated by Switzerland, 1-0. What was more impressive was that several Spanish media declared that the goal that sealed the Swiss victory was the fault of goalkeeper Iker Casillas and his girlfriend, the beautiful Telecinco journalist Sara Carbonero. The controversy broke out when the British newspaper *The Times* published a photograph in which Carbonero was seen with her microphone in her hand behind the goal defended by Casillas, in the sector reserved for the press. It was suggested that a mistake made by the goalkeeper seconds before the Swiss goal could have been because he was distracted by the beautiful reporter. The president of the Madrid Press Association, Fernando González Urbaneja, considered the relationship between goalkeeper and journalist "a shame." "As a journalist, she should know that it is not necessary to get emotionally involved in the stories that are told. If she wants to be a great professional, she should not be tempted by the bad practices of journalism," said the severe González Urbaneja. For other, less rigorous commentators, perhaps dazzled by the green eyes of their beautiful young colleague, well, Spain had only lost a soccer game. In the end, the setback did not prevent Spain's historic campaign, nor did Casillas, who sealed the enormous victory with a sweet kiss to his girlfriend in front of everyone's cameras.

North Koreans

On the day North Korea debuted in the tournament against Brazil in Johannesburg, a hundred fans dressed in red cheered the players with overflowing passion. The boys displayed flags and did not stop cheering despite the defeat—surprisingly close, by the way, 2-1. However, it was soon after discovered that the handful of fanatics did not include a single person born in the communist nation. As the Pyongyang government had banned fans from leaving the country, the leaders had a brilliant idea so that their team would not be alone inside the stadium: to hire a claque of Chinese workers living in South Africa. Covered in a jersey, scarf and hat, the hundred of Chinese jumped and sang as if they had been born on the other side of the Yellow Sea. The "rent" of the fans was the work of the company China Sports Management Group, to which the Koreans gave a thousand tickets for each game (did they pay the "fans" with the resale of the 900 they did not use?). North Korea had the worst World Cup performance, with three defeats, twelve goals surrendered and just one scored. The claque had no opportunity to work overtime in the round of 16.

How religious!

On the peaceful afternoon of Sunday, June 13, David Makoeya—a 61-year-old man in the South African province of Limpopo—wanted to enjoy good German soccer. But when he appeared in the living room of his home, he sadly discovered that his wife and his two children had beaten him and had already tuned into a religious channel on the only television in the house. Makoeya asked permission to watch the game, but his family, fervent fans of gospel shows, flatly rejected him. The man did not settle for "no" and, after their refusal, tried to take the remote control of the device from the woman. The struggle soon turned into a fierce fight: in one corner, Makoeya; in the other, his 68-year-old wife and his eldest son, 36. As a spectator, their 23-year-old daughter. With numerical superiority, mother and son easily defeated their opponent: Makoeya died in a nearby hospital from serious head injuries and the family was detained by the police, charged with the murder.

Crazy about soccer

It is commonly asserted that there are many people who do not make sacrifices to improve their quality of life or help family and friends, but are willing to commit anything crazy in order to attend a World Cup match, especially if that game is the final. The marriage of Maurice and Nicole Meyer is proof of the extremes people will go to. The couple, from the city of Nelspruit, in the northeast of South Africa, decided to participate in an unusual contest organized by the program "Just plain breakfast" on the local radio station Jacaranda 94.2: whoever performed the most original feat won a VIP ticket for the grand final at Soccer City Stadium in Johannesburg, valued at $13,000. After listening to the different suggestions from the audience, Maurice convinced his wife with a deranged idea. "We win for sure," he said. The woman thought her husband's plan—swimming across the "Crocodile River"—was crazy, not so much because of its cold temperatures, but because, as its name implies, it is full of hungry crocodiles. "I was listening to the proposals that came to [host] Darren Scott and they all seemed quite poor. I have no idea how I came up with swimming in the Crocodile River, it just appeared inside my head," said Maurice. And there they went, brave and foolish, husband and wife. Why both, if there was only one ticket at stake? "To have a better chance of winning," Maurice said. To prove they did it, the couple asked Maurice's brother Gert to videotape the experience, which was quickly uploaded to YouTube.com. Gert also played the role of bodyguard: he took a rifle with him, in case the reptiles dared to make the couple their lunch. "Anyway," said Maurice, "I'm not quite sure what Gert would have done: kill the crocodile or kill me to avoid my agony." Not a single shot was fired, though there was anguish for a few days, until Scott announced that the wacky couple were the rightful winner of the award.

Live robbery

All referees made, make and will make mistakes during a soccer game. None was as exposed as the Italian referee Roberto Rosetti, who was in charge of the game Mexico-Argentina game at the Soccer City Stadium in Johannesburg for the second round of South Africa

2010. At 26 minutes, after two attacks of the Tricolor that miraculously did not reach the Argentine net—a shot by Andrés Guardado came out kissing the right post and a shot by Carlos Salcido hit the crossbar of Sergio Romero's goal—the blue and white magician Leonel Messi fed Carlos Tevez. A quick move by Aztec goalkeeper Óscar Pérez cut off that advance at the penalty spot, but the ball returned to Messi, who launched a high and deep pass to Tevez who sent a header to the goal, guarded by Mexican defenders Francisco Rodríguez and Efraín Juárez. Linesman Paolo Calcagno, somewhat hesitant, walked towards the middle of the field, as a sign that the goal, from his point of view, had been valid. After consulting his partner through the intercom, Rosetti extended his right index finger to the center circle. While the Argentine players celebrated, the Mexicans pounced on Calcagno to demand he tell the referee that Tevez had scored in an obvious offside position. Rosetti approached the group and, while they argued about whether it was offside, the giant screens of the stadium replayed the controversial action. The judges, the players from both teams, the two substitute benches and the 84,000 people who packed the stands were able to corroborate that, indeed, the striker had headed from a prohibited position. There was no doubt. But the rules did not allow the referee to rely on external elements to review a decision, so Rosetti had to validate a goal that made him an accomplice to an injustice. The Mexican team was rattled, and Argentina scored twice more to settle the match. Javier Chicharito Hernández's goal came too late. Argentina won.

The next day, FIFA president, Joseph Blatter, apologized to the Mexican delegation and spoke on the issue of using technology to help referees in key situations. "It would be foolish not to worry. We have to re-discuss this issue. Personally, I am sorry when you see obvious referee errors, but this is not the end of the competition or the end of soccer. These are things that can happen," said the diplomatic Swiss leader who, a few months later, would be dismissed for

Spain celebrates its 2010 World Cup victory.

his alleged links to cases of sports corruption. Meanwhile, the referee Rosetti was kicked out of the World Cup due to his failure and FIFA ordered the operators of the giant screens at the stadiums not to show "conflicting actions" again, as spokesman Nicolas Maingo described them. All very nice, but these measures in no way remedied the enormous injustice that contributed to Mexico's dismissal from South Africa.

As in 1966 . . .

As happens in each edition of the Cup, South Africa 2010 was not exempt from serious referee errors. There were two clear offside goals—in addition to the Argentine goal against Mexico was another by the Netherlands in the semi-final against Uruguay, which ended 3- 2—and two legitimate goals annulled as supposedly offside—one by the United States against Slovenia and another against Italy, which could have qualified the Azzurri team against Slovakia. However, the biggest injustice of the tournament, by far, occurred on June 27 at the Free State Stadium in Bloemfontein, when Germany and England met. In the 52nd minute, with the score 2-1 for the Germans, the England's Frank Lampard took the ball outside the rival area and shot. The ball beat goalkeeper Manuel Neuer, hit the crossbar and bounced inside the goal, about 60 centimeters behind from the line. But the ball, capricious, left the goal and was immediately taken by Neuer. Neither the Uruguayan referee Jorge Larrionda nor the linesman and compatriot Emanuel Espinosa realized that Lampard had scored a legitimate goal, and ordered the continuation of the game, despite the protests of the English players. They never recovered, and were finally humiliated 4-1 by their rivals.

The scene immediately brought to mind what happened at Wembley during the extension of the 1966 final, coincidentally between England and Germany, although this resolution was exactly the opposite way: in London, local striker Geoff Hurst's shot had bounced off the crossbar and had come out after bouncing on the line, without crossing it. On that occasion, it was considered a goal by the Swiss referee Gottfried Dienst, also unfairly. In South Africa, at least, for the victims there was a consolation: FIFA president Joseph Blatter announced the organization would study the possibility of using technology, like television cameras, to avoid this kind of unjustifiable event. "Personally, I regret when obvious referee errors are seen, although they are things that can happen. I apologized to the English, who thanked us and accepted that sometimes you win and sometimes you lose," said Blatter. In England, meanwhile, the bookmakers were the center of attention again. As in 1986—when it was decided to return the money to those who had bet on the tie between England and Argentina, after the "hand of God"—the Ladbrokes and William Hill agencies paid those players who bet that Lampard would score a goal in that match. "Everybody could see it was a goal," explained William Hill's spokesman. With this measure, each gambling establishment lost about 100,000 sterling pounds but gained much more in credibility.

An eight-legged star

There is no rational explanation for the incredible performance of the octopus Paul, the greatest star of the World Cup in South Africa. The cephalopod mollusk (male or female?) guessed, from an aquarium located in Germany, the eight World Cup matches for which it was consulted, including the final. The system of the eccentric oracle was simple: before each game played by the German team, the caretakers of the Sea Life Park in the town of Oberhausen offered Paul—who had been born in Weymouth, England—two acrylic containers, one with the flag from Germany and another with that of its rival, and a succulent clam inside each. The octopus came down and wrapped its tentacles around one of the two cubes, which was taken as its prediction. Paul did not miss a single one: he even anticipated Germany's two defeats, against Serbia (in the first round) and Spain (in the semi-final).

After Germany was eliminated, Paul's custodians went for more and asked who would be the champion. The octopus, without hesitation, pounced on the container that carried the Spanish flag and swallowed its clam in a few seconds. The invertebrate's fame generated all kinds of analysis and comments, and it was even said that it had received death threats. The owners of sports betting houses, for example, wanted to see it out of the fish tank and in a pot. Another who might have desired an octopus lunch was the leopard Zakumi, the official mascot of the tournament. The poor feline disappeared from the scene, humiliated by Paul, who had become the exotic star of South Africa 2010.

Brazil 2014

The catastrophic history repeated itself. Brazil, winner of more World Cups—five—than any other nation, and an exceptional performer in all editions, again received a hard slap (in truth, seven) at its own home, which forced it to become for the second time a spectator at someone else's victory lap. The blows that knocked the host out of the twentieth World Cup were not, this time, from fellow South Americans but from Europeans. Germany, dressed in a shirt identical to that of the Clube de Regatas do Flamengo, the most popular local team, humiliated the host nation with a shocking 7-1 score in the semi-final, played at the Mineirão stadium in Belo Horizonte.

Never before had Brazil suffered so much in its twenty cup appearances. Never before had a country organizing a World Cup suffered such disgrace. Only Switzerland, in 1954, had endured seven goals in a single game, albeit in an electrifying 7-5 quarter-final los. In the history of the competition, the most goals Brazil had surrendered in a game was five, to Poland in 1938, but that contest ended with a 6-5 victory. They had never lost by more than three goals. The German win also had no antecedents in a World Cup semi-final: the widest scores had occurred in Uruguay 1930, when both Argentina and Uruguay beat the United States and Yugoslavia

6-1, respectively. Brazil, to add insult to injury, became the host country that gave up the most goals in a World—14.

The Germans took over two other prestigious marks that were in the hands of Brazilians, thanks to Miroslav Klose: with the goals he scored against Brazil and Ghana, the Polish-born striker made it 16 and unseated Ronaldo Luís Nazário de Lima as the top scorer in the history of the World Cup. Klose, who had scored five goals in Korea-Japan 2002, another five in Germany 2006 and three in South Africa 2010, surpassed the Carioca attacker by one. Likewise, the gunner surpassed Brazilian right back Marcos Evangelista de Morães, famous by the nickname of Cafú, in matches won in the World Cup: 17 to 16.

In the grand finale, Germany dispatched a tepid Argentina in extra time, with a lone goal from Mario Götze. They were familar antagonists: before Brazil 2014, they had starred in the final of the championship in Mexico 1986 (Argentina won 3-2) and Italy 1990 (German victory 1-0). Argentina and Germany also equaled the cup record for matches, matching Brazil-Sweden, with seven games. As if all these notable marks were not enough, the German team also became the one that starred in the most finals: eight (four won, four lost).

Some more soccer pearls: Brazil 2014 equaled the World Cup record that had been held alone by France 1998 for most goals, with 171. With four games refereed in this tournament, the Uzbek Ravshan Irmatov reached nine (he had five in South Africa 2010) and established himself as the referee with the most matches worked in the entire history of the World Cup. For the first time, two African teams (Nigeria and Algeria) qualified for the round of 16. The Netherlands, meanwhile, became the first team to use all 23 players on its official list. The orange squad, which played seven games from the debut to the bronze medal match, surpassed that of France, which in Argentina 1978 had also used all its players. The difference was that, until the 2002 Korea-Japan edition, the teams could enlist 22 men.

The Spanish team, defending champions and winners in the two previous European Cups, was out of the competition in the initial round after playing only two games: they lost 5-1 to the Netherlands and 2-0 to Chile. It said goodbye with a 3-0 win over Australia that didn't help. Colombian goalkeeper Faryd Mondragón played just over six minutes against Japan, replacing David Ospina, enough to become the oldest World Cup's footballer, at 43 years and three days. Finally, in this tournament, FIFA accepted the incorporation of two technological elements to improve control over certain situations: the evanescent spray that prevents defenders from creeping up on a free kick, and the "hawk's eye," a system of cameras that allow for the determination if a ball crossed the goal line or not. This system was used for the first time in the match between France and Honduras, to confirm that a ball from the Frenchman Karim Benzema had crossed the Central American goal after bouncing off a post and on goalkeeper Noel Valladares.

At the organizational level, Brazil suffered tremendous headaches. The tournament started with 35 infrastructure works that were not completed on time. Some suffered delays, others were paralyzed and, most strikingly, some never started! The Estádio das Dunas of Natal got approval from the fire department just a couple of hours before the first whistle of the clash between Mexico and Cameroon, on the first date of Group A. Strange tragedies also occurred, such as the collapse of a road bridge in Belo Horizonte that crushed a passenger bus and killed two people. A few weeks before the ball started rolling, FIFA Secretary General Jérôme Valcke said during an interview that Brazil needed "a kick in the ass" to speed up the work. "In Brazil, things are usually done at the last minute," complained Valcke who, just a year later, would be expelled from the organization and arrested, accused of reselling tickets for the Cup matches. What a gem!

The high cost of remodeling stadiums, airports, highways and other projects earned the hatred of millions of people, who took to the streets to complain about alleged acts of corruption and demand that the local government invest less money in the championship and more on quality public services. According to international consultants, Japan and Korea spent about $3.5 billion to build or renovate all of their stadiums for the 2002 Cup; Germany, $2.2 billion; South Africa, $2 billion; Brazil, $6,700 billion. But to that amount must be added another $7 billion to rebuild airports, roads and other works to flesh out the most expensive tournament in the world.

Poker of brothers

During the Oceania qualifying round, there was a singular case in World Cup history: four brothers scored goals in the same match. The unique event took place on June 1, 2012, when Samoa played Tahiti at the Lawson Tama Stadium in Honiara, capital of the Solomon Islands, for the second round of qualifying. The Tahitian starting team, armed by the French coach Eddy Etaeta, included three of the Tehau brothers: Lorenzo scored four goals, Alvin two and Jonathan another two. The ninth family goal was achieved by Teaonui, who had replaced Alvin. The prolific production of the Tehau allowed Tahiti to prevail 10 to 1 (Steevy Chong Hue had the honor of scoring the only goal that wasn't in the fraternal count). The brothers kept scoring n subsequent games, though never in such a forceful way (Jonathan, Alvin and Teaonui all met again on the scoreboard in a 4-1 win over Vanuatu, for example) and Tahiti managed to go to the final. But, in that defining moment, the effectiveness of the Tehau brothers evaporated and Tahiti was no match for New Zealand, the winner of the zone who would go to a playoff with the fourth of CONCACAF finisher, Mexico.

315

Thank you, manito Yankee

The road Mexico took to Brazil 2014 was almost dramatic. In the final hexagonal of CONCACAF, which it shared with the United States, Costa Rica, Honduras, Panama and Jamaica, the "tricolor" boat lost its way and was soon to be capsized in the dark waters of humiliation. The unusually poor campaign—nine goals scored in ten games, eleven conceded and only two wins, against Jamaica and Panama—did not end in a resounding failure thanks to the help of substitute soccer players from the United States. In the last game of the group, Mexico fell to Costa Rica in San José and Panama was winning at home, after 90 minutes, 2 to 1 to the Americans. With this combination of results, Panama would be awarded a place in the playoff against the representative of Oceania, New Zealand. But the American stormed back with two goals, from Graham Zusi at 92 minutes and Aron Johannsson at 93. Back to life thanks to the miraculous help of their northern neighbors, the tricolores, led by a new coach, Miguel Piojo Herrera, crushed the New Zealanders (5-1 at Azteca, 4-2 at Wellington) to be, one once again, in the great World Cup event.

Uncorruptible?

Jonas Eriksson, a Swedish journalist and businessman, owned 15 percent of a company dedicated to the commercialization of sports rights worldwide, called IEC in Sports. In 2007, the company was sold to a French corporation, Lagardère, which allowed Eriksson to collect more than ten million euros in exchange for his small package of shares. From that moment on, the journalist decided to dedicate himself completely to his true passion: refereeing. After participating with great success in World Cup qualification matches, the Champions League, the Europa League and international youth tournaments, FIFA appointed Eriksson to perform in

Brazil 2014. The Swede worked the Ghana-United States game and Cameroon-Brazil, both in the first pase, and Argentina-Switzerland in the quarter-finals. FIFA was very satisfied with his performance, the most reliable of the referees in the World Cup. With more than ten million euros in the bank, Eriksson was obviously a very difficult judge to bribe.

Opposed

Brazil 2014 is not the World Cup with the highest number of own goals (that black record belongs to France 1998, with six), but two of its unfortunate goals have remained in history. In the first, the one scored by Marcelo Vieira da Silva (Rio's left-back known simply as Marcelo), came in the opening match June 12, 2014 between Brazil and Croatia at the São Paulo Arena. Never before has a World Cup started with an own goal. It is fair to say that Marcelo's score, which occurred after eleven minutes of play, had more misfortune than clumsiness: Croatian Ivica Olić sent a low and powerful cross from

Not all of Marcelo's moments in the 2014 world cup were this pretty.

317

the left, which passed between many legs, including those of two defenders, before bouncing off the left-back's right foot, who had come rushing to protect Júlio César Soares Espíndola's goal. (The only officially recorded own goal in an opening match before that was scored by Tom Boyd on June 10, 1998, at the Stade de France coliseum in Paris. In this case, the fateful action did not break the zero but rather tied Brazil and Scotland at one.)

The second famous own goal was the work of Bosnian Sead Kolašinac, who broke the zero against Argentina on June 15, 2014, at the Maracanã stadium. In truth, Kolašinac also had bad luck: a cross from Lionel Messi, later headed by Marcos Rojo, chanced to hit the legs of the European defender, who could not avoid the contact, or Argentina winning that day two to one. Why is this so much more famous? Because it happened 130 seconds into the game and it became the fastest in World Cup history. The previous one had been scored by Carlos Gamarra 166 seconds into the match between Paraguay and England in Germany 2006.

The bite

Group D was called "the group of death," an exaggerated expression highlighting that it had more soccer heavyweights than other groups—former champions England, Italy and Uruguay, along with the supposedly weaker Costa Rica. The competition began with a surprise Central American victory over Uruguay, 3-1, and a thrilling Italian triumph over England. On the second date, Uruguay recovered and eliminated England, while Costa Rica once again moved its fans with another glorious day, against Italy, by establishing itself as the first of the survivors of the tricky quartet. In this context, on June 24, at the Estádio das Dunas in the city of Natal, South Americans and Azzurri got together to play a game hotter than the Brazilian climate, which that day raised the mercury to 33 degrees Celsius.

The Europeans had the advantage of having a better goal differential, so a draw was enough for them to move on. The encounter was tense, sizzling. In the second half, with the score still tied at zero, Mexican referee Marco Rodríguez sent off Italian Claudio Marchisio for a violent kick to the right leg of Egidio Arévalo Ríos. The tension did not dissipate and, ten minutes before the end, the defender Giorgio Chiellini and the forward Luis Suárez collided and fell together within the Azzurri penalty area. Rodríguez whistled a free kick for Italy while the defender wriggled in pain. The referee let the injury claim pass since he had not noticed anything, nor had his collaborators. The game continued and, a minute later, the Uruguayan Diego Godín scored the only goal of the match with a header. After the final whistle, the eliminated Italians complained about the referee's leniency towards Suárez and raised a protest.

FIFA took up the case and analyzed the images of the match. The Uruguayan had a history in the matter. In 2010, when he was a member of the Dutch club Ajax, he received a seven-game suspension matches for biting a player from PSV Eindhoven; in April 2013, during his time with the English team Liverpool FC, he did the same to a Chelsea FC defender and was punished with another ten games. FIFA decided to disqualify Suárez ex officio for nine official matches with his national team after finding him guilty of "having committed an offense to sportsmanship against another player." The World Cup ended for the striker, but the punishment was not limited only to playing: "For four months, Luis Suárez is prohibited from engaging in any kind of activity related to soccer, administrative, sports or of any other kind," which vetoed his training sessions with Liverpool, and also "entering the venues of all stadiums during the period of the ban." "The player will not be allowed to enter the premises of the stadium where the Uruguayan team plays a match while they are serving the nine suspension matches," continued the ruling, which also imposed a fine of 100,000 Swiss francs. The controversial case was known around the world, and transcended the bounds of soccer. In several countries, bottle openers appeared with the player's face and his prominent teeth as a lever. In Sweden, the sex toy store Oliver & Eva launched the "Suárez nipple clamps," a very creative product to stimulate and enhance pleasure. "Maybe we should send him a sample. He might be proud to spread a bit of pleasure and love, despite his mistake on the field," said the store director Tobias Lundqvist.

Perhaps the most curious thing about the case was that 167 people from twenty countries bet through the website Betsafe, before the start of the competition, that the Uruguayan striker would use his teeth to attack an opponent. The winners pocketed a prize equal to 175 times their wager.

Once the suspension was completed, Suárez went to FC Barcelona. Three years later, he met Chiellini again on a pitch when the Catalan team met Juventus of Italy in the quarter-finals of the Champions League. The players, this time, treated each other with enormous respect and, when the competition ended, they exchanged their jerseys.

The Boateng II

The strange fraternal duel between Kevin-Prince and Jerome Boateng was repeated at the World Cup on June 21, 2014, at the Castelão stadium in Fortaleza. In this case, the teams from Germany and Ghana—united by chance in the starting Group G—tied 2-2 and the brothers were together only during the first half, because Jerome was replaced during the break by Shkodran Mustafi. The draw allowed the European squad to finish in first place in the group, but the African team was last, and eliminated.

Team Germany celebrates with the 2014 World Cup

In the line of fire

Although a 3-2 loss against Argentina would not affect the Nigeria's classification—both teams had enough points to advance to the second round—the African team pressed the accelerator to get closer to Sergio Romero's goal and try to tie up the match at the Beira-Rio stadium in Porto Alegre. At 58 minutes, midfielder Ogenyi Onazi sent a strong shot towards the Argentine target. However, the ball crashed into his teammate Michael Babatunde, who was struck down. The doctors of the Nigerian squad realized the very violent ball had fractured the radius bone of Babatunde's right arm, and he was immediately replaced by Okechukwu Uchebo. The injured player was operated on a few hours later in a Brazilian clinic, although he was unable to continue in the Cup. Onazi, meanwhile, joked that "it would have been a sure goal if it weren't for his hand." Another favorable hand on the Argentine road to a World Cup final.

321

Red card for a press officer

The round-of-16 match between Brazil and Chile was as dramatic as it was hot. The 1-1 draw after ninety minutes forced. In the final moments of that period, Chilean forward Mauricio Pinilla had the victory on his right foot, but his shot bounced off the crossbar of the goal defended by Júlio César and left the host's box. In the penalty shootout, Brazil won 3-2 and went on to the next round. The most dramatic part of this South American duel may have been halftime: as the two teams headed to the locker rooms, Brazilian forward Frederico Fred Chaves Guedes had a heated discussion with Chilean defender Gary Medel. The exchange of words led to the swirling of slaps and the intervention of several players to separate the contestants. In the middle of the skirmish, the press officer of the Brazilian Soccer Confederation (CBF), Rodrigo Paiva, hit Pinilla in the face. The men in black saw the incident, and English referee Howard Webb immediately showed the red card to the spokesman. FIFA condemned Paiva's action with a four-match suspension matches and a fine of 10,000 Swiss francs. The CBF was even more blunt: it fired him immediately.

The strange case of Dr. Van Gaal

The intense quarter-final duel between the Netherlands and Costa Rica on July 5, at the Arena Fonte Nova in Salvador, ended miraculously without goals: the teams had attacked each other without stopping during the two hours of play. A minute before the final whistle of the extra time, the Dutch coach, Louis van Gaal, played a definitive card: he took advantage of the last change he had left to replace goalkeeper Jasper Cillessen with one of the substitute netminders, Tim Krul, who had closely studied the Costa Rican players who had participated in a round-of-16 penalty shoot-out against Greece. The move was a success. Krul saved two shots and the Netherlands prevailed 4-3. When the Dutch went up against Argentina in the semi-final, Van Gaal exhausted his substitutions and could not bring Krul in. Cillessen failed to stop a shot when the game went to penalites, and Argentina went on to the final thanks to two saves from goalkeeper Sergio Romero. "I was the one who taught him to stop penalties, that's why it hurts," complained the coach after the game. When Romero went from Racing Club in Argentina to AZ Alkmaar in the Netherlands in 2007, the European club's coach was . . . Van Gaal.

Twice with the same stone

Joedir Belmont moved heaven and earth to get one of the 174,000 tickets that were put on sale for the culminating match of the 1950 World Cup, in the then lush Maracanã stadium. But when the big day arrived, poor Joedir decided to miss the duel between Brazil and Uruguay to stay with his mother Alicia, who was dying in her bed due to a sudden illness. Joedir kept his ticket intact for 64 years until, a few weeks before the start of the second Brazilian World Cup, he proposed to FIFA that he donate that ticket to its Soccer Museum in Zurich, in exchange for another two for the final of 2014, which he hadn't been able to get because they were sold out. FIFA accepted the exchange and gave him two tickets during a brief ceremony held in the Maracanã, once again the scene of the great outcome. The 85-year-old was excited, eager to fulfill his dream of seeing a final. But fate, perhaps chance, intruded again. During the trip back to his house, Don Joedir . . . lost his tickets! Maybe the third time will be the charm and Belmont can finally witness the final of a World Cup if Brazil is chosen to host again in 64 years.

RUSSIA 2018

The World Cup had been played once in two countries (South Korea and Japan, in 2002) but never before had a single tournament had been played on two continents. The choice of Russia as the host country—a giant that occupies a large portion of Eastern Europe and almost a third of Asia—made this curious scenario possible. Sixty matches of the 2018 World Cup were decided in eleven European coliseums in Moscow (the only city with two venues, Luzhniki and Otkrytie Arena), Saint Petersburg, Kaliningrad, Kazan, Nizhny Novgorod, Rostov-on-Don, Samara, Saransk, Sochi and Volgograd, and four (all from the first phase) on Asian soil, in the Central Stadium of Yekaterinburg, a city located on the other side of the Ural Mountains, the natural border between the two continents.

France team won its second Cup, against Croatia, supported by the versatility of the skillful Antoine Griezmann and the dizzying runs of the striker Kylian Mbappé, a 19-year-old boy chosen as the best young player in the tournament. The champion coach, Didier Deschamps, who had already lifted the Cup as a player in 1998, joined the small and select group who'd won as both player and coach, until that moment consisting only of the Brazilian Mário Zagallo and Germany's Franz Beckenbauer.

Russian president Vladimir Putin with the 2018 World Cup

This edition also saw the controversial of the VAR (or Video Assistant Referee), which little by little would begin to spread throughout the professional soccer world. The first use intervention of the system occurred on June 16 at the Arena of Kazan, during the first round duel between France and Australia: the referee analysts called the Uruguayan referee Andrés Cunha to indicate that Griezmann had been hit by defender Josh Ridson inside the Australian penalty area. Cunha, who had not noticed the infraction, reviewed it on a monitor and sanctioned the first World Cup penalty kick via VAR, which Griezmann himself transformed into a goal. The technological assistance the cameras provided meant the Russian Cup saw the highest number of penalties in history, with 29, eleven more than the tournaments of Italy 1990, France 1998 and Korea-Japan 2002. Under another new rule, FIFA authorized the teams to make a fourth substitution, but only in the event of overtime. Russian coach Stanislav Cherchesov was the first to use this resource: 97 minutes into the round-of-16 match against Spain at the Luzhniki Olympic Stadium in Moscow, the local manager took out Daler Kuzyaev and sent Aleksandr Erokhin to the pitch. Russia finally won the penalty shootout. Japan, meanwhile, became the first World Cup team to go to the second round of a World Cup by tiebreaker, through Fair Play. The Asian squad and Senegal, members of Group H, had equaled in points, goals scored and goals conceded. They had also drawn their duel in Yekaterinburg 2-2. However, Japan advanced to the next round having collected four yellow cards, two fewer than their African rival.

Mexico's Jesús Gallardo stamped his name in the record books when he was cautioned thirteen seconds into the first phase match against Sweden, for hitting his Scandinavian opponent Ola Toivonen. In other cautionary tales, the Argentine Javier Mascherano reached seven yellow cards in 20 World Cup games, a mark that surpassed the six that the French Zinedine Zidane, the Brazilian Cafu and the Mexican Rafael Márquez had accumulated. Márquez, meantime, not only equaled his compatriot Antonio Carbajal and German Lothar Matthäus in the number of World Cups played—five—but also became the first player to be captain of his team in five editions of the Cup. His 17 games as captain of his squad also surpassed the record held by Argentine Diego Maradona, by one. At the same time, the Egyptian goalkeeper Essam El-Hadary shattered the mark that Colombian Faryd Mondragón had achieved four years earlier: on June 25, at the Volgograd Arena, the North African became the oldest soccer player to participate in a World Cup match when he played against Saudi Arabia at 45 years and 161 days. Another "old man," Panamanian Felipe Baloy, broke the record for the oldest debutant to score a goal, a mark which had belonged to Argentine Martín Palermo. Baloy scored against England at 37 years and 120 days. (The score was not enough to reverse a 6-1 defeat, but it was able to at least earn a place in the record book.)

Russia 2018 did not see the most goals scored in a World Cup—it registered two less than France 1998 and Brazil 2014—nor did it come close to the average of Switzerland 1954: it had 2.64 goals per game, far from the Swiss 5.38. However, an interesting and obscure fact is that every team in this tournament scored at least two goals. Another colorful data point: the Russian cup was the fifth in which all the semi-finalists were European (France, Croatia, Belgium and England), after Italy 1934, England 1966, Spain 1982 and Germany 2006.

It came as a surprise that the German team, the defending champion of Brazil 2014, were eliminated in the first phase. Not because it was the first defending champion to fail that way—Brazil, France, Italy and Spain had already suffered this contingency—but because the German squad had never been eliminated in the first round since the current system was introduced in 1950. Still, it was striking that the last three champions (Italy in 2010, Spain in 2014 and Germany in 2018) were shipwrecked in their bid to retain their crown.

The twenty-first World Cup edition added two new participating nations: Panama and Iceland. The latter was also the country with the smallest population ever to play in a World Cup. England finally managed to win a round of penalty kicks. It beat Colombia that way in the round of 16 and broke its streak of three disappointments (against Germany in 1990, Argentina in 1998 and Portugal in 2006). Croatia, a finalist for the first time in a World Cup, reached the big event after playing three overtime periods: in the round of 16, it beat Denmark on penalties, in the quarter-finals it did the same against Russia and in the semi-finals it defeated England 2-1, thanks to a goal by Mario Mandžukić in the 109th minute. And speaking of Mandžukić, in the final against France on July 15, he pulled off something that had been done just once before: he scored a goal and an own-goal in the same match. (The previous case had been the work of the Netherlands's Ernie Brandts in 1978, against Italy in the semi-final group stage.) Mandžukić's unfortunate marker was the twelfth of the tournament, setting another record for Russia 2018: never before have so many own goals been scored.

I only ask God

Afflicted by the absence of his national team in eight consecutive World Cups, the president of Peru, Ollanta Humala, took advantage of a visit to the Vatican to make an unusual request of Pope Francis. "Knowing about your soccer passion, I give you the shirt of the Peruvian team and I ask you help us with the Heavenly Father so that Peru can be in the World Cup again," Humala told the Pontiff during their meeting at the Holy See. The Pope must have been successful because, to the happiness of Humala and all his people, Peru managed to qualify for the World Cup after 36 years of absence. The wthite-and-red squad arrived in Russia thanks to the intercontinental play-off against New Zealand . . . and the invaluable divine intervention.

The Phantom Goal and the Nosy Granny

Panama achieved the first World Cup berth in its history thanks to a phantom goal and the unusual performance of a grandmother. The nonexistent goal occurred in the 53rd minute of the last match of CONCACAF qualifying, when Panama was losing 1-0 to Costa Rica, a team that was already qualified for Russia. Aníbal Godoy took a corner kick from the left, the ball passed visiting goalkeeper Patrick Pemberton and bounced off Panamanian striker Gabriel Torres. The ball rolled towards the goal and, despite Blas Pérez's effort to push it into the net, it was rejected by the Costa Rican defender Ronald Matarrita. Guatemalan referee Walter López, confused by his linesman, pointed to the center circle to concede a non-existent goal. A tie, however, was not enough for Panama to make it to Russia, despite the fact that, in that moment, Trinidad and Tobago was beating the United States by two to one. Panama needed three points to overcome the Americans. At 88 minutes, Román Torres beat Pemberton with a strong shot that broke the draw and would put his country in a World Cup for the first time.

There were several additional minutes left, however, before the dream could come true. While the stands of the Rommel Fernández stadium in the Panamanian capital boiled, a grandmother named Elida de Mitchell overcame the protective fences and jumped onto the grass. The lady, known in her neighborhood as "La Fula," interfered to stop the action and accelerate the end of the meeting. Disoriented, the referee López called the police to remove the intruder, but "La Fula" remained on the field. First, with a devastating argument for the Panamanian officers: "If you take me out, damn it, we are not going to the World Cup." Second, by simulating a faint that unleashed the celebration of the fans. The referee, overcome by the farce and unbothered by the lukewarm response of the Costa Ricans, who were little affected by the result, whistled the end of the most extravagant match of the Russian qualifiers.

Betrayal and punishment

"We are not going to make a revolution, we are going to make an evolution," promised Julen Lopetegui when he took over as the coach of Spain in July 2016, replacing the 2010 South African champion coach Vicente del Bosque. Lopetegui partially kept his word: Spain qualified undefeated for the World Cup in Russia and added twenty games without a loss in a period in which they faced top-level teams such as Italy, England, Argentina, France and Germany. Before traveling to the 2018 World Cup, the Basque coach signed an extension of his contract with the national squad until 2020. However, just two days before the debut against Portugal, the president of the Royal Spanish Federation, Luis Rubiales, announced Lopetegui's dismissal. This strange occurrence was based on the fact that, a few hours after his departure for Russia, the Real Madrid club announced they were hiring him to take control of the club after the tournament. Rubiales, offended by the attitude, threw Lopetegui from the squad camp in the city of Krasnodar and appointed the federation's sports director, the former defender Fernando Hierro, as his successor. "The national squad is the team of all Spaniards and there are decisions that we are obliged to make based on a way of acting," Rubiales said, annoyed that the negotiation between Lopetegui and Real Madrid had taken place behind his back and at a decisive moment for the national team. "Madrid is looking for a coach, and it is permissible for them to seek the best for their interests. God forbid me to have an opinion on the way Madrid acts. But the Federation has an obligation: the coach is a worker of the Federation, and whoever who led him into a negotiation has been wrong," insisted Rubiales.

The Spanish team passed the first phase of the Cup and was eliminated in the round of 16 against Russia, losing on penalty kicks. Lopetegui managed Real Madrid for just four months and 16 games. A historical streak of 481 minutes without scoring a goal and six defeats, the last against FC Barcelona 5-1—without its star Lionel Messi—put an end to his stay at the White House.

Intercontinental

The Belgian team, third in this Cup, achieved a curious mark: defeating teams from five different continental federations in a single tournament. In the first phase, the squad led by the Spanish coach Roberto Martínez beat England (UEFA), Tunisia (African Confederation) and Panama (CONCACAF). In the round of 16,

Belgium defeated Japan (Asian Confederation) and in the quarter-finals, Brazil (CONMEBOL).

Belgium only needed to subdue a representative of the Confederation of Oceania to complete a global record, but none qualified for the World Cup in Russia (Australia, which did play the tournament, resigned from its continental federation in 2006 and has competed in the Asian one ever since).

Newborn

Their 1-0 victory over Peru put the Danes in high spirits. So much so that the Nordic boys decided to raise money and pay for their teammate Jonas Knudsen to have a private plane ride home to meet his newborn daughter. Knudsen, who had not played against the South American squad, flew with the consent of coach Åge Hareide, gave the baby a kiss, another to his wife, and returned immediately—and very proud—to the camp in Russia.

Controversial award

Although Egypt lost its debut to Uruguay, 1-0 in Yekaterinburg, FIFA chose African goalkeeper Mohamed El-Shennawy as the best player of the match. As he left the field, a FIFA manager approached him to present the award, but El-Shennawy courteously rejected it. Why? Because the award was sponsored by the American brewery Budweiser and the goalkeeper, faithful to the ban on alcohol promoted by most Muslim religious orders, refused to be photographed with a pint-shaped trophy, decorated with the name of the beer company. FIFA took note and modified the protocols for awarding the prize: it accepted that a player could reject it and removed the Budweiser name for broadcast on television when the winners were the Moroccan Amine Harit, the Senegalese Mbaye Niang and the

Egyptian Mohamed Salah. The Danish Yussuf Poulsen, on the other hand, had no problem toasting his trophy.

Never dreamed-of injury

Brazil's third game in the initial phase—against Serbia on June 27 at the Otkrytie Arena in Moscow—started with a setback: A few moments after the beginning, left-back Marcelo asked for a change. The Mexican referee, César Ramos, stopped the action and Marcelo left his place to Filipe Luís. The fans worried that the defender could barely walk, and he crawled into the locker room supported by the Brazilian doctor, Rodrigo Lasmar. After clinical tests, Lasmar informed the press that the soccer player had suffered "spasms in the stabilizing muscles of the spine," presumably when running during a play. But the most striking thing was the cause cited by the doctor who blamed . . . the hotel mattress! Marcelo also missed the round-of-16 match against Mexico, and just returned to the team for the quarter-final match, against Belgium in Kazan. But Brazil lost and for Marcelo, and for the whole Verdeamarela squad, the dream of a championship vanished.

Messianic divorce

They met thanks to soccer, in a bar in the city of Chelyabinsk, while the Russian team played in the 2002 World Cup of South Korea and Japan. They divorced because of a player, four World Cups later. The marriage of Arsen and Ludmyla was broken after fourteen years by a "third Wheel," Argentine star Lionel Messi. The FC Barcelona hero was not the woman's lover—in fact, he did not even know the couple—but he was the recipient of affection from Arsen. According to the Moscow newspaper *Argumenty i Fakty*, Arsen professed an inordinate admiration for the talented Argentine player. His wife, perhaps jealous, perhaps a Cristiano Ronaldo fan, scoffed when Messi missed a penalty against Iceland, and even more so when Croatia beat Argentina 3-0 in their first round match. When the blue and white squad defeated Nigeria and secured its passage to the second phase of the tournament, Arsen retaliated with expletives that offended Ludmyla and ignited a fierce verbal dispute that culminated with Arsen packing up his most precious belongings and abandoning their home forever. The next day, Arsen went to the civil registry and filed for divorce. What soccer had united, a soccer player had torn apart.

Rejected medal

After the final, FIFA distributed 23 gold medals for the French winners and another 23 silver for the Croatian runners-up. However, one of the awards was left without an owner following a conflict between Croatian striker Nikola Kalinić and coach Zlatko Dalić.

Team France celebrates with the 2018 World Cup.

During the opening match against Nigeria, Dalić called up Kalinić, who was warming up with the rest of the substitutes, to replace Mario Mandžukić in the 86th minute, with the score favoring the Europeans by two to zero. The substitute, unhappy because he was not a starter and annoyed at being told to play for just a few minutes, refused to enter. The coach, furious, kicked Kalinić out of the squad camp and sent him back home. At a press conference, Dalić explained that Kalinić had already made similar gestures in a friendly against Brazil and in a training session. Croatia continued in the Cup with one player less than the rest of the participating teams, a disadvantage that did not prevent them from reaching the final. After the fall to France and the distribution of the awards, a manager took the one that corresponded to Kalinić and took it to Croatia, but the player rejected it. "I do not want the medal because I did not contribute during the tournament, I did not share the team's achievement," said the disobedient player. Dalić took note and did not call Kalinić to play for the National Team again.

Qatar 2022

Splashy facilities await players and fans alike in Doha, Qatar, 2022.

All World Cup records

Teams

- Country with the highest number of World Cup titles: Brazil, with five. They won in Sweden 1958, Chile 1962, Mexico 1970, United States 1994 and Korea-Japan 2002.
- Country with the most finals played: Germany, with eight (they won in 1954, 1974, 1990 and 2014, lost in 1966, 1982, 1986 and 2002).
- Country with the highest number of participations: Brazil is the only team that participated in all editions of the World Cup, 21, up to Russia 2018.
- Country with the highest number of matches played: Germany and Brazil, with 109.
- Country with the lowest number of games played: Dutch East Indies (now Indonesia) barely played one game, which they lost 6-0.
- Country with the highest number of wins: Brazil, with 73.
- Country with the highest number of ties: Italy and England, with 21.

- Country with the highest number of defeats: Mexico, with 27.
- World Cup with the fewest participants: Uruguay 1930 and Brazil 1950 had only thirteen participant squads.
- World Cups with the largest number of participants: since the France '98 edition, the Cup has had 32 countries distributed in eight initial groups of four teams each.
- Most games played in fewer days: Italy played three World Cup matches in four days, between May 31 and June 3, 1934. They drew their first match against Spain, and won the remaining two: the tiebreaker against the Iberian team and the clash against Austria in the semi-finals.
- First team eliminated from a World Cup without having lost: Scotland, who in 1974 beat Zaire and drew with Yugoslavia and Brazil. They were left out of the second round on goal differential.
- Only champion not to play the next edition of a World Cup: Uruguay, winner in 1930, did not participate in Italy in 1934.
- First country to become consecutive World Champion: Italy, after winning the 1934 and 1938 cups. Brazil repeated this in 1958 and 1962.
- Longest unbeaten streak: The Brazilian team was undefeated for 13 games, from their debut in Sweden 1958 until their defeat against Hungary in the first round of England 1966.
- Biggest winning streak: Brazil won eleven consecutive matches between their debut in Korea-Japan 2002 to the Germany 2006 quarter-finals, when they lost to France.
- Longest losing streak: Mexico lost nine games in a row between Uruguay 1930 and Sweden 1958. They finally managed a draw against Wales (1-1) on June 11, 1958.
- Longest winless streak: Bulgaria did not win in 17 games, from their debut in 1962 until their victory over Greece 4-0 in USA 1994.
- Most ineffective defending champions: In Korea-Japan 2002, France, who had been crowned four years earlier, was eliminated

in the first round without scoring a single goal. The blue squad drew with Uruguay and fell to Senegal (1-0) and Denmark (2-0).

- Most repeated match between teams: the Brazil-Sweden and Argentina-Germany clashes were played seven times each.
- Most repeated final match: Germany and Argentina starred in three World Cup finals: 1986, 1990 and 2014.

Goals

- World Cup with the most goals: France 1998 and Brazil 2014, with 171 goals in 64 games.
- World Cup with the highest goal average: Switzerland 1954, with 5.38 goals per game (140 scores in only 26 clashes).
- World Cup with fewest goals: Uruguay 1930 and Italy 1934 equaled with just 70.
- World Cup with the worst goal average: Italy '90 averaged just 2.2 goals per game.
- Top scorer of the World Cup: German Miroslav Klose scored 16 goals between the 2002, 2006, 2010 and 2014 World Cups.
- Player with the most goals in a single World Cup: Frenchman Just Fontaine scored 13 times in the six games he played in Switzerland 1954.
- Highest-scoring team in history: Brazil, with 229.
- Lowest-scoring teams in history: Canada, China, Trinidad and Tobago, and Zaire did not score in three games each. Dutch East Indies (now Indonesia) also did not score in its only game played in 1938.
- Team that gave up the most goals in World Cup history: Germany, with 125.
- Team with the most goals in a single tournament: Hungary scored 27 goals in six games played during the 1954 Swiss Cup. However, they were not champions.

- Most scored against team in a World Cup: South Korea gave up 16 goals in just two games in Switzerland 1954. They are also the team with the worst goal difference in a tournament (-16), because they failed to score.
- Highest-scoring champion: Germany scored 25 goals in six games in Switzerland 1954.
- Champion with the fewest goals: Spain, who in South Africa 2010 scored just 8 goals in 7 games.
- Champion who gave up the fewest goals: France (1998), Italy (2006) and Spain (2010), with 2.
- Most scored against champion: Germany surrendered 14 goals in Switzerland 1954.
- World Cup match with the most goals: Austria 7-Switzerland 5, played on June 26, 1954 in Lausanne.
- Biggest World Cup win: Hungary beat El Salvador 10 to 1 on June 15, 1982, in Group 3. Despite the remarkable feat, the Magyar squad did not pass the first round (they were third behind Belgium and Argentina).
- Biggest win in a qualifier game: Australia smashed American Samoa 31-0 on April 11, 2001.
- Player with the most goals in a World Cup match: Russian Oleg Salenko scored five times against Cameroon on June 28, 1998. The match ended 6-1.
- Top scorer in a final: English Geoffrey Hurst scored three times against Germany in 1966.
- Top scorers in finals: Brazilians Edvaldo Isidio Neto "Vavá" and Edson Arantes do Nascimento "Pelé", Englishman Geoff Hurst and Frenchman Zinedine Zidane scored three goals in World Cup finals.
- Top scorers in more World Cup finals: Brazilians Edvaldo Isidro Neto "Vavá" (1958 and 1962) and Edson Arantes do Nascimento "Pelé" (1958 and 1970); German Paul Breitner (1974 and 1982)

and Frenchman Zinedine Zidane (1998 and 2006) scored in two finals. Vavá is the only one to do it in consecutive finals.

- Team that scored the most goals in a final: Brazil scored five times against Sweden in 1958.
- Player with the most goals in a qualifier game: Australian Archie Thompson scored thirteen goals against American Samoa on April 11, 2001.
- Highest-scoring substitute player in a game: Laszlo Kiss, who replaced Andras Torocsik in the 55 minute, scored three goals against El Salvador on June 15, 1982.
- Players who scored in the most consecutive games at a World Cup: Frenchman Just Fontaine and Brazilian Jair Ventura Filho "Jairzinho." Fontaine scored in all six of his team's games at the 1958 World Cup in Sweden, while Jairzinho repeated in the six in Brazil in Mexico 1970.
- Player with the highest goal average: Polish Ernest Wilimowski has an average of four goals per game, although he played only one, on June 5, 1938 against Brazil. His team lost 6 to 5.
- Most scored against goalkeeper: Mohamed Al Deayea (Saudi Arabia) gave up 25 goals between 1994 and 2002.
- Fastest double: Germany's Toni Kroos scored two goals against Brazil in the 2014 semi-final in just 69 seconds.
- First World Cup hat trick: American Bert Patenaude scored three goals against Paraguay on July 17, 1930.
- More hat-tricks: four players scored three goals in two different World Cup matches: Sándor Kocsis (1954), Just Fontaine (1958), Gerd Müller (1970) and Gabriel Batistuta, who is the only one who achieved it in different World Cups (1994 and 1998).
- Fastest hat-trick: In 1982, Hungarian László Kiss scored three goals against El Salvador in just seven minutes.
- Fastest goal: Turkish Hakan Sukur scored at 10.8 seconds of the

match for third place that his team and South Korea played on June 29, 2002. Turkey won 3-2.

- Fastest goal in an opening match: César Sampaio of Brazil scored four minutes from the initial whistle against Scotland on June 10, 1998.
- Fastest goal in a final: Dutch Johan Neeskens scored from the penalty spot 87 seconds from the beginning of the final against Germany in 1974.
- Fastest goal scored by a substitute: the Danish Ebbe Sand beat Nigeria's goalkeeper 16 seconds after replacing his teammate Peter Moller, 59 minutes into the match played on June 28, 1998.
- First own goal: Mexican Manuel Rosas Sánchez score on his own team when playing against Chile on July 16, 1930.
- Fastest own goal: Bosnian Sead Kolašinac defeated his own goalkeeper 130 seconds into the match against Argentina on June 15, 2014. The European team lost 2-1.
- Match with the most own goals: the one between the United States and Portugal on June 16, 2002, with two, scored by the American Jeff Agoos and the Portuguese Jorge Costa. The Americans triumphed 3-2.
- World Cup with the most own goals: Russia 2018, with twelve.
- Player who scored the most own goals in World Cup history: Bulgarian Ivan Vutsov scored two own goals in England 1966: one against Portugal, one against Hungary. FIFA awarded Ivan Davidov the second, although television footage clearly shows that the ball bounced on Vutsov before entering the goal.
- Goalkeeper with the longest goalless streak: Italian Walter Zenga kept his goal at zero for 517 minutes in Italy 1990. Argentine Claudio Caniggia ended his streak in the 67th minute of the semi-final.
- Country with the longest undefeated goal: Switzerland kept its goal scoreless for 559 minutes, between USA 1994, Germany 2006 and the South Africa 2010 cups.

- Team that spent the most consecutive minutes without scoring a goal: Bolivia spent 517 minutes without scoring between its appearances in Uruguay 1930, Brazil 1950 and USA 1994. Erwin Sánchez scored the first and only Bolivian goal in World Cup history against Spain, after five games and 67 minutes without success.
- First World Cup goal: it was scored by the Frenchman Lucien Laurent, 19 minutes after the beginning of the clash between France and Mexico, July 13, 1930.
- First goalless draw: it was on June 11, 1958, when Brazil and England faced each other (in the sixth edition of the Cup and after 115 games).
- First substitute to score a goal: on June 7, 1970, the Mexican Ignacio Basaguren replaced Jaime López in the 76th minute and in the 83rd minute he got the fourth and final goal against El Salvador.
- Youngest player to score a World Cup goal: Pelé was 17 years and 239 days old on June 19, 1958, when he put the ball in the back of the Welsh net.
- Oldest player to score a goal: On June 28, 1994, against Russia, Cameroonian Albert Roger Miller (known as Roger Milla) became the oldest scorer (42 years and 39 days) in the Cup history.
- Oldest rookie to score a goal: Panamanian Felipe Baloy scored against England at 37 years and 120 days, in Russia 2018.
- First player to score goals at the World Cups for two different teams: Robert Prosinecki scored a goal for Yugoslavia against the United Arab Emirates in Italy 1990, and then scored for Croatia against Jamaica and the Netherlands in France 1998.
- First squad that did not score goals in a Cup final: Argentina lost 1-0 against Germany in the Italy 1990 final.
- Only goalless final: Brazil and Italy tied the culminating USA 1994 match without scoring after 120 minutes. Brazil won on penalties, 3-2.

- Winner of a group with the worst goal difference: Cameroon, in 1990, became the only team to finish first in its group with a negative goal difference (-2). The African squad defeated Argentina (1-0), Romania (2-1) and lost to the former Soviet Union (4-0).
- Tournament with the highest number of top scorers: in South Africa 2010, the German Thomas Müller, the Spanish David Villa, the Dutch Wesley Sneijder and the Uruguayan Diego Forlan equalized in the first place of the table of "top scorers", with five goals each.
- Organizing country who gave up the most goals: Brazil, in 2014, at 14 goals.

Players

- Player with the highest number of World Cups played: German Lothar Matthäus (1982, 1986, 1990, 1994, 1998), Mexican Antonio Carbajal (1950, 1954, 1958, 1962, 1966) and the also Mexican Rafael Márquez (2002, 2006 , 2010, 2014, 2018) took part in five World Cups.
- Player who won the World Cup the most times: Edson Arantes do Nascimento "Pelé" is the only one to become champion three times, in Sweden 1958, Chile 1962, and Mexico 1970.
- Player with the most consecutive finals played: Marcos Evangelista de Moraes, "Cafú," with three (1994, 1998 and 2002).
- Footballer with the most games played: German Lothar Matthäus played 25 games, with 15 wins, 4 losses and 6 draws.
- Player with the most games as captain: Mexican Rafael Márquez, with 17.
- Player with the highest number of minutes played: Italian Paolo Maldini played 2,217 minutes in 23 World Cup matches corresponding to the 1990, 1994, 1998 and 2002 Cups.
- Youngest player to participate in a World Cup: Brazilian Edu

was 16 years, 11 months and 6 days old at the start of the 1966 England Cup. However, he did not appear in any of his team's three matches.

- Youngest player to perform in a World Cup match: Northern Irishman Norman Whiteside became the youngest in the World Cup facing Yugoslavia at the age of 17 years and 41 days on June 17, 1982.
- Oldest Player: Egyptian goalkeeper Essam El-Hadary was 45 years and 161 days old when he faced Saudi Arabia on June 25, 2018 at the Russian Volgograd Arena.
- Youngest player to win a World Cup: Brazilian Pelé became champion in Sweden 1958 when he was just 17 years and 237 days old.
- Oldest player to win a World Cup: Italian goalkeeper Dino Zoff was 40 years and 4 months old when Italy won the Spain 1982 edition.
- Youngest player in a qualifier match: Souleymane Mamam of Togo was 13 years and 310 days old when he played in the clash against Zambia on May 6, 2001.
- Oldest player in a qualifier game: MacDonald Taylor of the US Virgin Islands was 46 years and 180 days old when he faced Saint Kitts and Nevis on February 18, 2004.
- Player with the most wins: the German Miroslav Klose was on the winning side in 17 of the 24 games he played between 2002 and 2014. With him, Germany tied another three and lost the remaining four matches.
- Player with most appearances as a substitute: Brazilian Denílson de Oliveira Araújo, with 11.
- Most players used by a team in a World Cup: in 2014, Holland used all 23 players in its seven games (bronze medal). In 1978, France used the 22 footballers then allowed in just three games, all in the opening round.

- Player who performed for more countries: Dejan Stankovic wore the jerseys of Yugoslavia in France 1998, Serbia and Montenegro in Germany 2006 and Serbia in South Africa 2010.

Coaches

- Coach with most titles: the Italian Vittorio Pozzo, with two World Cups won in 1934 and 1938.
- Coach with most consecutive wins: Luiz Felipe Scolari won 12 games in a row, 7 with Brazil in Korea-Japan 2002 and 5 with Portugal in Germany 2006.
- Coach with most matches: The German Helmut Schoen completed 25 World Cup matches, all with Germany, in the 1966, 1970, 1974 and 1978 editions.
- Coach with most World Cups: Brazilian Carlos Alberto Parreira as coach in Spain 1982 (with Kuwait), Italy 1990 (United Arab Emirates), United States 1994 (Brazil), France 1998 (Saudi Arabia), Germany 2006 (Brazil) and South Africa 2010 (South Africa).
- Coach of the most teams: Serbian Velibor "Bora" Milutinovic was coach of Mexico in 1986, Costa Rica in 1990, United States in 1994, Nigeria in 1998 and China in 2002; Carlos Alberto Parreira, of Kuwait in 1982, the Arab Emirates in 1990, Brazil in 1994 and 2006, Saudi Arabia in 1998 and South Africa in 2010.
- Champions as players and coaches: Brazilian Mario Zagalo lifted the World Cup as a footballer in 1958 and 1962, and as a coach in 1970. He was equaled only by German Franz Beckenbauer in 1974 and 1990, and French Didier Deschamps in 1998 and 2018, respectively. Beckenbauer has another record, but a negative one: he lost a final as a player (1966) and another as a coach (1986).
- The only pair of brothers who were coaches of the same national team in different World Cups: Aymoré and Alfredo Zezé Moreira led Brazil in Switzerland '54 and Chile '62, respectively.

- First coach fired in the middle of a World Cup: Brazilian Carlos Alberto Parreira was fired from the Saudi Arabia squad after his team's second defeat, against France 4-0, on June 18, 1998. Saudi Arabia had already lost in their debut against Denmark, 1-0, and although they had been eliminated, they still had to face South Africa.

Referees

- The referee with most matches: Uzbek Ravshan Irmatov participated in nine World Cup matches between the editions of South Africa 2010 and Brazil 2014.
- The youngest referee: the Uruguayan Francisco Mateucci was 27 years and 62 days old when he managed the Yugoslavia-Bolivia match on July 17, 1930 in the Central Park of Montevideo.
- The oldest referee: Englishman George Reader was 53 years and 236 days old when he umpired the final of Brazil 1950 that Uruguay won.
- Most matches refereed in a single tournament: a record shared by Argentines Horacio Elizondo and Néstor Pitana, and Mexican Benito Archundia, with five. Elizondo and Pitana also had the honor of refereeing the opening match and the final match of the same Cup (Germany 2006 and Russia 2018, respectively).

Cautions and ejections

- Faster player sent off: Uruguayan José Batista saw the red card 53 seconds into the match against Scotland, on June 13, 1986, in Group E, for an alleged violent foul called by French referee Joel Quiniou. The match ended 0-0 and allowed the South American team to go to the next round.
- Faster warning: Mexico's Jesús Gallardo was booked thirteen

seconds into the match against Sweden in the first round of Russia 2018.

- First player sent off in a World Cup: according to FIFA, the Peruvian Placido Galindo was the first and only player expelled from the 1930 Uruguay Cup. It happened on July 14, against Romania. Some sources assure that the man who was sent off was actually Mario de las Casas.

- First goalkeeper sent off: Italian Gianluca Pagliuca was the first goalkeeper to see the red card in a World Cup. It happened 21 minutes after the start of the clash on June 23, 1994, between Italy and Norway. Despite playing with one man down almost the entire match, the squad won 1-0.

- First coach sent off: Paraguayan Cayetano Ré was the first coach sent off in World Cup history, on June 11, 1986, against Belgium. The Bulgarian referee Bogdan Dotchev showed him the red card for insulting.

- First player sent off in a final: Argentine Pedro Monzón, on July 8, 1990 against Germany. The Uruguayan nationalized Mexican referee Edgardo Codesal showed him the red for a strong foul on Juergen Klinsmann. Monzón was joined 22 minutes later by his compatriot Gustavo Dezotti.

- Most sanctioned player: Frenchman Zinedine Zidane received four yellow cards and two red cards in 12 World Cup matches, between 1998, 2002, and 2006.

- Players with most red cards: Cameroonian Rigobert Song and Frenchman Zinedine Zidane, with two.

- Player with most cautions: Javier Mascherano, with seven in 20 games between 2006 and 2018.

- Referee with most send offs: Mexican Arturo Brizio Carter showed seven red cards at the 1994 and 1998 World Cups.

- Record cards in a match: Russian referee Valentin Ivanov showed 16 yellows and 4 reds on June 25, 2006, when Portugal and the

Netherlands met in the round of 16. It was also the game with the most players sent off, and the most cautioned in World Cup history.

- Record cards in a final: During the 2010 Spain-Netherlands clash in South Africa, English referee Howard Webb showed 14 yellows and one red.
- Tournament with the highest number of players cautioned and sent off: in Germany 2006 there were 28 reds and 345 yellows.
- The fastest caution for a substitute: On June 4, 2002, Korean Doo-Ri Cha replaced Ki Hyeon Seol 89 minutes into the match against Poland, and twenty seconds later he received a yellow card from Colombian referee Oscar Ruiz for kicking a rival player.
- Fastest substitute to be sent off: Bolivian Marco Antonio Etcheverry saw the red card three minutes after replacing Luis Ramallo in the 1994 opening game against Germany, on June 17.
- First player to be sent off in two consecutive World Cups: Cameroonian Rigobert Song saw the red card against Brazil in United States 1994 and against Chile in France 1998.
- Youngest player to be sent off: again the African Rigobert Song. He was 17 years and 358 days old when he saw the red on June 24, 1994, against Brazil.
- Oldest player to be sent off: American Fernando Clavijo saw the red at 37 years old on July 4 1994, in a match against Brazil.
- First caution: Soviet Evgeni Lovchev was the first player to see the yellow card in the opening match between his country and Mexico, on May 31, 1970. (The yellow and red cards came into effect in Mexico 1970)
- First substitute to be sent off: on June 18, 1978, against Germany, Dutchman Dick Nanninga replaced Pieter Wildschut in the 79th minute, and at 88 he saw the red. Substitutions were first approved for the 1970 Mexico Cup.

- Champion with the highest number of players sent off: France, in 1998, suffered three ejections. Marcel Desailly, Zinedine Zidane and Laurent Blanc saw the red card.

Penalties

- Most goals from penalties in a single game: the Dutch Johan Neeskens (against Bulgaria in 1974) and Nicolaus Robert Rensenbrink (Iran in 1978), and the English Gary Lineker (Cameroon in 1990), all with two.
- Most missed penalties in a single game: Hungary's Istvan Avar missed two penalties against Austria on May 31, 1934.
- First player to miss penalties in two consecutive World Cups: Ghanaian Asamoah Gyan missed a penalty on June 17, 2006 against the Czech Republic and another on July 2, 2010 in Johannesburg, against Uruguay.
- Most penalties sanctioned in a single match: Bolivian referee Ulises Saucedo whistled three penalties on July 19, 1930, when Argentina defeated Mexico 6-3 (two went to the loser). Italian Francesco Mattea repeated the record on May 31, 1934, when Hungary and Austria collided in Bologna. In this case, all three favored the Magyar squad, but only one was converted.
- Most penalties saved by one goalkeeper in a World Cup shoot-out: the Portuguese Ricardo stopped three shots in the series against England on July 1, 2006 for the quarter-finals. Croatian Danijel Subašić repeated the feat also on July 1, but 2018, against Denmark, for the round of 16.
- Most penalties saved in a World Cup shoot-out: five. On July 1, 2018, at the Nizhny Novgorod Stadium, Croatian goalkeeper Danijel Subašić blocked three penalties and Danish rival Kasper Schmeichel two. Croatia won three to two.
- First shoot-out: Germany-France, on July 8, 1982, after equaling

3 to 3 for the semi-finals. The series was won by the German squad 5-4.

- Team that participated in the most penalty shoot-outs in World Cups: Argentina, with five: four wins and one loss.
- Team that won most shoot-outs in World Cups: Germany won the four shoot-outs it has played (France in 1982, Mexico in 1986, England in 1990 and Argentina in 2006). Argentina also added four victories, but in five opportunities.
- Team that lost most penalty shoot-outs in World Cups: Italy and England, with three.

Fans

- World Cup with the highest average attendance: United States 1994, with 68,991 spectators per game.
- World Cup with the lowest average attendance: France 1938, with 20,872 spectators per game.
- World Cup with the highest total attendance: United States 1994, with 3,587,538 spectators.
- World Cup with the lowest public attendance: Italy 34, with just 358,000 spectators.
- Match with the largest audience: for the final of Brazil 1950, between the host team and Uruguay, 174,000 tickets were sold, but it is estimated that the audience reached 200,000 people (including guests and gate crashers).
- Match with the smallest crowd: Romania-Peru barely gathered around 300 people when they played on July 14, 1930 at the Peñarol stadium in Montevideo.
- Qualifing match with the largest number of spectators: 183,341 tickets were sold for the clash between Brazil and Paraguay on August 31, 1969, at the Maracanã stadium.

Various records

- First qualifier match: Sweden and Estonia inaugurated the World Cup qualification system on June 11, 1933. The Scandinavian team won 6-2.
- First World Cup match that was decided in extra time: Austria 3-France 2, played in Turin on May 27, 1934 for the round of 16 (first round).
- First final decided in extra time: Italy 2-Czechoslovakia 1, played on June 10, 1934.
- Only host country that did not pass the first round: South Africa in 2010.
- First player substitution: occurred on May 31, 1970 when Soviet Anatoli Puzach replaced Viktor Serebrjanikov at halftime of the opening match against Mexico.
- The fastest substitution: Italian Giuseppe Bergomi replaced Alessandro Nesta four minutes after the beginning of the match against Austria on June 23, 1998.
- Most replaced captain: Tunisian Riadh Bouazizi was replaced in the three games his team played in Germany 2006.
- First World Cup in which the numbers were used on the shirts: Brazil 1950.
- First World Cup with televised live matches: Switzerland '54.
- First nation to become champion with a pair of brothers in their team: Germany, in Switzerland '54, had Fritz and Ottmar Walter (later they would be joined by England, with Bobby and Jack Charlton, in 1966).
- First champion to be eliminated in the first round of the following World Cup: Italy, champion in 1938, was eliminated in 1950 after they lost 3-2 against Sweden and beat Paraguay 2-0. The triumph was not enough to qualify for the next stage (Sweden and Paraguay equalized 2-2).

- First player to participate in the World Cups with two different teams: Argentine Luis Monti wore the white and blue colors in Uruguay 1930 and the Azzurri jersey for Italy in 1934.
- First squad to include a chef on its staff: Spain brought Francisco Blanch to the 1934 Italian Cup, who prepared Basque and Catalan dishes.
- First final not played in the host country's capital city: On July 7, 1974, the game between West Germany and the Netherlands was played at the Olympic stadium in Munich, Federal Republic of Germany. The West German capital city was Bonn at that time.
- First positive doping test: Haitian Ernst Jean-Joseph, after his team lost against Italy 3-1, on June 15 in Munich, in 1974. Traces of ephedrine were found in his urine sample and Jean-Joseph was immediately expelled from the Cup.
- First "golden goal" in World Cup history: French defender Laurent Blanc scored the winning goal against Paraguay 113 minutes into the match on June 28, 1998. It was the only game of that edition that was resolved by that route, sometimes known as sudden-death overtime. There were three others in Korea-Japan. Later, FIFA eliminated that rule.
- First pair of brothers to face each others on two different teams: Kevin-Prince Boateng and Jerome Boateng, who played for Ghana and Germany, respectively, in the match that took place on June 23, 2010 at Soccer City Stadium of Johannesburg, for Group D of the World Cup in South Africa. The strange episode was repeated in Brazil 2014.

Bibliography

Books

"ABC Diccionario Enciclopédico del Fútbol." *Sport Newspaper Olé*, Buenos Aires, 2000.

Ash, Russell, y Morrison, Ian; *Top ten of football*. Hamlyn, London, 2010.

Baingo, Andreas; *100 moments forts de la Coupe du Monde de football*. Chantecler, Aartselaar, 1998.

Ball, Phil; *Morbo: the story of Spanish football*. WSC Books Limited, London, 2003.

Barret, Norman; *The Daily Telegraph chronicle of football*. Carlton Books, London, 2001.

Biblioteca total del fútbol, el deporte de los cinco continentes. Editorial Océano, Madrid, 1982.

Biblioteca total del fútbol, de los orígenes al Mundial. Editorial Océano, Madrid, 1982.

Bilardo, Carlos; *Así ganamos*. Sudamericana/Planeta, Buenos Aires, 1986.

Bilardo, Carlos; *Doctor y campeón*. Editorial Planeta, Buenos Aires, 2014.

Carlisle, Jeff; *Soccer's most wanted II*. Potomac Books, Virginia, 2009.

Crossan, Rob; *Football extreme*. John Blake Publishing Ltd., London, 2011.

Cruyff, Johan; *14. La autobiografía*. Editorial Planeta, Buenos Aires, 2017.

Dély, Renaud; *Brèves de football*. François Bourin Editeur, Paris, 2010.

Diario La Nación; *Historia del fútbol argentino*. Diario La Nación, Buenos Aires, 1994.

Díaz, Juan Manuel, y otros; *La pelota nunca se cansa*. Editorial Base, Barcelona, 2007.

Editorial Abril; *El libro del fútbol*. Editorial Abril, Buenos Aires, 1976.

El libro de oro del Mundial. Diario Clarín, Buenos Aires, 1998.

Etchandy, Alfredo; *El mundo y los mundiales*. Ediciones del Caballo Perdido, Montevideo, 2008.

Foer, Franklin; *How soccer explains the world*. Harper Collins, New York, 2004.

Foot, John; *Calcio, A History of Italian Football*. Harper Perennial, London, 2007.

Galeano, Eduardo; *El fútbol a sol y sombra*. Catálogos, Buenos Aires, 1995.

Galvis Ramírez, Alberto; *100 años de fútbol en Colombia*. Planeta, Bogotá, 2008.

Glanville, Brian; *Historia de los Mundiales de fútbol*. TyB Editores, Madrid, 2006.

Goldblatt, David; *The ball is round*. Penguin Books, London, 2006.

Hesse-Lichtenberger, Ulrich; *Tor! The story of German football*. WSC Books, London, 2003.

Hirshey, David, y Bennett, Roger; *The ESPN World Cup companion*. Ballantine Books, New York, 2010.

Historia El Gráfico de la selección argentina. Revista El Gráfico, Buenos Aires, 1997.

Historia del Fútbol Argentino. Fascículos del diario La Nación, Buenos Aires, 1994.

Historia del fútbol argentino. Editorial Eiffel, Buenos Aires, 1955.

Hofmarcher, Arnaud; *Carton rouge*. Le Cherche Midi, Paris, 2010.

Inglis, Simon; *The football grounds of Great Britain*. Willow Books, London, 1987.

Lauduique-Hamez, Sylvie; *Les incroyables du football*. Calmann-Levy, Paris, 2006.

Les miscellanées du foot. Éditions Solar, Paris, 2009.

Lodge, Robert; *1001 bizarre football stories*. Carlton Books, London, 2010.

Lowndes, William; *The story of football*. The Sportsmans Book Club, London, 1964.

Los Mundiales (1930-1994)" Colección de la Agrupación de Diarios del Interior (ADISA), Buenos Aires, 1997.

Ludden, John; Los partidos del siglo. TyB Editores, Madrid, 2010.

Matthews, Tony; *Football oddities*. The History Press, Stroud, 2009.

Mini Enciclopedia del Fútbol. Lareousse-Diario El País, Montevideo, 1990.

Murray, Colin; *A random history of football*. Orion Books, London, 2010.

Prats, Luis; *La crónica celeste*. Fin de Siglo, Montevideo, 2010.

Radnedge, Keir; *Histoire de la Coupe du Monde*. Gründ, Paris, 2006.

Relaño, Alfredo; *366 historias del fútbol mundial que deberías saber*. Ediciones Martínez Roca, Madrid, 2010.

Rice, Jonathan; *Curiosities of football*. Pavilion Books, London, 1996.

Risolo, Donn; *Soccer stories*. University of Nebraska Press, Lincoln, 2010.

Roland, Thierry; *La fabuleuse histoire de la Coupe du Monde*. Minerva, Paris, 2002.

Seddon, Peter; *The World Cup's strangest moments*. Portico, London, 2005.

Señorans, Jorge; *Son cosas del fútbol*. Fin de Siglo, Montevideo, 2014.

Sharpe, Graham; *500 strangest football stories*. Racing Post Books, Compton, 2009.

Snyder, John; *Soccer's most wanted*. Potomac Books, Virginia, 2001.

Southgate, Vera; *The story of football*. Ladybird Books, London, 2012.

Spurling, Jon; *Death or glory, the dark history of the World Cup*. Vision Sports Publishing, London, 2010.

Thomson, Gordon; *The man in black*. Prion Books Limited, London, 1998.

Venegas Traverso, Cristián; Fuera de juego. Editorial Forja, Santiago de Chile, 2013.

Ward, Andrew; *Football's strangest matches*. Portico, London, 2002.

Wernicke, Luciano; *Curiosidades Futboleras*. Editorial Sudamericana, Buenos Aires, 1996.

Wernicke, Luciano; *Curiosidades Futboleras II*. Editorial Sudamericana, Buenos Aires, 1997.

Wernicke, Luciano; *Fútbol increíble*. Ediciones de la Flor, Buenos Aires, 2001.

Wernicke, Luciano; *Nuevas curiosidades futboleras*. Ediciones Al Arco, Buenos Aires, 2008.

Wilson, Jonathan; *Inverting the pyramid*. Orion Books, London, 2009.

Wilson, Jonathan; *The outsider, a history of the goalkeeper*. Orion Books, London, 2012.

Newspapers

Argentina: *Clarín, La Nación, Olé, Diario Popular, Crónica, La Argentina.*

Brasil: *O Estado, Lance, Folha de Sao Paulo.*

Chile: *La Tercera, El Mercurio.*

Colombia: *El Tiempo, El País.*

Ecuador: *Hoy, El Telégrafo.*

Spain: *As, Marca, El Mundo, El País, La Vanguardia, Mundo Deportivo, ABC de Sevilla.*

United States of America: *New York Times, New York Post, Los Angeles Times, Los Angeles Sentinel.*

France: *L'Équipe, Le Dauphiné.*

Italy: *Corriere Della Sera, La Repubblica, Gazzetta dello Sport, La Stampa.*

Mexico: *El Informador, El Siglo de Torreón, El Universal, Excelsior, Jornada.*

Paraguay: *ABC Color.*

Perú: *El Comercio, El Nacional.*

United Kingdon: *Daily Mail, The Times, Evening Stardard, Daily Telegraph, Daily Mirror, The Independent, Herald Scotland,* "WalesOnLine."

Uruguay: *El País, El Observador.*

Venezuela: *El Universal.*

Magazines

El Gráfico (Argentina), *Sport* (Argentina), *La Cancha* (Argentina), *Mística* (Argentina), *Todofútbol* (Argentina), *Superfútbol* (Argentina), *FIFA Magazine* (Switzerland), *FourFourTwo* (United Kingdom), *Total Football* (United Kingdom), *Revista de la Confederación Sudamericana de Fútbol* (Paraguay), *Libero International of the IFFHS* (Germany).

News agencies

Diarios y Noticias (Argentina), Télam (Argentina), Reuters (United Kingdom), Deutsche Presse-Agentur (DPA), Agencia Española de Prensa (EFE), Agence France Presse (AFP), Agenzia Nazionale Stampa Associata (ANSA), United Press International (UPI).